Collins

Cambridge IGCSE®

Accounting

TEACHER'S GUIDE

Also for Cambridge O Level

David Horner, Leanna Oliver

Collins

William Collins' dream of knowledge for all began with the publication of his first book in 1819.

A self-educated mill worker, he not only enriched millions of lives, but also founded a flourishing publishing house. Today, staying true to this spirit, Collins books are packed with inspiration, innovation and practical expertise. They place you at the centre of a world of possibility and give you exactly what you need to explore it.

Collins. Freedom to teach.

Published by Collins
An imprint of HarperCollins*Publishers*
The News Building
1 London Bridge Street
London
SE1 9GF

HarperCollins *Publishers*
1st Floor
Watermarque Building
Ringsend Road
Dublin 4
Ireland

Browse the complete Collins catalogue at

www.collins.co.uk

10 9 8 7 6 5 4 3

ISBN 978-0-00-825413-1

British Library Cataloguing in Publication Data

A catalogue record for this publication is available from the British Library.

Author: David Horner, Leanna Oliver

Development editor: Penny Nicholson

Commissioning editor: Lucy Cooper

In-house editors: Alexander Rutherford, Letitia Luff

Project manager: Amanda Harman

Copyeditor: Joan Miller

Proofreader: Piers Maddox

Cover designers: Kevin Robbins and Gordon MacGilp

Cover illustrator: Maria Herbert-Liew

Internal designer / Typesetter: Jouve India

Production controller: Tina Paul

All exam-style questions and sample answers in this title were written by the authors. In examinations, the way marks are awarded may be different.

Contents

Suggested teaching times

Cambridge IGCSE syllabuses are designed on the assumption that learners have about 130 guided learning hours per subject over the duration of the course, but this is for guidance only. The following is a suggestion as to how this time may be divided among the units of the course. However, the number of hours required to complete the course may vary according to local curricular practice, the particular circumstances of your school and the learners' prior experience of the subject.

Unit		Hours
1.1	The purpose of accounting	2
1.2	The accounting equation	4
2.1	The double entry system of book-keeping	9
2.2	Business documents	3
2.3	Books of prime entry	8
3.1	The trial balance	3
3.2	Correction of errors	6
3.3	Bank reconciliation	5
3.4	Control accounts	5
4.1	Capital and revenue expenditure and receipts	2
4.2	Accounting for depreciation and disposal of non-current assets	6
4.3	Other payables and other receivables	6
4.4	Irrecoverable debts and provision for doubtful debts	5
4.5	Valuation of inventory	2
5.1	Sole traders	7
5.2	Partnerships	7
5.3	Limited companies	8
5.4	Clubs and societies	6
5.5	Manufacturing accounts	6
5.6	Incomplete records	8
6.1	Calculation and understanding of ratios	6
6.2	Interpretation of accounting ratios	4
6.3	Inter-firm comparison	2
6.4	Interested parties	3
6.5	Limitations of accounting statements	2
7.1	Accounting principles	3
7.2	Accounting policies	2
		130

Introduction

The *Collins Cambridge IGCSE Accounting Teacher's Guide* has been written to support the teaching and learning of the Cambridge IGCSE® Accounting syllabus 0452 and Cambridge O level syllabus 7707. It is intended to be used alongside the Student's Book as a tool for enhancing the learning experience. The Teacher's Guide has been matched unit by unit to the Student's Book to allow easy cross-referencing between the books. The material within each unit also follows the order of the material within the Student's Book. Photocopiable materials supporting delivery of the course and Answers to the Knowledge check questions, Chapter review questions and the questions in the Workbook are collated at the end of the book for easy reference and printing.

The course is based on a discovery model of learning. Students are encouraged to explore their prior knowledge through discussion in the **Starting point** sections at the beginning of each unit in the Student's Book. Students are then encouraged to explore the unit topic for themselves, discovering solutions and developing understanding in their own way in the **Exploring** sections. There are questions throughout the **Developing** sections to encourage active learning. Students apply the skills and knowledge they have acquired in the **Applying** and **Knowledge check** sections. They are then encouraged to reflect on their understanding in the **Check your progress** sections. Additional practice is provided in the **Chapter reviews** in the Student's Book, to encourage deep learning, and further differentiated activities are provided in the Workbook and Teacher's Guide to enhance students' achievement.

The suggestions for teaching and the additional activities are provided to help teachers prepare their lessons. However, it is assumed that teachers will use and adapt the material in whatever way would work best for their class.

Getting the most from this book

This Teacher's Guide is divided into seven chapters and each chapter is divided into units, in the same way as the Student's Book. Each of the units is organised in the same way and has the following features.

The **Learning objectives** and **key terms** from the Student's Book are included at the start of each unit in the Teacher's Guide. The definitions of the key terms are shown in margin boxes in the Student's Book in the unit where the term is first introduced and can also be found in the glossary at the back of the Student's Book. In addition, there is a list of the **resources** provided to support your teaching of the unit.

Language support

It is important that students are able to communicate their ideas clearly and accurately, both verbally and in writing. This can be particularly challenging for students who do not have English as their first language.

The Student's Book uses a wide range of accounting vocabulary; frequent practice of this vocabulary is useful to ensure students are confident with it. There is a glossary of key terms in the Student's Book. In addition the key terms and their definitions are provided on **photocopiable resource sheets** in the Teacher's Guide and these can be used to help students learn them.

Strategies to support students with verbal communication

- Allow students sufficient thinking time when asking them to respond to questions in class. As non-native English speaking students are having to think about what to say as well as how to say it, it can take them more than a few seconds to formulate a response to a question.
- Give students an opportunity to discuss their ideas in the safety of pairs or small groups before reporting back or presenting to the whole class.

Strategies to support students with written communication

- Use exemplar written responses and analyse them with students in terms of language used. For example, when interpreting ratios ask students to analyse the use of comparatives and highlight the words used to link cause and effect, such as *due to* and *leads to*.
- Provide students with writing templates which scaffold them in terms of the structure and the organisation of their written work.
- Model written responses for students by writing them on the whiteboard or large sheets of poster paper with input from students.

Starting point: The questions in this section encourage students to reflect on prior knowledge. They may make links to students' own experience or they might relate to a familiar context. They can be used to refresh or reinforce material from previous units. These questions should take no longer than ten minutes to complete. Allow students a few minutes to discuss the content of the questions, in pairs. Brief notes could be made. After this, nominate students to share their answers with the whole class. Take this opportunity to identify and correct any misconceptions.

Exploring: The questions in this section are open questions designed to stimulate interest in and thought about the content of the unit ahead, building on what they already know. Allow students about five minutes to discuss the content of the questions, in pairs. Again, brief notes could be made. Then bring students together to discuss the questions as a class. Bear in mind that these questions are designed to prepare students for the concepts they will be encountering in the unit so they are not expected to know all of the answers. Ask questions to develop the discussion if necessary but resist the urge to provide them with all of the relevant information at this point. Allow them to discover for themselves the information they need as they work though the **Developing** section of the unit. You can use their answers to gauge the areas of the unit that students may find more difficult or that may need additional explanation. Students could use the **Exploring** questions as revision before their final examinations, once they have completed all of the taught content.

The two sets of questions can be used together as the starter activity for the first lesson on the unit. The Teacher's Guide provides guidance on how to develop the discussion if necessary, as well as **suggested answers**.

Developing: This section includes suggestions for how to teach each unit. These might highlight common misconceptions and errors or outline a suggested approach.

The Student's Book includes **questions** within the text of each unit. They are intended to allow students to check their understanding of key concepts or to encourage them to come up with an answer before it is explained in the text. The Teacher's Guide provides guidance on using these questions and **suggested answers**.

Eliciting responses from students

Providing responses to questions and participating in discussions allow students to engage both with the content and with their peers. These are important aspects of any taught session. However, students need to feel comfortable to interact with the class and participate in discussions.

- Allow students sufficient thinking time when asking them to respond to questions in class. A period of silence is important, even if it is tempting to provide the answer yourself.
- If it seems that students still need more time to think, ask them to turn to a classmate and discuss some responses to the question.
- For a less confident class, after asking a question you could try giving students one or two minutes to write down their thoughts. This will allow them time to formulate their response without feeling under pressure to provide an answer. This is particularly important for more complex material. It also reinforces the use of writing to process and order thoughts and ideas.
- For individual students who are not confident about speaking in front of the class, you could use a buddy system. The student could let their buddy know their thoughts, which can then be fed into the discussion.

It is important to ensure that all students have the opportunity to contribute in class.

- You can call for volunteers to start a discussion. However, do avoid asking the same students all of the time.
- You can then invite individuals to comment on another student's answer or ask if they agree with it.
- You can nominate students to answer questions, based on your knowledge of the students' understanding. However, especially when covering material with which students should be confident, you could try using some kind of random name generator to select the student to respond. For example, write the names of all the students on lollypop sticks and draw one at random from a cup or a bag.

The Teacher's Guide also includes suggestions for **additional activities** to use during lessons to support students' understanding of the content of the course. Where appropriate, **photocopiable resource sheets** are provided at the end of the book. These can be photocopied and distributed among students.

Each unit in the Student's Book ends with an **Applying** section that provides an opportunity for students to bring together their learning through discussion with their peers. It often involves a **task** designed to be done by students working in pairs. Working alongside their peers allows students to benefit from peer teaching, clarify their ideas and enhance their accounting skills as well as gaining independent working experience. These tasks also provide suitable opportunities for assessment and will allow you to provide individual and group support where required. The Teacher's Guide includes **suggested answers** for the tasks and discussion questions in this section.

Using the Applying tasks

The tasks in the **Applying** section are designed to be completed by students working in pairs. Students working with their peers are engaged in active learning, while enhancing their own learning and understanding of the topics being considered. Students will progress on their own educational journey and help each other to understand the course content. Teamwork is one of the most valued skills in the accounting job market. Accountants need to know how to work together to solve complex problems and be able to work as a team with management, other peers and clients.

Students work in pairs to discuss and produce the answer. Monitor the students as they work, to assess their understanding and provide additional support if necessary. The answer could be checked against a handout or you could go over the answer in class if there were any problems or misunderstandings common to the class. Pairs could be asked to contribute at this stage. For the later chapters, there are also opportunities for students to prepare presentations of their results.

The **Knowledge check** questions could be completed as an 'unseen' test at the end of the unit. They could be self-marked or marked by the teacher. Less able students might be allowed to use the textbook but should be encouraged to paraphrase the text where appropriate. Alternatively, teachers could use the **Knowledge check** questions at relevant points during the unit. **Photocopiable resource sheets** are available, with blank pro-forma accounting documents and partially completed accounting documents that can be photocopied and distributed in class, if you wish.

Check your progress encourages students to reflect on each of the learning objectives. Students should self-assess their knowledge of the unit and consider which of the following statements best reflects their level of knowledge:

- *I struggle with this and need more practice.*
- *I can do this reasonably well.*
- *I can do this with confidence.*

The Workbook provides a table that students can use for this purpose.

For some of the units, students could also test each other verbally on their knowledge of the unit, in pairs, using the learning objectives as question prompts.

The Workbook focuses on providing differentiated practice of the calculations and the techniques for preparing accounting documents required by the syllabus. There are **Support**, **Practice** and **Stretch** questions for each unit in the Student's Book. The **Support** questions are aimed particularly at those students who are struggling with the topic, providing lower-level questions to help them with the basic knowledge required and to build their confidence. Those students who felt they understood the work of the unit reasonably well or were confident of their understanding will work through these quickly or could omit these questions. The **Stretch** questions challenge those students who found the work of the unit easy or finish quickly.

The Teacher's Guide also provides **Support**, **Consolidation** and **Stretch questions and activities** to help you to provide activities tailored to all ability levels in your class.

Teaching mixed ability classes

It is important to differentiate lessons so that individual students of all abilities are sufficiently challenged to achieve to their full potential. Some strategies which can be used to differentiate learning include:

- Conduct a needs analysis. You can consider learning styles and strategies, language needs, learning environments and enjoyment, motivation, strengths and weaknesses.
- During small pair or group work, move among the groups, monitoring student progress. Help to scaffold the learning of less able students and stretch more able students through the use of questioning and dialogue.
- Group students of different abilities so that higher ability learners can model and scaffold concepts and processes for those of lower ability.
- Group students of similar abilities so that the task can be completed at different levels. For example, lower-ability students could use prompt cards for topics such as the rules of double entry book-keeping, the accounting equation, the rules for dealing with inventory, the types of errors. Higher ability groups could be given a different level or number of tasks. This will stretch and challenge the most able students.
- In **small** group work, one student could act as the teacher, delivering a small section of a topic to the rest of the group. In many cases, explaining a concept to another person aids the individual to understand the work themselves.

The **Chapter reviews** provide exam-style questions drawing on material from across the chapter. The Workbook provides an additional **Chapter review exercise**, which could also be used when a chapter has been completed, either in class, for assessment or for homework; alternatively, it could be reserved for revision.

The Teacher's Guide also includes two additional sections.

- There is a bank of **photocopiable materials**. The layout of accounting documents is important and must follow international guidelines. There are therefore several **blank pro-formas** of accounting documents, which can be used to produce double entry accounts, journals, income statements and other accounting documents in the correct format. There are also **resource sheets** for use with the additional activities suggested in this book or to save time when answering the Knowledge check and Chapter review questions.
- **Answers** to the Knowledge check and Chapter review questions are found at the end of the Teacher's Guide, along with guidance about how to allocate marks to the students' answers to the exam-style questions.

We hope that you enjoy teaching the course and find these resources useful.

1 The fundamentals of accounting

This chapter explains the background to the accounting function in a business. The role of accounting is explored, along with some other aspects of financial terminology. Basic numerical techniques for recording financial transactions are also explored.

Prior knowledge

As this is the first unit, there is no prior knowledge.

Background for non-subject specialists

There is a lot of terminology and jargon in an accounting course. Much of the terminology uses language that may be difficult to grasp in early periods of study. Rote learning of the terms is a useful way of ensuring that the correct terminology is used appropriately. Precision in the usage of the terms and the methods used for accounting is crucial.

Accounting is a numerical subject. However, the amount of mathematical ability required is limited to being comfortable dealing with numbers. The mathematical content of the course simply comprises basic arithmetic and some manipulation of numbers, such as rearranging simple equations and calculating percentage changes.

1.1 The purpose of accounting

Learning objectives

By the end of this unit, students should be able to:

- understand and explain the difference between book-keeping and accounting
- state the purposes of measuring business profit and loss
- explain the role of accounting in providing information for monitoring progress and decision-making.

Resources

- Student's Book pages 2–7
- Workbook page 1
- Resource 1.1A
- Resource 1.1B

Key terms

Book-keeping, Accounting, Financial statements, Profit maximisation, Profit, Accounting period, Income statement, Management accounting

STARTING POINT

It may take time to generate responses to question 1. The task is designed to get students to put themselves into the position of running a business.

Question 2 is likely to focus on two main aspects.

- accounting knowledge/qualifications – depending on your students and their personal experience, it may be worth elaborating on the professional qualifications available
- mathematical ability – you might need to emphasise that it is not mathematics that is being assessed in this course but the ability to record, process and interpret numerical information.

Suggested answers

1 For tax calculations; legal requirements; to make it easier to borrow money, for example, from a bank; to measure performance, that is to calculate profit; to help the organisation of the business – knowing how much money is available and who the business owes (or is owed) money to (by).

2 Accounting knowledge/qualifications, mathematical ability, problem solving, people skills.

EXPLORING

Students are generally familiar with the concept of profit and loss, and many will be able to state how it is calculated (difference between revenue and expenses). Students are often aware that profit is seen as a main measure of successful performance. If the group quickly arrives at the notion of profit as an indicator of performance, the discussion can be extended with additional questions, for example:

- *If profit is used to judge performance, how much profit would be a sign of satisfactory or good performance?*
- *Can profit ever not be a good thing? For example, does it matter how profit is made?*
- *Do all businesses wish to be judged by the profit that they earn?*

For measures of performance such as sales, students may refer either to quantity (volume) or value, although they may not use these terms. Some students may also suggest size of market share, although this is not part of the course.

For those who have difficulty with the concept of profit, using prompt questions to elicit the measures of business performance can help, for example:

- *If you ran your own business, what would be your goal for the first year?*
- *Once your own business is well established, would your goals for the business change?*
- *If your business had many close rivals/competitors, how would you know that your business was performing better than your rivals?*
- *In a competitive market, what would you be pleased with in terms of business performance?*

Suggested answer

1 Profit is the most common measure of business performance. Other measures include sales, market share, growth and social, environmental and charitable goals.

Question 2 follows on from the first question, since it is likely to be centred around the concept of profit. The idea of business objectives (goals) can be introduced at this point. Students should not find objectives a difficult concept.

Where students identify growth as an objective, elicit what is meant by 'business growth'. Ask students to suggest ways in which growth can be measured. Ensure they recognise that there may be different ways of measuring growth: either by value measured in monetary terms, such as dollars, or volume measured in units of output sold.

Suggested answer

2 Possible goals for a business include:

- survival
- profit (maximisation)
- sales targets (either in $ or in volume)
- market share (percentage of market a business achieves in sales)
- non-financial objectives (social, environmental or charitable goals).

DEVELOPING

The purpose of this unit is to introduce the role of accounting and to consider the accounting function.

At this early stage, much of the terminology and concepts are likely to be new to most (or all) students. To help students familiarise themselves with terms and concepts, encourage them to set up a list of key terms or a glossary in the back of their books.

Introduce question 1 from the perspective of a business start-up. Elicit how a newly started business will focus on survival and growth during the first few years of trading, and how objectives may change over time, once the business is established, to profit maximising.

Suggested answer

1 Reasons may include:

- Difficult economic conditions may mean a business focuses on survival rather than profit maximisation.
- As a business increases in size it may move away from simple survival and focus more on profit maximisation.
- In a competitive environment, growth may become a more important objective.
- Change in legal ownership means greater focus on profits (e.g. conversion into a limited company).

Activity: Calculation of profit

This activity is designed to support students who find calculations difficult. It can also be used to assess students' ability to carry out numerical calculations. The activity gives practice in calculating profit.

Approximate time required: 20 minutes

Resources: Resource 1.1A

Before the lesson: Print one set of profit calculations and answers cards for each group. Cut out and shuffle the cards.

Pair/group work: Students match the correct profit calculation to the information provided. Calculators can be used.

Question 2 highlights the fact that many companies (especially those in the UK) have an accounting year that starts in April each year and ends the following March. Some students will know that this is due to the tax year in some countries also beginning in April and ending in March of the following year.

Suggested answer

2 In many countries the tax year starts at the beginning of April. Hundreds of years ago, the new year was celebrated around the start of April and the current start of the tax year is likely to be connected to this. As 1 January is a national holiday in many countries, business owners may wish to avoid having the start of the financial year coinciding with a period when the business is closed.

Question 3 will help students to understand how businesses do not operate in isolation and introduces them to the notion of stakeholders (groups that take an interest in the business, for example workers, managers, directors, shareholders/owners, customers, suppliers, lenders, competitors, local community/pressure groups, local and national government). Ensure students understand that statements of the business can be used by all stakeholders, such as banks, to monitor the progress of the business and obtain information for their own goals.

Suggested answer

3 A business may apply for a loan from a bank. The bank will take an interest in the progress of the business and will only lend money to a business that it considers is not at risk of failure.

APPLYING

These questions focus on how accounting information applies to the real world of businesses operating in a dynamic environment. Question 1 encourages students to consider how profit can be used by one stakeholder group – workers.

Question 2 allows students to identify possible reasons why not all businesses aim to achieve profits. Discuss that charities and other social organisations may have other objectives.

Suggested answers

1 Reasons may include:

- Job security – employment positions are more likely to be secure if the business is profitable. Profits are a clear sign of success and may mean that the business will survive and possibly grow in the future. Redundancies are also less likely (or business closure). Profits do not guarantee job security but are a good indicator.
- Pay awards – increased pay for workers has to come from a business's resources, usually its profits. An increase in profits is often seen as an encouraging sign that a business may increase workers' pay. Pay increases can also come from rising productivity. This too indicates a profitable business.

- Bonuses – some workers will be paid in full or in part, according to satisfactory levels of performance. Profit-related pay is often used as a method of motivating workers to be productive. Therefore, rising profits may indicate potential for workers' bonuses.
- Job satisfaction – workers may see rising profits (or profits, in general) as a sign of their positive impact on business performance. Workers may take pride in seeing their efforts result in profits of the business.

2 Businesses that have profit as their main objective may still see rising profits are unsatisfactory for a number of reasons, including:
- Profits may have risen from a very low level and are seen as inadequate for certain businesses.
- Rival companies may have faster growth in profits.
- Economic performance may mean that a business should have been performing better, with higher profits.
- Shareholders (for limited companies) may demand higher profits so as to maximise their own returns.
- Directors may have set targets for a minimum acceptable level of profit that is not fulfilled.

Knowledge check

- **Answers**: See page 215

Check your progress

Ask students to complete the **Check your progress** section in the Student's Book.

Support

- To reinforce the concepts of book-keeping and accounting, ask some whole-group questions such as those below. Record answers on the board or in students' notes. For example:
  - *What do you think an accountant does?*
  - *What do you think book-keeping means?*
  - *What are the 'books' that book-keeping refers to?*
- **Workbook 1.1 Support**

Consolidation

- Students prepare revision cards for the unit. They write a key term from the unit on one side of the card and the definition on the other side. Students can then work in pairs and take turns identifying a key term from the definition or providing a definition, given the key term.
- **Resources**: Resource 1.1B
  Alternatively or in addition, you can use the resource provided and students can match the key terms to the definitions. You can use this matching activity as a starter activity for lessons in this unit.
- **Workbook 1.1 Practice**

Stretch

- Download a set of financial accounts for a public limited company, or ask students to do this. Alternatively, you or they could use personal contacts or write to a local business to request copies of their financial statements (although many businesses may be unwilling to release their information). Note that these could also be used in later chapters. If you wish to use the stretch activity in Unit 6.3, students will also need a set of financial accounts from a second company that is similar in nature to the first.
- Students research the business objectives of the companies and answer these questions.
  - Does the company aim to make a profit?
  - If so, do the reports indicate the level of profit they aim to achieve?
  - Does the company distinguish between short-term and long-term business objectives?
  - Have they achieved previously set targets?
- **Workbook 1.1 Stretch**

1.2 The accounting equation

Learning objectives

By the end of this unit, students should be able to:

- explain the meaning of assets, liabilities and owner's equity
- explain and apply the accounting equation.

Resources

- Student's Book pages 8–16
- Workbook pages 2–3
- Resource 1.2A
- Resource 1.2B
- Resource 1.2C
- Pro-forma 1

Key terms

Duality principle, Assets, Liabilities, Owner's equity, Statement of financial position, Liquidity, Inventory, Trade payable, Trade payables, Trade receivable, Trade receivables

STARTING POINT

Question 1 is straightforward. Most students will be able to suggest some basic responses in terms of owner's equity and liabilities. For those having difficulty with the question, prompt questions can help, for example:

- *Why do businesses need money to start with?*
- *Is it possible to start a business with no money being provided by the owner?*
- *Where does the money to start a business come from?*

For question 2, prompt questions can help to stimulate ideas, for example:

- *If a business owner has none, where could they get go to get money?*
- *If a business wants to expand quickly, how could it finance the expansion?*
- *Are there reasons you would refuse an investment into a business from a potential business partner?*

For question 3, students may be aware that businesses borrow money, before being formally introduced to this in the teaching of this unit. Most recognise that businesses borrow money from banks and other financial institutions but may be unaware of the difficulties in obtaining borrowed funds.

Suggested answers

1 Business start-ups are likely to use a combination of owner's equity and borrowed money in the following forms.
   - Owner's equity, including:
     - owner's own savings
     - amounts given by family members
     - amounts given by friends.
   - Liabilities, including:
     - loans from friends and family
     - bank loans
     - mortgages.

2 Reasons include:
   - to finance assets needed to start the business
   - to expand the business

- to finance a period where cash flow is insufficient to continue trading
- to acquire other businesses.

3 Reasons include:
- Considered too much of a risk by banks and other financial institutions, who decide not lend money.
- Interest rates are set at a high level on any loans taken by the business.
- Unable to provide financial records, which are often asked for by lenders when deciding whether or not to lend money.
- No credit history (this is similar to the previous answer).
- No experience in obtaining borrowed money, so not knowing the methods available.

EXPLORING

Question 1 is straightforward.

For question 2, prompt questions can help to promote discussion, for example:

- *Does it matter if asset values are not up to date?*
- *How would you decide on the current market value of an asset?*
- *How subjective is it to provide a market value for an asset?*
- *Do all assets lose value over time?*

Students may suggest various methods, including market value (the value the asset could currently be sold for) or replacement cost (how much it would cost to replace the asset if damaged, destroyed or stolen). Ensure students understand that from an accounting point of view, only a method based on cost (the price paid for the asset) is considered to be correct.

Suggested answers

1 Reasons include:
- For legal (including tax) purposes, well-organised records of all items of income and expenditure must be kept.
- Obtaining finance from any financial institution (such as a bank) usually requires a business to produce a credible set of financial records. Any business without full records will find it more difficult to convince any lender that they are worthy of borrowing money.
- Business management – running a successful business depends on knowing how much money is available. A business can spend money it doesn't have for a short period of time if it uses trade credit. However, it will need to keep records of who it owes money to (and who it is owed money by) if the business is to survive.

2 At this stage, students may suggest:
- cost – the price paid for the asset
- market value – the value the asset could currently be sold for
- replacement cost – how much it would cost to replace the asset if damaged, destroyed or stolen.

DEVELOPING

The purpose of this unit is to ensure that students are familiar with the terms 'assets', 'liabilities' and 'capital' and how these are applied to the accounting equation.

Much of accounting is based on the principle of duality and encountering the equation is the first time students are introduced to this concept. As with Unit 1.1, there is plenty of new terminology. Ensure plenty of practice until you are certain all students are familiar with the terms.

Encourage students to be confident when distinguishing between assets, liabilities and owner's equity. These elements are a fundamental part of the accounting equation, which underpins much of the work in the following chapters.

Activity: Classifying assets, liabilities and owner's equity

Use this activity after introducing the key terms of assets, liabilities and owner's equity. It may also be used as a support activity.

Approximate time required: 15 minutes

Resources: Resource 1.2A

Before the lesson: Print one set of assets/liabilities/owner's equity cards for each group. Cut out and shuffle the cards.

Group/pair work: Students classify each card as assets, liabilities or owner's equity.

Answers

Assets: business premises, bank balance, trade receivables, computer, cash in till, fixtures, inventory, amount owed by customer, office equipment

Liabilities: trade payables, bank overdraft, bank loan, mortgage, amount owing to supplier

Owner's equity: owner's car introduced to business, money placed in business by owner, profit, loss

Students need plenty of practice to ensure they are able to calculate the value of groups of items, such as the value of assets for a business, given values of liabilities and owner's equity. It is essential to spend time ensuring that students understand the accounting equation – without solid foundations, further development is difficult.

Question 1 is based on the manipulation of the accounting equation. This question can be used once the equation has been introduced, and as a precursor to introducing the concept of rearranging the accounting equation so as to ascertain 'missing figures', including ascertaining the value of liabilities if only assets and owner's equity are known.

Activity: Using the accounting equation

Use this activity after the work on rearranging the accounting equation. It may also be used as a support activity.

Approximate time required: 15 minutes

Resources: Resource 1.2B

Before the lesson: Print sufficient copies of the resource sheet for the class.

Individual work: Students calculate the missing figure in each accounting equation. Calculators may be used.

Answers

Assets ($)	Liabilities ($)	Owner's equity ($)
4324	3212	1112
5654	1311	4343
15280	7840	7440
26770	9945	16825
12311	4141	8170
21010	7860	13150
16670	9999	6671
89793	23123	66670
124500	34550	89950
80500	23677	56823

Question 2 is more difficult. Before introducing the question, consider a few examples of how the statement of financial position is altered by transactions. Guide students towards answering what they know, that is:

- inventory (an asset) is sold, so the total of assets will decrease
- the selling price of the inventory (either as trade receivables – if on credit, or bank or cash) will increase the value of assets – by more than the decrease in inventory.

Students may not be aware of the key information: the profit on the sale is added to the owner's equity. (As this is developed further in chapter 5, a lengthy discussion is not needed at this stage.)

For question 3, either display a copy of Worked example 7 on the board, or ensure students all have it available in front of them. Rather than allowing students to work on this question by themselves, it may be more effective to discuss what changes as a result of the transaction. (There will be two changes to the statement – duality.)

Reinforce students' understanding of the concept of the duality principle of business transactions. Use the accounting equation to help you do this. For those having difficulty with the concept, prompt questions can help; for example, ask students to decide what side of the equation is affected in each of the following transactions.

- An owner introduces more of their own money into the business.
- A car is being purchased for business use but financed by a bank loan.
- Office furniture is being sold for cash.
- Repayment of a loan is made from funds in the business bank account.
- Machinery is sold on credit to a customer. (If students are not familiar with the concept of credit then replace this example with 'sold for cash'.)

APPLYING

The principle of duality appears in other topics. Students may find it helpful to think of every transaction as having two effects on the business.

Students may find question 2 difficult, though it is likely that some will be able to work out how to deal with losses. It may help to refer students to their responses to question 2 on page 13. As with the earlier question, clarify what has changed (assets has decreased due to sale of asset; trade receivables or bank or cash – also an asset – has increased by a smaller amount). The key aspect for students is to appreciate how the accounting equation deals with the discrepancy in the values.

Suggested answers

1 The statement of financial position is essentially a statement of the accounting equation applied to actual business transactions that have taken place in a business. The statement has to balance, as the accounting equation shows the same items but viewed from two different perspectives: the resources used by the business and how those resources were financed (namely, from owner's equity or liabilities).

2 A sale of an asset reduces the 'asset' side of the accounting equation by the cost value of the asset. The 'asset' side increases by the amount the asset is sold for. Due to it being sold for a loss, the decrease in the assets is greater than the increase in assets.

The loss on the sale is the difference between the cost value of the asset and the selling price of the assets (depreciation of assets is covered in Unit 4.2). The 'owner's equity and liabilities' side of the accounting equation is reduced by the amount of loss on the asset's sale. The value of owner's equity is reduced as the loss represents a loss in the owner's investment in the business.

Use the task to ensure students have understood the meaning of assets, liabilities and owner's equity.

Answer

Henwood Ltd Statement of financial position as at 10 May 2018			
Assets	**$**	**Owner's equity and Liabilities**	**$**
Laptop	1000	Owner's equity	25000
Office equipment	240	Bank loan	10000
Inventory	1190	Trade payables (Sabkha)	1190
Bank	33440		
Cash	320		
	36190		36190

Knowledge check

- **Resources:** Pro-forma 1
- **Answers**: See page 215

Check your progress

Ask students to complete the **Check your progress** section in the Student's Book.

Support

- **Resources**: Resource 1.2A, Resource 1.2B
  - **Resource 1.2A**: To give students practice in classifying items into assets, liabilities and owner's equity.
  - **Resource 1.2B**: For students who need support with numerical work. Students use the accounting equation to fill in the missing figures.
- **Workbook 1.2 Support**

Consolidation

- Students work in pairs. One member of the pair writes down three simple transactions. From these transactions, the other member produces a statement of financial position to record the three transactions.
- Students prepare revision cards for the unit. They write a key term from the unit on one side of the card and the definition on the other side. Students can then work in pairs and take turns identifying a key term from the definition or providing a definition given the key term.

  Alternatively or in addition, you can use the resource provided and students can match the key terms to the definitions. You can use this matching activity as a starter activity for lessons in this unit. You may also want to include key terms from earlier units.
- **Resources**: Resource 1.2C
- **Workbook 1.2 Practice**

Stretch

- Students produce their own statements of financial position. For each one they write an additional two or three transactions that take place after the date of the construction of the statement of financial position. This is then passed on to the group to 'solve'. The task involves updating the statement of financial position based on the additional transactions that have occurred.
- **Workbook 1.2 Stretch**

Chapter review

- **Answers:** See page 215
- **Workbook: Chapter 1 review**

2 Sources and recording of data

Double entry book-keeping, introduced in this chapter, is the foundation for most of the course. Knowledge of the rules of double entry book-keeping is fundamental to all financial accounting. Chapters 3, 4 and 5 build on the work introduced here.

Prior knowledge

Knowledge gained in Chapter 1 is necessary for the study of this chapter. Students should be familiar with assets, liabilities, owners' equity and the accounting equation.

Background for non-subject specialists

Book-keeping is key to nearly all that follows in the world of accounting. Therefore, it is essential that the rules of double entry book-keeping are understood. At first appearance, they may appear unusual. In fact, the system is both simple and effective in ensuring that transactions are correctly recorded and that the information found in the accounts has further uses, such as the construction of the financial statements.

The rules of book-keeping must be followed consistently, otherwise any mistakes will be discovered when the accounts are balanced and the trial balance is produced (the trial balance is introduced in Unit 3.1).

2.1 The double entry system of book-keeping

Learning objectives

By the end of this unit, students should be able to:

- outline the double entry system of book-keeping
- process accounting data using the double entry system
- prepare ledger accounts
- post transactions to the ledger accounts
- balance ledger accounts as required and make transfers to financial statements
- interpret ledger accounts and their balances
- recognise the division of the ledger into the sales ledger, the purchases ledger and the nominal (general ledger).

Resources

- Student's Book pages 18–35
- Workbook pages 6–8
- Resource 2.1A
- Resource 2.1B
- Resource 2.1C
- Resource 2.1D
- Pro-forma 1
- Pro-forma 2

Key terms

Double entry book-keeping, Trader, Purchases, Sales, Purchases returns, Sales returns, Drawings, Balance (of an account), Personal accounts, Sales ledger, Purchases ledger, Nominal ledger

STARTING POINT

The purpose of the questions is to get students thinking about the practicalities of the early transactions likely to appear in a business, and to introduce them to the idea of owner's equity, assets and liabilities. Students do not require technical knowledge to be able to respond.

Suggested answer

1 Resources may include:

- money – from the owner or from other personal sources (such as friends or family)
- borrowed money (from banks or financial institutions)
- resources owned or borrowed by owner that can be used in business (such as property, equipment, vehicles)
- skills and experience of owner
- personal characteristics (such as determination, resilience, calculated risk taker).

In regard to question 2, it would be surprising, although not impossible, to find any financial institution that was willing to lend money to a business for which no money was provided from the owner(s). A compromise would be for someone the owner knows to provide money, as a form of guarantor. Another possible way in which no initial money is needed is if the business is bought as a going concern (one that already exists) and requires an injection of cash to keep it running, although it would be surprising to find people willing to lend such a business money.

Suggested answer

2 Most people who start a business will use their own savings or money given to them by family or friends – this may be lent or given. In addition, some form of borrowing from a bank or financial institution as a loan, overdraft or mortgage is likely.

Students may need support when answering question 3. It may be helpful to use prompt questions, for example:

- *Would you lend a stranger money?*
- *What would you want in return for lending money to someone who may not be able to pay you back?*
- *How much interest (if any) would you want on any money you lent?*
- *What evidence would you want that the business can repay?*

At this stage, students may describe financial documents, such as cash flow forecasts, forecast income statements, and so on, rather than referring to the documents by name.

Suggested answer

3 A business may need to:

- produce evidence of its ability to repay the loan, such as cash flow forecasts, forecast income statements, sales forecasts
- show the records of the business, including past data relating to sales, profits, and so on
- offer security on any borrowing (for example, an asset that can be repossessed by the lender if the business fails to keep up with repayments).

EXPLORING

Initially, students may struggle with question 1. Some may guess that 'double entry' involves 'two entries' without any genuine understanding of the term. If students continue to have difficulty with the concept, recap Unit 1.2 and the accounting equation.

Before introducing question 2, briefly discuss with the group the different legal structures that exist for businesses, such as:

- sole trader
- partnership (students need to know about general partnerships but not limited liability partnerships – LLPs)
- limited company – public and private
- charities – which are often set up as limited companies.
- nationalised or government owned enterprises.

In most cases, students should recognise that many businesses have multiple owners and that this may lead to difficulties in terms of record keeping.

Suggested answers

1 'Double entry' refers to the process whereby every transaction requires two entries to be made in the books of the business. This is because each transaction has two effects on the business (see the accounting equation in Unit 1.2).

2 Difficulties may include:

- who has authority to spend money in the business
- how often records will be updated
- how close (geographically, or personally) the multiple owners are
- how much decision making may occur independently of other owners.

DEVELOPING

The purpose of this unit is familiarise students with the process of double entry book-keeping.

A useful approach is to focus on examples of transactions on the bank or cash account of a business. Students generally find it straightforward to see that money coming in is debited and money going out is credited to these accounts.

Bank and Cash accounts	
Debit	**Credit**
Money coming in	Money going out

Build on this knowledge by eliciting that transactions must always have one debit entry and one credit entry in the books of the business. You could prompt with an example: *A cash payment to a credit supplier is credited to the cash account. Where does the other half of the entry appear?* (a debit entry in the supplier's account)

Activity: Applying the rules of double entry book-keeping for asset, liability and owner's equity accounts

This activity is designed to enable students to practise the application of the rules of double entry book-keeping.

Approximate time required: 15 minutes

Resources: Resource 2.1A

Before the lesson: Print sufficient copies of the resource sheet for the class

Individual/pair work: Students identify the account to be debited or credited for a range of transactions. If working in pairs, students should discuss answers before recording them on their own resource sheet.

Answers

	Account to be debited	Account to be credited
Owner introduces cash into business bank account	Bank	Owner's equity
Cash is deposited in the business bank account	Bank	Cash
Equipment is purchased on credit from Hunter	Equipment	Hunter
Motor vehicle sold – payment received by cheque	Bank	Motor vehicle
Amount owing to Faisal paid in cash	Faisal	Cash
Owner brings own computer into business use	Computer	Owner's equity
A customer – Maria – pays amount owing in cash	Cash	Maria
Fixtures and fittings purchased on credit from Usman	Fixtures and fittings	Usman
Office equipment bought on credit from Rashmi – returned due to unsuitability	Rashmi	Office equipment
Van sold on credit to Herbert returned to us due to it being unsafe	Van	Herbert
Shanaya – a credit supplier – is paid by cheque	Shanaya	Bank
Ester – a credit customer – pays in cash	Cash	Ester
Bank loan obtained from Nanchester Bank	Bank	Nanchester Bank
Cash borrowed from Alex	Cash	Alex
Loan from Leyla repaid in cash	Leyla	Cash
Car sold on credit to Kalim	Kalim	Car
Machinery sold for cash	Cash	Machinery
Van purchased and payment made by cheque.	Van	Bank

For question 1, most students will comprehend that profits are earned on the trade in inventory (inventory is covered in Unit 1.2). They should also consider why inventory might be sold for less than its original cost (that is a loss is made on the inventory).

Suggested answer

1 The inventory is likely to be sold for a higher price than was paid for it. This is how businesses make profits.

Question 2 can be introduced once the techniques for accounting for inventory have been covered. Students may find it difficult to understand the need for four separate inventory accounts in the double entry system. Take time to reinforce this. The activity below is useful for further practice.

Suggested answer

2 It is useful to know the value of returns. If these are simply off-set against sales and purchases it would not be possible to find out the size of any returns. Not recording returns separately may also make it more likely that the correct action (e.g. the issue of a credit note) does not happen.

Activity: Applying the rules of double entry book-keeping for inventory, expense and income transactions

This activity is designed to enable students to practise the application of the rules of double entry book-keeping.

Approximate time required: 15 minutes

Resources: Resource 2.1B

Before the lesson: Print sufficient copies of the resource sheet for the class.

Individual/pair work: Students identify which account should be debited or credited for a series of transactions. If working in pairs, students should discuss answers before recording them on their own resource sheet.

Answers

	Account to be debited	Account to be credited
1 Goods sold on credit to Oliver	Oliver	Sales
2 Equipment sold on credit to Irena	Irena	Equipment
3 Goods sold on credit to George are returned to business	Sales returns	George
4 Inventory purchased on credit from Janine	Purchases	Janine
5 Goods sold for cash	Cash	Sales
6 Purchases paid by cheque	Purchases	Bank
7 Purchases returned to credit supplier – Reyansh	Reyansh	Purchases returns
8 Motor vehicle purchased for resale paid by cheque	Purchases	Bank
9 Purchases on credit from Beatriz	Purchases	Beatriz
10 Machinery sold as inventory on credit to Lau	Sales	Lau
11 Amount owing to Loukas – a credit supplier - paid in cash	Loukas	Cash
12 Sundry expenses paid in cash	Sundry expenses	Cash
13 Rent paid by cheque	Rent	Bank
14 Commission received by cheque	Bank	Commission received
15 Wages paid in cash	Wages	Cash
16 Money taken from bank by owner for private use	Drawings	Bank
17 Rent received by cheque	Bank	Rent received
18 Owner takes furniture out of business for own use	Drawings	Furniture

Question 3 can be introduced when covering the topic of book-keeping for incomes and expenses. It provides scope to consider some of the contradictions in book-keeping. Explain that while the need to keep incomes and expenses separate is usually clear, this rule is relaxed for accounts such as general expenses or sundry expenses or 'heating and lighting'. If students have difficulty with the question it may help to use prompt questions, for example:

- *What happens if expenses are greater than incomes in value?*
- *Can a business have expenses greater than incomes for a prolonged period?*
- *How might a business deal with a situation where expenses are greater than incomes?* (If the response is that expenses should be reduced, follow up with *Which ones?* or *How do you know you are spending too much?)*

Suggested answer

3 Separate accounts are used for each type of income and expense, so that categories of expenses can be monitored closely. This ensures that unnecessarily high expenses are noticed. A reasonable level of cash flow is needed within the business to pay bills, trade payables, and so on. Running out of cash is a common source of business failure. Taking assets from the business means they can no longer be used for profit-making activities within the business.

Question 4 is reasonably straightforward. Explore why profits are useful for a sole trader. You could link this to the idea of an individual using their personal savings to reduce the need to take out a loan, when purchasing a large item such as a car or a holiday. You could also consider the benefits to a business of no drawings being taken. A prompt question may be helpful: *If all profits are reinvested within a business, what advantages does the business benefit from?* (More resources available, for example, to pay off any liabilities early, reduce the need for further liabilities, purchase new assets without the need for borrowing.)

Suggested answer

4 Drawings should not be excessive as this takes resources away from the business, which reduces its ability to use profits to finance expansion.

Question 5 can only be introduced once students have encountered drawings as a topic. As tghey result in a reduction in capital, students will often jump to the conclusion that drawings are debited to the owner's equity account. If students have difficulty with this it may help to use prompt question(s), for example:

- *Is it important to know the size of the owner's stake in the business?*
- *If drawings are equal to the balance on the owner's equity account, what would be the balance on the owner's equity account?*
- *Is it useful to know how much is taken as drawings each year?*

Suggested answer

5 Keeping drawings and owner's equity separate allows the owner to check that the drawings taken out of the business are not excessively high.

Question 6 encourages students to practise the skill of locating transactions in the correct ledger.

Suggested answer

6 Sales ledger: Hassan; Alex

Purchases ledger: James; Luis

Nominal ledger: Bank; Owner's equity; Equipment; Computer; Mehdi*; Purchases; Sales; Purchases returns; Sales returns; Rent received; Insurance; Drawings; Wages

* Mehdi' account could also be in the Purchases ledger but this depends on whether the computer(s) purchased on credit from Mehdi were for resale or for business use. The purchases ledger is used for suppliers of goods for resale.

APPLYING

The double entry book-keeping here is not difficult but the balancing of the accounts requires care and precision. Use the task to ensure that students can do this confidently. Students should be careful when preparing their answers. For example, if working on paper, they will need to ensure that they leave enough space for each account. A common mistake is to leave insufficient space between accounts underneath each other. A good rule is to make an estimate of how many entries are to be made in each account (remembering that the balancing of the account will take a number of lines of space). Proforma 1 provides enough lines for all of these accounts.

Answers

Wages					
		$			$
Jan 22	Bank	5400	Jan 31	Balance c/d	5400
Feb 1	Balance b/d	5400			

Bank					
		$			$
Jan 31	Balance c/d	6150	Jan 22	Wages	5400
			Jan 27	Kobi	250
			Jan 29	Insurance	500
		6150			6150
			Feb 1	Balance b/d	6150

Purchases					
		$			$
Jan 23	Akpo	590	Jan 31	Balance c/d	1000
Jan 23	Kobi	410			
		1000			1000
Feb 1	Balance b/d	1000			

Akpo					
		$			$
Jan 25	Purchases returns	150	Jan 23	Purchases	590
Jan 31	Balance c/d	440			
		590			590
			Feb 1	Balance b/d	440

Kobi					
		$			$
Jan 27	Bank	250	Jan 23	Purchases	410
Jan 31	Balance c/d	160			
		410			410
			Feb 1	Balance b/d	160

Purchases returns					
		$			$
Jan 31	Balance c/d	150	Jan 25	Akpo	150
			Feb 1	Balance b/d	150

Insurance					
		$			$
Jan 29	Bank	500	Jan 31	Balance c/d	500
Feb 1	Balance b/d	500			

Sales					
		$			$
Jan 31	Balance c/d	330	Jan 30	Garcia	330
			Feb 1	Balance b/d	330

Garcia					
		$			$
Jan 30	Sales	330	Jan 31	Balance c/d	330
Feb 1	Balance b/d	330			

List of balances

	Debit balances ($)	Credit balances ($)
Wages	5400	
Bank		6150
Purchases	1000	
Akpo		440
Kobi		160
Purchases returns		150
Insurance	500	
Sales		330
Garcia	330	
Totals	**7230**	**7230**

Knowledge check

- **Resources**: Pro-forma 1, Pro-forma 2
- **Answers**: See pages 216–219

Check your progress

Ask students to complete the Check your progress section in the Student's Book.

Support

- **Resources**: Resource 2.1C

  Students complete the resource sheet with the rules of double entry book-keeping. (The answers can be found in Unit 2.1 of the Student's Book.) They can use the completed sheet to help them complete questions successfully.
- **Workbook 2.1 Support**

Consolidation

- Students prepare revision cards for the unit. They write a key term from the unit on one side of the card and the definition on the other side. Students can then work in pairs and take turns identifying a key term from the definition or providing a definition given the key term.
- **Resources**: Resource 2.1D
- Alternatively or in addition, you can use the resource provided and students can match the key terms to the definitions. You can use this matching activity as a starter activity for lessons in this unit. You may also want to include key terms from earlier units.

- Build on students' understanding of double entry book-keeping by focusing on examples surrounding individual credit customers and credit suppliers. It can help students if they imagine the supplier's and customer's accounts appear as follows:

Credit supplier	
Debit	**Credit**
How the amount owing to suppliers is settled	Money owed to suppliers and increase in amounts owed

Credit customer	
Debit	**Credit**
How much is owed to business by customer and increases in amounts owed	How the amount owing to business is settled

  Then ask them to suggest what transactions would affect these accounts – credit sales and purchases, returns, cash paid and received (and discounts once covered in Unit 2.3).
  Students could make a revision card (or cards) from these templates, which they can use when working through related exercises.
- **Workbook 2.1 Practice**

Stretch

- Students who are interested in the origins of double entry book-keeping may wish to research its use through the ages. Internet sources will give them the history of this topic – and how Luca Paciola formalised the rules that are still in use today.
- **Workbook 2.1 Stretch**

2.2 Business documents

Learning objectives

By the end of this unit, students should be able to:

- recognise and understand the following business documents: invoice, debit note, credit note, statement of account, cheque, receipt
- complete pro-forma business documents
- understand the use of business documents as sources of information: invoice, credit note, cheque counterfoil, paying-in slip, receipt, bank statement.

Resources

- Student's Book pages 36–48
- Workbook pages 9–10
- Resource 2.2A
- Resource 2.2B
- Resource 2.2C
- Resource 2.2D

Key terms

Business document, Invoice, Trade discount, Debit note, Credit note, Statement of account, Cheque, Cheque counterfoil, Payer, Payee, Paying-in slip, Receipt, Bank statement

STARTING POINT

Most students will be familiar with the idea of a bank statement, and some may have received bank statements of their own. Students may come up with other valid ideas in response to question 1, such as a bank book (though these are rare in today's banking system). Some may mention online banking.

Question 2 will generate a range of responses. Students are not expected to know the formal names of business documents at this stage, although some might.

If students find these questions difficult, it may help to use prompt questions, for example:

- *How does a business know when it has made a payment from its own bank account?*
- *How does a business know when a sale is made? What proof does it have of the goods being ordered?*
- *What evidence does a business keep to show it has paid money to a person or to another business?*
- *What records does a business keep relating to bills, such as electricity and phone bills?*

Suggested answers

1 Bank statements, paying-in slips, cheque books, bank books, receipts from ATMs ('cash points')

2 Written and electronic records (orders, emails, online ordering, receipts, and so on)

EXPLORING

Before students look at question 1, recap the distinction between cash sales and credit sales as an introduction. As a stretch task, ask students to consider the problems of allowing credit sales. (Problems include irrecoverable debts, risk of delays in payment and problems with cash flow.)

If students find question 2 difficult, it may help to use prompt questions, for example:

- *Why do mistakes occur in the financial records when a person uses a computer to keep these records?*
- *What mistakes could be made when entering information into a computer?*

The errors elicited in answer to question 2 are explored in Chapter 3.

Suggested answers

1 Generates further sales; generates loyalty; may mean the business is allowed credit from other businesses.

2 Human error – inputting transactions incorrectly, such as getting the names of the customer or supplier wrong; entering incorrect amounts; not entering some transactions.

DEVELOPING

The purpose of this unit is to put double entry accounting, introduced in Unit 2.1, into the context of the business documents used as part of business trading. Double entry transactions are triggered by the business documents created out of the various transactions that a business undertakes.

The pro-forma documents used by businesses vary between businesses but share common basic information. The information contained within the business document is used to record the double entry transaction. Examples of pro-forma documents can be presented to the class individually and with discussion focused on what information is shown and how it is used to make entries in the double entry accounts.

Frequent simple questions used as a starter exercise in lessons help students understand the link between documents and transactions. For example:

- What document is created from cash sales?
- What double entry accounts will be used once a purchases invoice is received?
- What would generate a credit note?

Sometimes debit notes cause confusion. Students may (mistakenly) believe that a debit note triggers an entry in the purchases returns account, which it does not – it is a request to be allowed to send goods back.

The in-text questions are designed to develop understanding of the business documents used within the business. Although the topic is knowledge based, understanding of the uses of the documents is needed for effective completion of exam-style questions.

The purpose of question 1 is to enable students to understand that two business documents – the sales invoice and the purchases invoice – are the same document. The difference arises because the same invoice is used by both a customer and a supplier.

Suggested answer

1 A credit sale by a business is a credit purchase for another business. A sales invoice and a purchases in voice are the same document. It is a sales invoice for the business selling goods on credit. It is a purchases invoice for the business making the credit purchase.

Question 2 is designed to show that the debit note, although a separate business document, does not generate an automatic entry in the double entry accounts (or the books of prime entry). It is a common misunderstanding that the debit note generates an entry in the sales returns account. This is not the case.

Suggested answers

2 A debit note is a request made by a business to be allowed to return goods to the original supplier. If accepted, the request generates a credit note issued by the business making the sale. The credit note generates an entry in the double entry accounts. The request made, via the debit note, to return goods may not be accepted by the business making the sale so it cannot be used to make an entry in the accounts.

Question 3 distinguishes between the 'common sense' understanding of bank balances and the accounting double entry understanding of the balance. In an everyday sense, a bank account with a credit balance means the customer has money in their bank account. This contradicts the rules of double entry accounting, which would expect a debit balance on the bank account. The contradiction is resolved by recognising that the balance on a bank account can be viewed from differing perspectives – the bank's perspective and the customer's perspective.

Suggested answer

3 The difference in the balances is the result of the bank account being viewed from two viewpoints – that of the bank and that of the customer. The bank owes money to any customer who has deposited money into a bank account. This means the bank balance is a liability of the bank and would be a credit balance in the bank's double entry accounts. From the viewpoint of the customer, the bank balance is an asset and a debit balance.

Activity: Producing documents for a set of transactions

Use this activity to give students practice in entering a set of transactions on pro-forma business documents. More able students could first generate their own transactions.

Approximate time required: The time taken will depend on the level of autonomy allowed to students. If students are provided with a set of transactions, allow 1 hour. Where students produce their own transactions, a longer period of time will be needed.

Resources: Resource 2.2A

Before the lesson: To save time in the lesson or for less-confident students, prepare a set of business transactions (see below) to be used with the pro-forma business documents (Resource 2.2B). Print sufficient copies of the business documents and transactions for each pair.

Pair work: Depending on the time available or the confidence of students, give each pair a set of transactions and the pro-forma business documents. More able students could generate their own set of transactions, although you may wish to check them. The set of transactions should relate to a number of transactions and be for the same business. They should include at least three of the following:

- a credit sale of goods
- a credit purchase of goods
- a request from a customer for the return of goods
- a return of goods to the original supplier
- a granting of permission for goods to be returned by a customer of the business
- payments made or received from any of these transactions.

More able students may also produce their own set of pro-forma business documents, either on paper or using ICT, and complete these with their own set of transactions. Business documents should include:

- an invoice – either as a sale made or as a purchase received by the business from its supplier
- a debit note – a request for returning some of the goods sold (or purchased)
- a credit note – the confirmation that the returns have been authorised by the business
- a statement of account – for the end of the month.

For less able students or to save time, the blank pro-forma documents on Resource 2.2A should be completed with the transactions provided.

Suggested answers

1 Students complete each pro-forma business document with their own transactions or those supplied.

APPLYING

These questions encourage reflective thinking on how business documents work. Use them to initiate a class discussion.

Question 1 considers a business that does not trade on credit. Although some documents would not be necessary (see suggested answers), those relating to payments and receipts would be required. Debit and credit notes would be needed in case of a return occurring.

Question 2 considers how bank accounts are often affected by automated transactions that may not have yet been recorded by the business in its double entry account for bank. Businesses will know of the transactions but may not know the exact timing of when they occur.

Suggested answers

1 Invoices may no longer be needed if the business is not engaged in credit sales and purchases. A statement of account is unlikely to be needed, though may still be used in case of a return being made.

2 Items may have been paid into and out of the bank account before the business is fully aware of the transactions. For example, interest, bank charges, standing orders and direct debits alter the bank balance before the business is aware that these transactions have been completed. Cheques paid out by the business will have been credited to the bank account before money actually leaves the bank account.

Knowledge check

- **Resources:** Resource 2.2B
- **Answers:** See pages 219–221

Check your progress

Ask students to complete the **Check your progress** section in the Student's Book.

Support

- **Resources:** Resource 2.2C
  Students complete the activity on the resource sheet. (The answers can be found in Unit 2.2 of the Student's Book.)
- **Workbook Unit 2.2 Support**

Consolidation

- Students prepare revision cards for the unit. They write a key term from the unit on one side of the card and the definition on the other side. Students can then work in pairs and take turns identifying a key term from the definition or providing a definition, given the key term.
- **Resources**: Resource 2.2D
- Alternatively or in addition, you can use the resource provided and students can match the key terms to the definitions. You can use this matching activity as a starter activity for lessons in this unit. You may also want to include key terms from earlier units.
- **Workbook Unit 2.2 Practice**

Stretch

- Ask students to try to find a set of business documents used by a real business. This could be through personal contacts or through the internet. Alternatively, students could write to a local business to request copies of documents used by the business – though a complete set may not be available.
- **Workbook Unit 2.2 Stretch**

2.3 Books of prime entry

Learning objectives

By the end of this unit, students should be able to:

- explain the advantage of using various books of prime entry
- explain the use of, and process, accounting data in the books of prime entry – cash book, petty cash book, sales journal, purchases journal, sales returns journal, purchases returns journal and the general journal
- post the ledger entries from the books of prime entry
- distinguish between and account for trade discount and cash discounts
- explain the dual function of the cash book as a book of prime entry and as a ledger account for bank and cash
- explain the use of and record payments and receipts made by bank transfers and other electronic means
- explain and apply the imprest system of petty cash.

Resources

- Student's Book pages 49–66
- Workbook pages 11–13
- Resource 2.3A
- Resource 2.3B
- Resource 2.3C
- Resource 2.3D
- Pro-forma 1
- Pro-forma 2
- Pro-forma 3
- Pro-forma 4
- Pro-forma 5

Key terms

Book of prime entry, Posting, Cash book, Cash discount, Discount allowed, Discount received, Petty cash book, Imprest system, Float, Sales journal, Purchases journal, Sales returns journal, Purchases returns journal, General journal, Narrative

STARTING POINT

The questions are designed to get students thinking further about the double entry system in practice.

Students should have had plenty of practice of entering transactions in ledger accounts but may not have an understanding of how they are completed in the world of business. This may be because practice questions are not necessarily always the same as the typical double entry transactions of a real business. At this stage, students will not have experience of more complex transactions such as those needed for depreciation, for correcting errors and for irrecoverable debts.

For those who may have difficulty answering question 1, break down the question as follows:

- *Which double entry accounts are likely to be used daily?*
- *Which accounts are likely to be used less often?*

Suggested answer

1 Accounts used less frequently include:

- occasional customers and occasional supplier (especially if a one-off customer/supplier)
- owner's equity – unless the owner is in the habit of making regular contributions from their own resources into the business
- assets that are bought infrequently and unlikely to be repeat purchases, for example, specific machinery or equipment.

Accounts used more frequently include:

- bank and cash
- regular customers and regular suppliers
- purchases and sales
- regular expenses – general expenses, rent, wages, utilities (gas, electricity, water), insurance.

Question 2 leads into the system of books of prime entry. Students have already been introduced to the idea of organising accounts when they studied the different ledgers used in business (Unit 2.1). Before students respond to the question, invite them to imagine they are running their own business and ask them to think about the best way to organise their own accounts. This approach will also support students who may not understand question 2.

Suggested answer

2 Possible methods include:

- in alphabetical order
- by region
- according to how often the accounts are used
- on the basis of types of accounts, for example collate all asset accounts together, all personal accounts together, and so on.

EXPLORING

These questions are concerned with the practicalities of double entry book-keeping and using books of prime entry in the real world. They will also prepare students for progression to Chapter 3, where systems and checks are introduced in the form of trial balances, bank reconciliation, correction of errors and control accounts.

Suggested answers

1 A lot of the errors made are human errors. Assuming the documents are correct but the information is not transferred correctly, then the following errors could occur:

- complete failure to record the transaction – this is possible if no one person is responsible for transferring the information into the accounts
- misreading the business documents and recording the wrong numerical information – the amounts are wrong
- misreading the business documents and recording the wrong personal information –entering amounts into the wrong customer account or wrong supplier account
- entering the information into the wrong account – for example, confusing the type of accounts to be entered.

2 For a sole trader, most of the jobs within a business have to be performed by the owner. In this case, all the financial records are maintained by one person. As the business expands, more people will be employed and specialisation of role is possible. If the business continues to expand, then multiple people may be needed for roles within the same functional area.

In accounting, people could be given different roles. These may include responsibility for:

- maintaining the cash book
- maintaining the petty cash book
- a ledger (sales or purchases or nominal)
- one or more of the books of prime entry
- checking the accuracy of the records.

DEVELOPING

The purpose of this unit is to introduce students to the additional system used to record accounting transactions alongside book-keeping entries. Students may think that the double entry system is sufficient on its own for recording transactions. In addition, the books of prime entry provide further order to the process of recording and storing transactions in the accounting records.

Students rarely have difficulty with the content of this topic. Cash books and petty cash books are generally seen as straightforward. However, you will need to be vigilant in the following areas to ensure students do not get into poor habits, when errors may become more widespread than they should be.

- Balancing the cash book correctly – especially when it is a three column cashbook. Here the potential for messy or incorrect presentation of the cash book is more likely when there are both debit and credit closing balances at the end of the period for which the cash book is being maintained. In addition, ensure that the discounts column in the cash book is totalled and not balanced.
- Petty cash books have a layout which is unique. Remind students of the importance of the presentation of the petty cash book, which must show precision and accuracy, as well as clarity.

Students may view books of prime entry as an unusual topic after the introduction of double entry book-keeping. In Unit 2.1, the topic was logical and forward looking, in that each extra piece of information built on the previous piece. With books of prime entry, students may think they are taking a step backwards, as the focus is on how transactions are initially recorded before the book-keeping occurs.

Ask students which book of prime entry and which ledger an entry appears in, when discussing any future double entry transactions – even though this is not an explicit requirement of the question. It may be helpful to recap some of the questions from Unit 2.1 to check if students would recognise the location of the account in terms of books of prime entry and ledgers. Alternatively, this approach could be used when covering double entry transactions from Chapter 3 onwards.

Question 1 is most effective if introduced when working through an example of a cash book that has a debit balance for cash and a credit balance for bank. This reinforces the issue of credit balances on cash accounts. It is possible that the issue of credit balances in cash books has already arisen when teaching Unit 2.1.

If students find question 1 difficult, it may help to use prompt questions, for example:

- *What does a debit balance on the bank account mean?* (The business has money in the bank.)
- *What does a credit balance on the bank account mean?* (The business has an overdrawn balance on the bank account.)
- *What does a debit balance on the cash account mean?* (The business has cash.)
- *What does a credit balance on the cash account mean?* (Students may suggest the business owes cash to someone. Emphasise that a credit balance on cash is not possible. The business can have some cash (a debit balance) or no cash (no balance) but a credit balance would indicate 'negative cash', an impossibility.)

Suggested answer

1 A debit balance for cash means the business has cash available. A credit balance for cash would mean a negative amount of cash is held. A business can have some cash or no cash but cannot have a negative amount of cash. (It can owe money, but that would be a liability, not a credit balance on the cash account.)

Question 2 relates to the methods of automated payments and receipts found on a bank statement. Use of cheques has declined in recent years. Asking students why this is so may be a challenge to them. A prompt question may be useful here: *Do you know anyone who does not use automated services from their own bank account and, if so, why not?*

Suggested answers

2 Reasons include:

- People or businesses may be unwilling to give out their bank account details.
- People or businesses may not want to use online or telephone banking services.
- Where the bank account details of the person or business being paid are not known.

Question 3 is straightforward and may be used once the books of prime entry (and the type of transaction recorded within) has been covered.

Suggested answer

3 It must appear in the general journal as it does not meet the criteria for any other journal.

Once students are familiar with what is recorded in each book of prime entry, they should be able to answer question 4. However, their response may be limited to 'buying and selling assets on credit terms'.

This prompt question may elicit a clearer response: *What transactions have you recorded that do not use monetary payment and receipt, or do not deal with inventory?*

Suggested answer

4 Taking assets out of the business for private use (as drawings).

Use one or both of the following activities to bring the work of the unit together.

Activity: Which book of prime entry?

This activity is designed as a support activity, although it could be used as a consolidation exercise.

Approximate time required: 20 minutes

Resources: Resource 2.3A

Before the lesson: Print sufficient copies of the resource sheet for the class and prepare a set of cards for each student.

Individual work: Students place the cards under the correct headings in the table.

Answers

See Resource 2.3A before it is cut into cards.

Activity: Linking the books of prime entry to the double entry accounts

This activity is designed to give students practice in classifying transactions according to which book of prime entry they belong to and how the transactions are then posted to the double entry accounts.

Approximate time required: 15 minutes

Resources: Resource 2.3B

Before the lesson: Print a resource sheet for each pair.

Pair work: Students complete the table with the appropriate book of prime entry for each transaction and state which accounts are to be debited and credited.

Answer

Transaction	Book of prime entry	Account to be debited	Account to be credited
1 Owner contributes money in bank for business use	Cash book	Bank (or cash book)	Owner's equity
2 Goods purchased on credit returned to Gabriel	Purchases returns	Gabriel	Purchases returns
3 Motor expenses paid in cash	Cash book	Motor expenses	Cash (book)
4 Owner takes equipment out of business for personal use	General journal	Drawings	Equipment
5 Sale of printer used in business, on credit to Lewis	General journal	Lewis	Printer
6 Rent received by cheque	Cash book	Bank (or cash book)	Rent received
7 Discount received, given by Leyla	Cash book	Leyla	Discount received
8 Purchase of office furniture on credit for business use, from Mariam	General journal	Office furniture	Mariam
9 Cash held in business deposited into bank account	Cash book	Cash book (bank column)	Cash book (cash column)
10 Goods sold on credit to Jon are returned to business	Sales returns	Sales returns	Jon
11 Machinery given to Nathan in return for debt owed to this credit supplier	General journal	Nathan	Machinery
12 Purchase of cash till by a baker, paid by cheque	Cash book	Cash till	Cash book (or Bank)

APPLYING

The work covered so far has been for businesses that are traders, which are businesses earning profits by buying and selling goods. In reality, many businesses are not traders. The system of books of prime entry does not fit together as neatly with non-trading organisations and this is covered in question 1.

The petty cash book is only used by certain businesses and this is covered in question 2.

Suggested answers

1 For a service provider, purchases of physical goods are unlikely, which probably means there is no need for a purchases journal or purchases returns journal. It is also probable – depending on the service – that there will be no sales journal or sales returns journal. For example, many service providers operate on sales for immediate payment and do not offer credit periods for customers.

2 A petty cash book is more likely to be used in the following circumstances.

- There are many items of expenditure paid into and out of the cash book.
- There are many small-value items paid into and out of the cash book.
- A business wishes to give experience of book-keeping to a junior member of staff.
- A business prefers to delegate the tasks for maintaining cash books and petty cash books across staff members of a business.

Use the task to ensure students are confident preparing journal entries and double entry accounts.

Answer

Purchases journal		
2018		**$**
1 July	Joseph	45
4 July	Markus	54
16 July	Olga	81
31 July	Total for month	180

Sales journal		
2018		**$**
5 July	Robert	165
18 July	Noah	145
31 July	Total for month	310

Purchases returns journal		
2018		**$**
8 July	Joseph	24
21 July	Olga	11
31 July	Total for month	35

Sales returns journal		
2018		**$**
11 July	Robert	31
18 July	Noah	32
31 July	Total for month	63

Purchases					
2018		**$**	**2018**		**$**
31 July	Total purchases for month	180			

Sales					
2018		**$**	**2018**		**$**
			31 July	Total sales for month	310

Purchases returns					
2018		**$**	**2018**		**$**
			31 July	Total purchases returns for month	35

Sales returns					
2018		**$**	**2018**		**$**
31 July	Total sales returns for month	63			

Knowledge check

- **Resources:** Resource 2.3C
- **Answers**: See pages 221–222

Check your progress

Ask students to complete the **Check your progress** section in the Student's Book.

Support

- Ask students for an example of a transaction contained within each of the six books of prime entry. To make it more interesting, ask the first student to nominate a book of prime entry and then move around the class, with each student describing a transaction belonging in the named book of prime entry, followed by them stating a new book of prime entry for the next person to give an example for.
- **Workbook 2.3 Support**

Consolidation

- Students prepare revision cards for the unit. They write the key terms from the unit on one side of the cards and the definition on the other side. Students can then work in pairs and take turns identifying a key term from the definition or providing a definition given the key term.
- **Resources**: Resource 2.3D
- Alternatively or in addition, you can use the resource provided and students can match the key terms to the definitions. You can use this matching activity as a starter activity for lessons in this unit. You may also want to include key terms from earlier units.
- **Workbook 2.3 Practice**

Stretch

- Students construct a flow chart that tracks transactions from the initial business document, through to the book of prime entry and finally to being posted in the correct ledger account. Students may require A3 paper and the chart should be planned carefully. Although students will probably think this is easy, it is surprisingly difficult to get the correct flow clearly presented.
- **Workbook 2.3 Stretch**

Chapter review

- **Resources:** Resource Ch2 review
- **Answers:** See pages 222–224
- **Workbook: Chapter 2 review**

3 Verification of accounting records

Previous chapters have considered the book-keeping processes that are used in businesses across the world.

It is inevitable that errors will occur when preparing any form of accounting records. The verification of accounting records is routinely completed using a variety of techniques and procedures. This chapter considers four main methods:

- a trial balance
- suspense accounts
- control accounts
- bank reconciliations.

The chapter further develops double entry principles, applying them to the verification of accounting records.

Numerical examples and tasks enable students to consider:

- the trial balance
- correction of errors
- bank reconciliation
- control accounts.

Prior knowledge

Students should already be able to:

- use the accounting equation and understand the purpose of accounting
- prepare double entry ledger accounts.

They should have a good understanding of double entry accounting processes, be proficient in manipulating financial data and able to apply the duality principle accurately.

Background for non-subject specialists

This chapter considers how the accounting statements of a business can be verified. There are accounting processes that try to ensure accounting records represent a true and fair view of the business and are free from error. These processes include the preparation of a trial balance, knowing how to correct errors that occur, bank reconciliations and the production of control accounts.

In particular, when preparing a trial balance, students need to be able to separate the debit balances and credit balances. It may be useful to remind them that:

- asset and expense accounts appear on the debit side of the trial balance
- liabilities, capital and income accounts appear on the credit side.

3.1 The trial balance

Learning objectives

By the end of this unit, students should be able to:

- understand that a trial balance is a statement of ledger balances on a particular date
- outline the uses and limitations of a trial balance
- prepare a trial balance from a given list of balances and amend a trial balance which contains errors
- identify and explain those errors which do not affect the trial balance – commission, compensating, complete reversal, omission, original entry, principle.

Resources

- Student's Book pages 71–79
- Workbook pages 17–19
- Resource 3.1A
- Resource 3.1B
- Resource 3.1C
- Pro-forma 7

Key terms

Trial balance, Revenue, Stock take,

Errors of: Commission, Compensating, Complete reversal, Omission, Original entry, Principle

STARTING POINT

The questions are designed to encourage students to think further about the double entry system in practice. Students should have completed plenty of practice in entering transactions in ledger accounts. They will require this knowledge when preparing a trial balance.

If students find question 1 difficult it may help to use prompt questions, for example:

- Which double entry accounts have you prepared where you have entered most of the entries on the debit side of the account? (trade receivables, purchases, expenses)
- Which double entry accounts have you prepared where you have entered most of the entries on the credit side of the account? (trade payables, sales, income)

Suggested answers

1 (a) Debit balance:

- trade receivables
- cash
- regular expenses – general expenses, rent, wages, utilities (gas, electricity, water), insurance
- purchases
- assets – premises, fixtures and fittings, motor vehicles
- inventory

(b) Credit balance:

- owner's equity/capital
- trade payables
- sales
- loan
- mortgage

2 Bank – debit balance (cash in the bank)/credit balance (bank overdraft)

Provision for irrecoverable debts

Asset disposal account

EXPLORING

These questions build on the work completed in chapters 1 and 2 and prepare students for the study of:

- bank reconciliations
- correction of errors
- control accounts.

Suggested answers

1 A list of balances:
   - is easier to read
   - enables a business to prepare its annual financial statements
   - assists in the identification of errors

2 As every debit entry has a credit entry when preparing the ledger accounts, the total of debit balances and the total of credit balances should be the same.

DEVELOPING

Students who have a good understanding of double entry book-keeping usually find this topic quite straightforward. For those students who have difficulty with the concept, the acronym PEARLS may assist.

Trial balance			
Debit entries		Credit entries	
P E A		R L S	

where:

P = purchases A = assets L = liabilities

E = expenses R = revenue (income) S = sales (revenue).

Activity: Trial balance – debit or credit?

This activity is designed to ensure students are confident in categorising items as debit or credit. Use as a starter activity.

Approximate time required: 20 minutes

Resources: Resource 3.1A, list of suggested debit/credit items (see below)

Before the lesson: Print sufficient copies of the resource sheet for the class. Prepare sets of two cards, one set per student.

Class work: Explain that you are going to call out various items that would appear in a trial balance (see suggested list below). Students identify whether the item would appear as a debit or credit in the trial balance by holding up either a debit or credit card.

Suggested items for debit or credit activity

Debit balances	Credit balances
Land and buildings	Liabilities
Purchases	Revenue (sales)
Sales returns	Purchases returns
Drawings	Owner's equity (capital)
Administration expenses	Commission received
Trade receivables	Provision for depreciation

Debit balances	Credit balances
Cash	Trade payables
Bank balance	Bank overdraft
Opening inventory	Mortgage
Motor vehicles	Loan

Question 1 allows students to consider the difference between debit and credit entries. For those having difficulty with the question, suggest that they think about the difference between a debit bank balance and a credit bank balance. From this, they should be able to make the link to cash.

Suggested answers

1 There is a mistake in the cash account entries. There can either be 'some cash' – a debit balance, or 'no cash' – a zero balance. There cannot be a negative cash balance, which is what a credit balance would imply. The business can borrow cash but this would be shown as a liability elsewhere in the accounts.

Activity: Preparing a trial balance

This activity is designed to ensure all students understand how a trial balance is prepared.

Approximate time required: 15 minutes

Resources required: Resource 3.1B

Before the lesson: Print sufficient copies of the resource sheet for the class

Individual work: Students complete the table to ensure the items are correctly categorised as either debit or credit in the trial balance.

Answer

Item	Debit	Credit
Revenue		✗
Purchases	✗	
Bank overdraft		✗
Land and buildings	✗	
Wages and salaries	✗	
Trade receivables	✗	
Trade payables		✗
Owner's equity		✗
Drawings	✗	
Rent received		✗
Sales returns	✗	
Purchases returns		✗
Bank loan		✗
Opening inventory	✗	

Question 2 reviews the use of a trial balance and also prepares students for the work that will be completed in Chapter 5.

Suggested answer

2 Yes, it can. All it needs is the entries from the ledger accounts. However, all the accounts would need to be balanced individually. There would be a risk that errors affecting the trial balance would not be detected. It would also take a long time to search through all the ledger accounts to find all the relevant balances.

Before they attempt to answer question 3, ensure that students fully understand errors and the trial balance. Clarify that there are two main categories of error. Then consider each type of error in turn. You could use the following activity.

Activity: Identifying errors

This activity allows you to check students' understanding of each of the errors.

Approximate time required: 5 minutes

Discussion: Give the class examples of errors that can occur and ask them to identify the error described. For example:

1 A business has omitted a payment of $2000 to a supplier.

2 Cash of $3140 paid to a supplier was posted as $3410.

3 Cash received from Loukas has been credited to the account of Lukas.

4 Credit purchases of $93 from Harper were debited to Harper's account and credited to Purchases.

5 Motor expenses of $75 was actually a payment made for the owner's private expenses.

6 If the non-current asset account is incorrectly totalled and understated by $550, and the heat and light account is incorrect totalled and overstated by $550, then the trial balance will still balance.

Answers

1 Error of omission

2 Error of original entry

3 Error of commission

4 Error of complete reversal

5 Error of principle

6 Compensating error

Question 3 provides a review question that could be used as a stretch task towards the end of the topic.

Suggested answer

3 If different amounts are added for the debit and credit entries of a transaction, the totals of the debit and credit columns of the trial balance will be different.

APPLYING

This task requires students to identify errors in a trial balance that has already been prepared. They will need to have a good understanding of the underlying principles in order to correct the errors.

Answers

	Dr	Cr
	$	$
Revenue		455000
Purchases	252521	

	Dr	Cr
	$	$
Sales returns	5451	
Purchases returns		4544
Premises	250000	
Commission received		12312
Heating and lighting	8989	
Machinery	26800	
Inventory at 1 January 2018	31313	
Trade payables		14519
Trade receivables	18908	
Bank	11808	
Wages	39800	
General expenses	8377	
Owner's equity		191000
Drawings	23408	
	677375	677375

Knowledge check

- **Resources**: Pro-forma 6
- **Answers**: See pages 224–225

Check your progress

Ask students to complete the Check your progress section in the Student's Book.

Support

- **Resources**: Resource 3.1A
- Ask students for examples of items in a trial balance. For each item, students decide whether it is a debit or credit entry. You could use the cards from Resource 3.1A for this.
- **Workbook 3.1 Support**

Consolidation

- Students prepare revision cards for the unit. They write a key term from the unit on one side of the card and the definition on the other side. Students can then work in pairs and take turns identifying a key term from the definition or providing a definition, given the key term.
- **Resources**: Resource 3.1C

  Alternatively or in addition, you can use the resource provided and students can match the key terms to the definitions. You can use this matching activity as a starter activity for lessons in this unit. You may also want to include key terms from earlier units.
- **Workbook 3.1 Practice**

Stretch

- Students revisit the double entry accounts they prepared in Unit 2.1 **Knowledge check** questions 7, 8 and 9 and prepare a trial balance. This allows them to see how the ledger accounts would be used.
- **Workbook 3.1 Stretch**

3.2 Correction of errors

Learning objectives

By the end of this unit, students should be able to:

- correct errors by means of journal entries
- explain the use of a suspense account as a temporary measure to balance the trial balance
- correct errors by means of suspense accounts
- adjust a profit or loss for an accounting period after the correction of errors
- understand the effect of correction of errors on a statement of financial position.

Resources

- Student's Book pages 80–90
- Workbook pages 20–22
- Resource 3.2A
- Pro-forma 1
- Pro-forma 5
- Pro-forma 8

Key terms

Undercasting, Overcasting, Transposition, Suspense account

STARTING POINT

This unit builds on the uses of a trial balance and the errors that do not affect a trial balance. The questions recap the work covered in Unit 3.1.

Suggested answers

1 Producing a trial balance is helpful for a business.

- It provides an arithmetic check on the accuracy of the double-entry book-keeping.
- It makes it easier to produce the financial statements of the business.

As a stretch task, ask students to identify the limitations of preparing a trial balance. (The time it takes to produce, the fact that even if the totals of the trial balance are the same, errors may exist in the accounts. Some types of error are not detected by the trial balance.)

Suggested answers

2 Errors include:

- commission
- compensating
- complete reversal
- omission
- original entry
- principle.

Check that students understand the definition of each error (see the glossary in the Student's Book).

EXPLORING

These questions build on the work completed in chapters 1 and 2 and prepare the students for study of:

- bank reconciliations
- control accounts.

Both questions consider the errors studied in Unit 3.1. Advise those students finding these questions difficult to revisit the work of the previous unit. For question 2, clarify that students understand the definition of each error.

Suggested answers

1 (b) and (c)

2 Types of error include:
   - the omission of one entry in a transaction
   - an error of calculation
   - multiple errors have occurred in the financial accounts.

DEVELOPING

Students who have a good understanding of how to prepare a trial balance should find the correction of errors quite straightforward. However, this is one of the most complex topics studied in accounting. Students require both mathematical skills and numerical dexterity in order to apply the concepts of double entry to correct the errors that have been identified. The topic is often referred to as a problem-solving topic.

When studying this topic, students should start by correcting errors that do not affect the trial balance. They should review the errors that they studied in Unit 3.1.

Activity: Errors that do not affect the trial balance

This activity reinforces understanding of errors that do not affect the trial balance.

Approximate time required: 30 minutes

Resources: Resource 3.1C (optional)

Pair/group work: Ask students to write a definition of each of the six errors that they met in Unit 3.1. Alternatively, use the cards relating to the six errors from Resource 3.1C for a matching activity.

Work through the worked examples in the Student Book.

Recap the activity on identifying errors given in Unit 3.1 (page 78), focusing this time on how students would correct the error. Then provide additional practical examples of how to correct each error. For extra practice, use the same errors but change the numbers throughout.

Question 1 allows students to consider how errors may be identified in practice. To introduce the task, ask students what is meant by an error of commission. Elicit examples.

Suggested answers

1 Errors may be discovered when a business:
   - sends a statement of account and a request for payment to a credit customer who is incorrectly identified as owing the business money, or owing more than they actually do
   - makes a payment to the wrong credit supplier.

Before the work on correcting those errors that do affect the trial balance, recap the format of the general journal (see Student's Book Unit 2.3, page 62), so students know how to record journal entries. Use practical examples to reinforce understanding. Explain the use of narratives in the general journal.

Question 2 reviews the purpose of a suspense account. This question should be used as a stretch task. The concepts involved here are quite complex.

Suggested answers

2 The suspense account deals with errors that affect the trial balance. Therefore, a suspense account that balances does not mean no errors are present. Any of the errors that do not affect the trial balance could still exist despite a suspense account having no outstanding balance.

Discuss how the correction of errors affects the financial statements of a business. Clarify that when all errors are located and corrected, the balance on the suspense account is cleared.

APPLYING

Use this activity to ensure students are confident with correcting errors and the calculation of revised profit for the year.

Answers

General journal extract		
	Dr	Cr
	$	$
Purchases returns	52	
Suspense		52
Expense originally overcast – now corrected		
Drawings	50	
Motor expenses		50
Error of principle – private expense included within business expenses, now corrected		
Wages	136	
Suspense		136
Incorrect entry – wrong total and wrong side of account, now corrected		
Jana	9	
Sales		9
Error of original entry – accounts corrected by adjustment of $9 in each account		

Suspense					
		$			$
	Balance b/d	188	Purchases returns		52
			Wages		136
		188			188

Wrightson Ltd Statement of corrected profit for the year ended 31 December 2018		
		$
Profit before adjustment		750
Less purchase returns		(52)
Add motor expenses		50
Less wages		(136)
Add sales		9
Corrected profit for the year		621

Knowledge check

- **Resources**: Pro-forma 1, Pro-forma 5, Pro-forma 8
- **Answers**: See pages 225–226

Check your progress

Ask students to complete the **Check your progress** section in the Student's Book.

Support

- Ask students for examples of errors that would not be identified by a trial balance.
- **Workbook 3.2 Support**

Consolidation

- Students prepare revision cards for the unit. They write a key term from the unit on one side of the card and the definition on the other side. Students can then work in pairs and take turns identifying a key term from the definition or providing a definition given the key term.
- **Resources**: Resource 3.2A

  Alternatively or in addition, you can use the resource provided and students can match the key terms to the definitions. You can use this matching activity as a starter activity for lessons in this unit. You may also want to include key terms from earlier units, particularly Unit 3.1.
- **Workbook 3.2 Practice**

Stretch

- Students construct a flow chart that demonstrates how different errors are corrected. Theys may require A3 paper and the chart should be planned carefully. Although students will probably think this is easy, it is surprisingly difficult to get the correct flow clearly presented.
- **Workbook 3.2 Stretch**

3.3 Bank reconciliation

Learning objectives

By the end of this unit, students should be able to:

- understand the use and purpose of a bank statement
- update the cash book for bank charges, bank interest paid and received, correction of errors, credit transfers, direct debits, dividends, and standing orders
- understand the purpose of, and prepare, a bank reconciliation statement to include bank errors, uncredited deposits and unpresented cheques.

Resources

- Student's Book pages 91–101
- Workbook pages 23–26
- Resource 3.3A
- Resource 3.3B
- Pro-forma 1
- Pro-forma 3
- Pro-forma 8

Key terms

Bank reconciliation, Credit transfer, Direct debits, Standing orders, Updated cash book, Bank reconciliation statement, Unpresented cheque, Uncredited deposit, Stale cheque, Dishonoured cheque

STARTING POINT

These questions recap the work from Chapters 1 and 2.

As a stretch task for question 1, ask students to identify entries that could occur in the cash book. As a research task, they could review the difference between a three column and two column cash book.

As a stretch task for question 2, students define each of the items on a bank statement. It might help students to look at actual bank statements that they may have at home.

Suggested answers

1 A cash book is a financial journal that contains all cash receipts and payments. This will include bank deposits and withdrawals.

Entries in the cash book are transferred and posted into the general ledger.

2 Items include:

- cash deposits
- cash withdrawals
- bank charges
- interest paid
- interest received
- credit transfers
- standing orders
- direct debits.

EXPLORING

The questions allow students to think about the purposes of bank statements and cash books in businesses. When completing question 1, students need to understand the difference between debit and credit balances.

Suggested answers

1 Reasons include:

- automated transactions
- timing differences

- errors have been made (either by the bank or, more likely, by the business)
- fraud or embezzlement has occurred.

2 The cash book contains both cash and bank transactions. Therefore, there are more transactions that potentially could have errors.

The cash book should contain all bank items. However, a number of these will be direct payments and receipts, which may be omitted, such as standing orders, direct debits, bank charges.

DEVELOPING

This unit focuses on updating the cash book and reconciliation of the bank statement. Students should know how to prepare a cash book. Give students who find cash book preparation difficult additional practice before commencing work on this unit.

Question 1 considers how contactless transactions would appear in the cash book of a business. Introduce the topic by asking: *What is a contactless transaction?* Discuss the benefits and problems of using contactless transactions. (Benefits – quick and convenient. Problems – relies on technology, possibility of fraud, not as secure as 'chip and pin' and not accepted everywhere.)

Suggested answer

1 They should appear as credit entries in the cash book.

Activity: Debit or credit?

This activity is designed to ensure students are confident in categorising items as debit or credit in the cashbook and the bank statement. Use as a starter activity.

Approximate time required: 20 minutes

Resources: Resource 3.3A; list of items appearing in a cash book/bank statement (see suggested list below)

Before the lesson: Print sufficient copies of the resource sheet for the class. Prepare sets of four cards, one set per student.

Class work: Explain that you are going to call out items that appear in a cash book and/or in a bank statement (see suggested list below). Students identify where the item should appear in the cash book and bank statement by holding up the correct cards.

Suggested items

	Cashbook	Bank statement
Dividends received	Debit	Credit
Bank charges	Credit	Debit
Cash received	Debit	Does not appear (students raise neither card)
Bank interest received	Debit	Credit
Direct debit paid	Credit	Debit
Standing order paid	Credit	Debit

Point out that the bank column of the business cash book and the bank statement issued by the bank should be the same, as they are a record of the same set of transactions.

Question 2 relates to the use of standing orders. Ask: *When might you or your family use a standing order?*

Suggested answer

2 This is used for making regular payments of the same amount to one person or business for example, monthly rent.

Before moving on to question 3, spend five minutes asking for definitions of key terms: bank reconciliation statement, unpresented cheque, uncredited deposit. Students may find question 3 challenging. Discuss which methods of payments are likely to be in use in 10 years' time.

Suggested answer

3 Largely, delays of days will disappear. There are still some delays in making electronic payments between two accounts but these are shorter – often hours rather than days. Some businesses take longer to log a payment than others, so the delays will not disappear entirely.

APPLYING

Use this task to ensure students are confident preparing updated cash books and bank reconciliation statements.

Answer

Updated cash book (bank columns only)					
1 Jul	Balance b/d	542	2 Jul	Marios	312
4 Jul	Althea	635	9 Jul	Interest	44
17 Jul	Credit transfer	180	10 Jul	Standing order: Baatar	275
18 Jul	Ivan	87	13 Jul	Direct debit: Insurance	112
20 Jul	Hao	190	20 Jul	Cheque dishonoured: Althea	635
29 Jul	Leyla	331	25 Jul	Bank charges	11
			22 Jul	Ranjit	143
			27 Jul	Carlos	240
			31 Jul	Balance c/d	193
		1965			1965

Bank reconciliation statement as at August 1	
	$
Balance on updated cashbook	193
Add unpresented cheques:	240
	433
Less uncredited deposits:	331
Balance on bank statement	102

Knowledge check

- **Resources**: Pro-forma 1, Pro-forma 3, Pro-forma 8
- **Answers**: See pages 226–227

Check your progress

Ask students to complete the **Check your progress** section in the Student's Book.

Support

- Ask students for examples of items that will appear in a business's cash book.
- **Workbook 3.3 Support**

Consolidation

- Students prepare revision cards for the unit. They write a key term related to bank reconciliation (see Resource 3.3B) on one side of the card and the definition on the other side. Students can then work in pairs and take turns identifying a term from the definition or providing a definition, given the term.
- **Resources**: Resource 3.3B
- Alternatively or in addition, you can use the resource provided and students can match the terms to the definitions. You can use this matching activity as a starter activity for lessons in this unit. You may also want to include key terms from earlier units.
- **Workbook 3.3 Practice**

Stretch

- Students construct a flow chart that demonstrates how the cash book, bank statement and bank reconciliation statement link together.
- **Workbook 3.3 Stretch**

3.4 Control accounts

Learning objectives

By the end of this unit, students should be able to:

- understand the purposes of purchases ledger and sales ledger control accounts
- identify the books of prime entry as sources of information for the control account entries
- prepare purchases ledger and sales ledger control accounts to include credit purchases and sales, receipts and payments, cash discounts, returns, irrecoverable debts, dishonoured cheques, interest on overdue accounts, contra entries, refunds, opening and closing balances (debit and credit within each account).

Resources

- Student's Book pages 102–114
- Workbook pages 27–30
- Resource 3.4A
- Resource 3.4B
- Resource 3.4C
- Pro-forma 1
- Pro-forma 7
- Pro-forma 8

Key terms

Sales ledger control account, Purchases ledger control account, Memorandum accounts, Irrecoverable debt, Written off, Contra entry

STARTING POINT

Students may find it helpful to revisit the work that they have covered in Chapters 1 and 2. Introduce the topic through a discussion of sources and recording of data.

As a stretch task for question 1, students could consider what is included in a purchases ledger.

Suggested answer

1 The sales ledger records the sales of a business, regardless of whether or not the business has received the money and how much the business is still owed. The sales ledger has an account for every business customer.

Activity: Books of prime entry

This activity will assist students to review the books of prime entry used in a business.

Approximate time required: 15 minutes

Resources: Resource 3.4A

Before the lesson: Print sufficient copies of the resource sheet for the class.

Individual work: Students complete the table by identifying the transactions that are recorded in each of the books of prime entry.

Answer

Book of prime entry	Transactions recorded
Cash book	All cash (and bank) transactions
Petty cash book	All small items of cash payment
Sales journal	All credit sales of goods
Purchases journal	All credit purchases of goods bought for resale
Sales returns journal	Sales returns of goods previously sold
Purchases returns journal	Purchases returns of goods previously purchased
General journal	Any transaction not covered by the other journals

The purpose of question 2 is for students to consider the reasons why a business allows trade credit.

Suggested answer

2 A business will allow trade credit to increase the number of customers that they currently have. Trade credit will act as a unique selling point for some businesses. This will allow a business to buy goods now and pay for them later.

EXPLORING

Question 1 could be linked to starting point question 1.

Suggested answers

1 The purchases ledger records the purchases of a business, regardless of whether or not the business has paid the money and how much the business still owes. The purchases ledger has an account for every business supplier.

2 The business would have no need to keep a sales ledger or purchases ledger as it only permits cash sales and purchases.

DEVELOPING

Understanding the books of prime entry forms the foundation of the work in this unit.

Activity: Control accounts

This activity is intended to introduce the topic of prime entry.

Approximate time required: 5 minutes

Discussion: Ask students to discuss the benefits of a business using books of prime entry.

Suggested answers

- Totals are posted from the books of prime entry instead of each individual entry. This means the double entry accounts are used less frequently and are easier to read as a result.
- The books of prime entry provide a back-up to information contained in the double entry accounts. This is useful when records are missing.
- Responsibility for maintaining the financial records can be delegated to different workers. Each person maintains a different book of prime entry.

Introduce the two main control accounts. Question 1 allows students to consider the methods of payment that can be used to settle business accounts.

Discuss different payment methods used in the past, currently and likely to be used in the near future. Consider the benefits and problems of the use of technology in payment systems.

Suggested answer

1 Normally, customers settle accounts by payment. Other ways include sales returns, discounts allowed (for partial settlement), irrecoverable debts – where the customer cannot settle so the business decides to settle that debt by cancelling it.

Activity: Control accounts

This activity illustrates the differences and similarities between the sales ledger control account and purchases ledger control account.

Approximate time required: 30 minutes

Resources: Resource 3.4B

Before the lesson: Print sufficent copies of the resource sheet for the class.

Pair/group work: Students complete the two tables to illustrate the difference between the two control accounts.

Answers

Information used in the sales ledger control account	
Item in the sales ledger control account	**Location of information**
Opening balance	Personal accounts in the sales ledger
Credit sales	Sales journal
Payments received	Cash book (bank column – debit side)
Discounts allowed	Cash book (discounts column – debit side)
Sales returns	Sales returns journal
Closing balance	Personal accounts in the sales ledger

Information used in purchases ledger control account	
Item in purchases ledger control account	**Location of information**
Opening balance	Personal accounts in the purchases ledger
Credit purchases	Purchases journal
Payments made to suppliers	Cash book (bank column – credit side)
Discounts received	Cash book (discounts column – credit side)
Purchases returns	Purchases returns journal
Interest due on overdue accounts owing to suppliers	Nominal ledger account for interest due
Closing balance	Personal accounts in the purchases ledger

Questions 2 and 3 could be used as homework or research questions. They encourage students to consider why interest is charged on overdue accounts and reviews when contra entries could be used in accounting.

Suggested answers

2 Interest can be charged on overdue accounts to encourage customers to settle their accounts promptly – the assumption being that customers will not want to incur interest added on to their debts.

3 A contra entry may appear in the cash book. This happens either when cash is banked (debiting bank but crediting the cash columns) or when cash is withdrawn from the bank (debiting cash but crediting the bank columns).

Before introducing question 4, examine the reasons for a credit balance in the sales ledger and reasons for a debit balances in the purchases ledger. Question 4 requires students to analyse why businesses may pay in advance for goods that they intend to purchase in the future but for which they have not yet placed an order.

Suggested answers

4 It may pay in advance:
- if it thinks the price may rise in the future
- If it thinks there is likely to be shortage
- If it is a requirement of the supplier.

APPLYING

Use these questions to review the topic of control accounts.

Suggested answers

1 Errors include:
- transactions that are not entered in a book of prime entry, which will also be omitted from both the individual account and the control account
- transactions that are entered incorrectly in the book of prime entry, which will be repeated in both the individual account and the control account
- casting errors (addition errors) in the book of prime entry, which will affect the control account but not the individual account
- transactions that are misposted from the prime record to the individual account, although the control account is not affected.

2 Businesses that have a considerable number of credit sales and purchases would benefit most from the production of control accounts. These tend to be large businesses in either the retail or manufacturing sectors. Students may make other appropriate business suggestions.

3 The use of accounting software reduces the benefits of preparing control accounts. For example, in a manual system, separate persons would prepare the control account and the ledger accounts. This would aid security in the business; however, in a computerised system, both will be prepared electronically.

Knowledge check

- **Resources**: Pro-forma 1
- **Answers**: See pages 227–228

Check your progress

Ask students to complete the **Check your progress** section in the Student's Book.

Support

- Ask students for examples of items that would appear in:
  - a sales ledger control account.
  - a purchases ledger control account
- **Workbook 3.4 Support**

Consolidation

- Students prepare revision cards for the unit. They write a key term from the unit on one side of the card and the definition on the other side. Students can then work in pairs and take turns identifying a key term from the definition or providing a definition, given the key term.
- **Resources**: Resource 3.4C

  Alternatively or in addition, you can use the resource provided and students can match the key terms to the definitions. You can use this matching activity as a starter activity for lessons in this unit. You may also want to include key terms from earlier units.
- **Workbook 3.4 Practice**

Stretch

- Students construct a flow chart that demonstrates how the sales ledger control account and purchases ledger control account link to the books of prime entry. This may require A3 paper and should be planned carefully.
- **Workbook 3.4 Stretch**

Chapter review

- **Resources:** Pro-forma 1, Pro-forma 7, Pro-forma 8
- **Answers:** See pages 229–231
- **Workbook: Chapter 3 review**

4 Accounting procedures

This chapter reviews five key accounting procedures:

- capital and revenue expenditure and receipts
- accounting for depreciation and disposal of non-current assets
- other payables and other receivables
- irrecoverable debts and provision for doubtful debts
- valuation of inventory.

The numerical examples and tasks enable students to acquire the skills required to apply these techniques to the preparation of financial statements in Chapter 6. They will also learn various procedures for adjusting double-entry accounts.

Prior knowledge

Students should already be able to:

- use the accounting equation and understand the purpose of accounting
- prepare double-entry ledger accounts.

Background for non-subject specialists

The chapter considers how income and expenditure are divided into different types. This classification impacts on the financial statements of a business. The chapter reviews how the depreciation of non-current assets is calculated and accounted for, together with the subsequent impact of this depreciation on the profit and asset valuations. How businesses account for being unable to collect debts owing to them is explored, as well as how a business accounts for the possibility of being unable to collect future amounts owing to them.

Finally, the chapter looks at adjustments made in the double entry accounts for expenses and incomes unpaid during the period or paid in advance of the period for which the accounts are prepared.

4.1 Capital and revenue expenditure and receipts

Learning objectives

By the end of this unit, students should be able to:

- distinguish between and account for capital expenditure and revenue expenditure
- distinguish between and account for capital receipts and revenue receipts
- calculate and comment on the effect on profit of incorrect treatment
- calculate and comment on the effect on asset valuations of incorrect treatment.

Resources

- Student's Book pages 121–128
- Workbook pages 34–36
- Resource 4.1A
- Resource 4.1B
- Resource 4.1C
- Resource 4.1D

Key terms

Capital expenditure, Revenue expenditure, Capital receipts, Revenue receipts

STARTING POINT

These questions consider the relationship between assets and profitability.

Question 1 reviews the use of the accounting equation (see Unit 1.2). Ask students to state the accounting equation before introducing the question $\left(\frac{\text{capital}}{\text{equity}} = \text{assests} - \text{liabilities}\right)$.

Question 2 prepares students for the work they are going to complete in Chapter 5.

Suggested answers

1 When assets are purchased on credit, the assets will increase and liabilities will increase due to the increase in trade payables. This means that the ratio $\frac{\text{capital}}{\text{equity}}$ of the business will remain unchanged.

2 Profit for an accounting period is calculated as gross profit *plus* additional income *less* expenses.

EXPLORING

These questions consider the impact of buying and selling assets on the business's profit.

Suggested answers

1 There will be no direct impact on the business's profit.

2 The sale of assets does not directly increase profits. The business needs to work out whether it has made a profit or loss on the sale of an asset. For example, if a business sells a piece of machinery that cost £50 000 for £25 000 cash, having depreciated it by £30 000, the business will make a profit on sale of £5000. This would increase the profit for the year by £5000. However, if a loss had been made on the sale of an asset, then the profit for the year would decrease.

DEVELOPING

Students generally find capital and revenue expenditure and receipts straightforward.

Activity: Capital vs revenue expenditure

This activity is designed to help students understand the difference between capital and revenue expenditure in practice.

Approximate time required: 30 minutes

Resources: Resource 4.1A

Before the lesson: Print sufficient copies of the resource sheet for the class.

Individual/pair work: Students complete the table with examples of capital and revenue expenditure relating to two different non-current assets.

Suggested answers

Example	Capital expenditure	Revenue expenditure
Delivery van	Purchase cost Delivery cost Modifications to the van Painting of the company logo on the van	Road tax Insurance Fuel Servicing Repairs
Machinery	Purchase cost Delivery cost Installation costs Testing costs Staff training costs	Power costs Insurance Servicing Repairs Maintenance

Question 1 considers the subjective nature of some accounting decision making, in particular, the classification of expenditure. Prior to introducing the question, clarify the meaning of **subjective** and **objective**.

Suggested answer

1 Different people will have different opinions about whether an item is capital or revenue expenditure. This means that the decision on classifying expenditure may be subjective. For example, for a very small business, an asset worth £1000 may be a capital expenditure but for a multinational company a £1000 item would be insignificant and be classified as an expense.

Question 2 reviews the difference between cash receipts and profit. As a stretch task, students could review the matching principle.

Suggested answer

2 Cash receipts are money that is actually received by a business such as cash from sales. Profit is calculated as revenue receipts *less* revenue expenditure.

Activity: Capital and revenue expenditure and receipts

This activity is designed to enable students to understand the difference between capital and revenue expenditure and receipts. Use as a plenary activity for this topic.

Approximate time required: 30 minutes

Resources: Resource 4.1B, list of capital and revenue items (see below)

Before the lesson: Print sufficient copies of the resource sheet for the class. Prepare sets of four cards, one set per student.

Class work: Explain that you are going to call out examples of capital and revenue items (see the list below). Students categorise the items by holding up the correct card.

Suggested capital and expenditure items

Capital expenditure	Revenue expenditure
Cost of buying assets	Maintenance and repairs
Delivery costs	Replacement parts
Import costs (if applicable)	Power costs (electricity, gas, fuel)
Cost of installation	Wages of the operators
Initial testing and safety certificate	Operating costs
Initial training of employees	Insurance
Legal costs of buying assets (e.g. solicitors fees for buying premises)	Rent
Capital receipts	**Revenue receipts**
Additions of money to the business from the owner	Sale of inventory
Loans and other long-term borrowing taken out by the business	Commission received
Sales of non-current assets	Rent received
Issue of shares (only for a limited company)	Profit on disposal of non-current assets

APPLYING

These questions explore how capital and revenue expenditure are applied in practice.

Suggested answers

1 Paper for an office printer should be treated as a revenue expenditure. It is a regular payment that a business makes and should be classified as an expense.

2 Business equipment, such as computers, is classified as capital expenditure and would be recorded as non-current assets in the statement of financial position.

Knowledge check

- **Answers**: See pages 231–232

Check your progress

Ask students to complete the **Check your progress** section in the Student's Book.

Support

- **Resources**: Resource 4.1C

  Ask students what type of error has been made when capital expenditure is treated as revenue expenditure (error of principle). Use the matching activity on the resource provided to review the effect of incorrect treatment of expenditure.

- **Workbook 4.1 Support**

Consolidation

- Students prepare revision cards for the unit. They write a key term from the unit on one side of the card and the definition on the other side. Students can then work in pairs and take turns identifying a key term from the definition or providing a definition given the key term.

- **Resources**: Resource 4.1D

  Alternatively or in addition, you can use the resource provided and students can match the key terms to the definitions. You can use this matching activity as a starter activity for lessons in this unit. You may also want to include key terms from earlier units.
- **Workbook 4.1 Practice**

Stretch

- Students choose a business with which they are familiar. They prepare a presentation that explains the difference between capital and revenue expenditure and income. The presentation should include practical examples from the business of their choice.
- **Workbook 4.1 Stretch**

4.2 Accounting for depreciation and disposal of non-current assets

Learning objectives

By the end of this unit, students should be able to:

- define depreciation
- explain the reasons for accounting for depreciation
- name and describe the straight line, reducing balance and revaluation methods of depreciation
- prepare ledger accounts and journal entries for the provision of depreciation
- prepare ledger accounts and journal entries to record the sale of non-current assets, including the use of disposal accounts.

Resources

- Student's Book pages 129–142
- Workbook pages 37–38
- Resource 4.2A
- Resource 4.2B
- Pro-forma 1
- Pro-forma 3
- Pro-forma 9

Key terms

Non-current asset, Depreciation, Provision, Straight line method of depreciation, Residual value, Reducing balance method of depreciation, Net book value, Revaluation method of depreciation, Asset disposal, Asset disposal account

STARTING POINT

These questions consider the assets that are used in a business. Introduce the topic by asking students to name the two types of asset (non-current and current).

Suggested answers

1 They are classified as non-current assets and appear in the statement of financial position.

2 Businesses purchase assets to enable the business to complete the operations of the business. For example, a car manufacturer may purchase a machine to attach doors to the car vehicles.

EXPLORING

Question 1 relates to the **historic cost principle**, which is studied in more detail in Chapter 7 (see Student's Book, page 348). At this stage students should be able to consider that businesses will want to be able to use an objective value rather than a subjective one.

Suggested answers

1 A business needs to value its assets at the original cost as this is an objective measure. If the business were to value its assets each year, the value would be subjective.

2 The business will need to use an estimate based on previous experience as to how long an asset is likely to last.

DEVELOPING

The topic of depreciation and disposal of assets underpins the preparation of financial statements, which students will undertake in Chapter 5.

Activity: Mind map of non-current assets

Use this as a starter activity.

Approximate time required: 10 minutes

Individual/pair work: Ask students to produce a mind map of non-current assets that would be found in a hotel.

Suggested answer

Students might include in their mind maps: premises, bedroom fixtures and fittings, kitchen equipment, motor vehicles, leisure centre equipment.

Question 1 considers the lifespan of non-current assets. Before introducing the question, elicit the meaning of depreciation and the factors affecting the useful economic life of assets (wear and tear, depletion, obsolescence). Remind students that not all non-current assets have a limited lifespan.

Suggested answer

1 In general, non-current assets, for example land, that do not have a limited lifespan are not depreciated.

Work through the three methods of depreciation. Advise students to learn the formulae for straight line and reducing balance depreciation. Use the worked examples in the Student's Book to highlight the differences between the methods. Follow up with a number of practical numerical examples for each of the methods, to ensure students are fully familiar with the calculations involved.

Suggested answers

2 The residual value is estimated as zero for an asset likely to be scrapped and disposed of at the end of its useful life.

3 Depreciation charge (per year) = $\frac{\$20\,000 - \$3000}{5 \text{ years}}$ = \$3400 each year

Activity: Which depreciation method is best?

This activity is designed to enable students to identify the advantages of all three methods of depreciation.

Approximate time required: 25 minutes

Resources: Resource 4.2A

Before the lesson: Print sufficient copies of the resource sheet for the class.

Individual/pair/group work: Students identify the advantages of each method of depreciation and complete the table. Ensure all student's books are closed to prevent copying from the text.

Answers

See Student Book, page 135.

Question 4 should prompt students to think about which method of depreciation is best. Emphasise that although the straight line method is the easiest to use, the most appropriate method should be selected.

Suggested answers

4 Using the reducing balance method, the amount of depreciation will decrease each year. This will be counter-balanced by the increase in maintenance and repair costs. Therefore, throughout the life of the vehicle the depreciation and maintenance costs together will remain relatively constant.

Question 5 considers the use of the general journal when accounting for non-current assets.

Suggested answer

5 The general journal is used to record the purchase and sale of non-current assets on credit.

Question 6 requires students to prepare a disposal account. Before they start the task, remind students of the format for the account and the meaning of the income statement entry in the account.

Suggested answers

6

Vehicle disposal account					
		$			$
	Vehicle	20000		Provision for depreciation of vehicle	15000
	Income statement	1000		Xia	6000
		21000			21000

Question 7 requires students to consider the meaning of a balanced disposal account.

Suggested answer

7 If an asset disposal account already balances before the entry for income statement is debited or credited to the account then the asset has made neither a profit nor a loss. This could be classed as break-even.

APPLYING

Use this task to ensure students are confident at preparing provision for depreciation accounts, including when assets are depreciated for fractions of a year.

Answers

Workings for 2018:

$40000 × 0.1 = $4000

Workings for 2019:

$40000 × 0.1 = $4000

$$\$50000 \times 0.1 \times \left(\frac{6}{12}\right) = \$2500$$

$$\$20000 \times 0.1 \times \left(\frac{3}{12}\right) = \$500$$

Total for 2019 = $7000

Provision for depreciation of machinery					
2018		**£**	**2018**		**£**
31 Dec	Balance c/d	4000	31 Dec	Income statement	4000
2019		£	2019		£
31 Dec	Balance c/d	11000	1 Jan	Balance b/d	4000
			31 Dec	Income statement	7000
		11000			11000
2020			2020		
			1 Jan	Balance b/d	11 000

Knowledge check

- **Resources**: Pro-forma 1, Pro-forma 9
- **Answers**: See pages 232–233

Check your progress

Ask students to complete the **Check your progress** section in the Student's Book.

Support

- Ask students for examples of non-current assets. For each non-current asset suggested, ask students which method of depreciation should be used.
- **Workbook 4.2 Support**

Consolidation

- Students prepare revision cards for the unit. They write a key term from the unit on one side of the card and the definition on the other side. Students can then work in pairs and take turns identifying a key term from the definition or providing a definition given the key term.
- **Resources**: Resource 4.2B

  Alternatively or in addition, you can use the resource provided and students can match the key terms to the definitions. You can use this matching activity as a starter activity for lessons in this unit. You may also want to include key terms from earlier units.
- **Workbook 4.2 Practice**

Stretch

- Students prepare a table of differences between the three methods of depreciation.
- **Workbook 4.2 Stretch**

4.3 Other payables and other receivables

Learning objectives

By the end of this unit, students should be able to:

- recognise the importance of matching costs and revenues
- prepare ledger accounts and journal entries to record accrued and prepaid expenses
- prepare ledger accounts and journal entries to record accrued and prepaid incomes.

Resources

- Student's Book pages 143–151
- Workbook pages 39–40
- Resource 4.3A
- Resource 4.3B
- Pro-forma 1
- Pro-forma 3

Key terms

Matching principle, In arrears, Accrued expenses, Prepaid expenses, Accrued incomes, Prepaid incomes

STARTING POINT

These questions recap the work covered in Chapters 1, 2 and 3.

Question 1 is a knowledge-based question about the trial balance. As a stretch task, ask students to identify other debit and credit entries in the trial balance.

Suggested answer

1 Profit appears as a credit entry in a business's trial balance.

Question 2 considers the matching principle and what happens to profit when an invoice remains unpaid. Students may suggest that profit would be increased. Clarify that the debt still needs to be paid and that the debt is for this financial year and not the next. As a research task, students could be asked to find out about the matching principle.

Suggested answer

2 A delayed payment would become an accrued expense. This would be added to the expenses in the income statement and therefore profit would be unaffected.

EXPLORING

The questions allow students to think about the application of the matching principle and how accruals and prepayments will be accounted for.

For question 1, advise students to assume that the business has a financial year that ends on 31 December each year.

Suggested answer

1 As the sale is made in December 2018, the sale would count towards the profit for the year ending 31 December 2018.

Question 2 considers prepaid expenses. Clarify what is meant by a prepayment before students attempt the question.

Suggested answer

2 This insurance has been prepaid. A prepaid expense is taken from the relevant expense in the income statement.

DEVELOPING

This unit covers two fundamental concepts that are required for the preparation of both ledger accounts and financial statements for businesses. It would be advantageous to link the first part of the unit with Chapter 7.

Once students understand the theory, they should start to work through the numerical examples and questions in the Student's Book. Extensive practice will aid students' understanding and confidence. The topic will be revisited in Chapter 5, allowing the students to develop their skills further.

Question 1 asks students to identify prepaid expenses.

Suggested answer

1 Rent paid, insurance, water rates, electricity and gas, business rates, and so on.

For question 2, students need to consider why accruals and prepayments are recorded in the general journal.

Suggested answer

2 The general journal records the amounts of accruals and prepayments in a book of prime entry and gives a bookkeeper the authority to record the transactions in the double entry accounts.

Activity: Identifying prepaid and accrued incomes and expenses

Use this as a starter activity for later lessons on this topic.

Approximate time required: 5 minutes

Discussion: Ask students to identify incomes and expenses that could be prepaid or accrued during a financial year.

Suggested answers

Incomes: commission received, rent received on premises

Expenses: rent paid on premises, insurance for a motor van, heat and lighting, business rates, electricity

APPLYING

Use this activity to ensure students are confident preparing ledger accounts to record prepayments and accruals.

Answers

Heating and lighting account for the year ended 31 December 2018					
2018		**$**	**2018**		**$**
1 Jan	Balance b/d (in advance)	64	1 Jan	Balance b/d	34
31 Dec	Bank	77			
31 Dec	Bank	432			
31 Dec	Bank	511			
31 Dec	Balance c/d (99 +31)	130	31 Dec	Income statement	1180
		1214			1214
2019			2019		
			1 Jan	Balance b/d	130

Knowledge check

- **Resources**: Pro-forma 1
- **Answers**: See pages 233–234

Check your progress

Ask students to complete the **Check your progress** section in the Student's Book.

Support

- Ask students to identify bills that are paid at home. Discuss whether each business expects their bill to be paid on time, in advance or in arrears.
- **Resources**: Resource 4.3A

  Students complete a summary of the principles involved in the recording of accrued and prepaid expenses and income. (Answers: 1 payable; 2 added; 3 current liabilities; 4 receivable; 5 deducted; 6 current assets; 7 deducted; 8 current liabilities; 9 added; 10 current assets) You could also use the completed table as part of a presentation to students or make it into a wall display for revision.
- **Workbook 4.3 Support**

Consolidation

[Note that some bullet points are followed by unbulleted but indentd paragraphs]

- Students prepare revision cards for the unit. They write a key term from the unit on one side of the card and the definition on the other side. Students can then work in pairs and take turns identifying a key term from the definition or providing a definition, given the key term.
- **Resources**: Resource 4.3B

  Alternatively or in addition, you can use the resource provided and students can match the key terms to the definitions. You can use this matching activity as a starter activity for lessons in this unit. You may also want to include key terms from earlier units.
- **Workbook 4.3 Practice**

Stretch

- Students prepare an information leaflet that could be provided to businesses. The leaflet should:
  - include definitions of accrued income and expenditure and prepaid income and expenditure
  - explain how these items are accounted for in ledger accounts
  - describe how these items are included in the income statement and statement of financial position
  - provide practical examples to illustrate the information.
- **Workbook 4.3 Stretch**

4.4 Irrecoverable debts and provision for doubtful debts

Learning objectives

By the end of this unit, students should be able to:

- understand the meaning of irrecoverable debts and recovery of debts written off
- prepare ledger accounts and journal entries to record irrecoverable debts
- prepare ledger accounts and journal entries to record recovery of debts written off
- explain the reasons for maintaining a provision for doubtful debts
- prepare ledger accounts and journal entries to record the creation of, and adjustments to, a provision for doubtful debts.

Resources

- Student's Book pages 152–160
- Workbook pages 41–42
- Resource 4.4A
- Pro-forma 1
- Pro-forma 3

Key terms

Recovery of debts, Credit control, Provision for doubtful debts

STARTING POINT

The questions consider the credit terms that businesses offer when selling goods to customers. Discuss 'buy now pay later' schemes that exist to encourage customers to purchase goods. As a stretch task, consider the ethical issues surrounding this, for example: *Is it appropriate to encourage people to go into debt for goods that they cannot afford?*

Suggested answers

1 Businesses offer credit terms to encourage people to purchase goods. By offering credit terms, a business may encourage a customer to purchase goods in bulk.

2 Since the business releases the goods to the customer before receiving any money, there is a risk that the customer will never pay. There is a possibility that the customer will go bankrupt and not be able to repay the debt.

EXPLORING

The questions consider the implications of failing to collect funds from trade receivables and allow students to consider how to avoid such situations.

Suggested answers

1 A business could offer cash only sales.

Alternatively, it could send regular statements to remind customers to pay, and follow up with reminder phone calls or charge interest on late payments, to encourage customers to pay earlier or on time. Some businesses offer discounts if a customer pays within a set number of days.

2 There will be an increase in expenses and reduction in the profit for the year.

Develop the discussion by eliciting reasons why an amount owing may fail to be collected by a business offering trade credit. Possible answers include: insolvency of the customer, the amount owing being disputed, refusal to pay, fraudulent purchases, poor credit control.

DEVELOPING

This unit investigates irrecoverable debts and provisions for doubtful debts. Students need to understand the difference between a debt that cannot be recovered and one that requires a provision but may be paid in the future. The principles used to prepare provision for depreciation accounts will be used when preparing provision for doubtful debt accounts.

Present the material and worked examples showing how to record irrecoverable debts and the recovery of debts written off.

Ask students to discuss the likely implications of the inability of a business to collect the amount of money owing to it (increase in irrecoverable debts, reduced profit for the year, a need to increase provision for doubtful debts). This leads into question 1, which considers how external factors may impact on the value of irrecoverable debts.

Suggested answer

1 External factors have a major impact on the value of irrecoverable debts each year – for example, if a country is in a recession, more businesses are likely to go into liquidation and be unable to pay their debts. If interest rates are increasing, businesses will have less disposable income after they have paid their priority debts (for example, mortgage payments) to pay other bills. They are likely to default on payments.

Question 2 requires students to consider what would happen if a debt that was deemed to be irrecoverable was then paid by the trade receivable.

Suggested answer

2 The business would need to ascertain the original reason for the debt not being paid. If the customer could provide evidence that any future payments would be made, then the business may consider allowing credit sales to that customer again.

Before introducing question 3, examine the idea of a provision for doubtful debts. Advise students that these debts are not yet irrecoverable. The adjustments that are studied here will be used again when preparing the financial statements in Chapter 5.

At this point, ask students how they might estimate the size of the provision for doubtful debts (how long debts have been outstanding; historical trends for irrecoverable debts in the industry of the business; economic factors – in economic downturns or recessions, business failure is more common and irrecoverable debts are more likely).

Question 3 is a problem-solving task, requiring students to consider how the age of a debt affects the likelihood of it becoming irrecoverable.

Suggested answer

3 Businesses tend to produce an aged trade receivables schedule. An example is shown below. The older the debt, the more likely it is that the debt will not be repaid. Therefore the percentage doubtful increases with age. In the example below debts less than one month old are 1% doubtful whereas debts over one year old are 20% doubtful.

Period owing	Amount ($)	% Doubtful	Provision ($)
Less than 1 month	2000	1	20
1–2 months	1000	3	30
2–3 months	400	4	16
3 months to 1 year	500	5	25
Over 1 year	100	20	20

Question 4 follows on from question 3 and asks students to consider the difference between an irrecoverable debt and a provision for doubtful debts.

Suggested answer

4 An irrecoverable debt is a debt that a business knows will not be repaid – this could be due to a customer going into liquidation. A provision for doubtful debts is a provision that is made to account for debts that a business perceives may not be paid.

APPLYING

Use this task to ensure students are confident in preparing ledger accounts to record the provision for doubtful debts for a number of consecutive years. Students will be able to review the increases and decreases in provision that occurred over time.

Answers

Provision for doubtful debts					
2018		**$**	**2018**		**$**
31 Dec	Balance c/d	1000	1 Jan	Balance b/d	0
			31 Dec	Income statement	1000
		1000			1000
2019			2019		
31 Dec	Income statement	216	1 Jan	Balance b/d	1000
31 Dec	Balance c/d	784			
		1000			1000
2020			2020		
31 Dec	Balance c/d	932	1 Jan	Balance b/d	784
			31 Dec	Income statement	148
		932			932
2021			2021		
			1 Jan	Balance b/d	932
31 Dec	Balance c/d	1119.20	31 Dec	Income statement	187.20
		1119. 20			1119.20
2022			2022		
			1 Jan	Balance b/d	1119. 20

Trade receivables as at 31 December 2021	
Trade receivables	$27 980.00
Less provision for doubtful debts	$1 119.20
	$26 860.80

Knowledge check

- **Resources**: Pro-forma 1
- **Answers**: See page 235

Check your progress

Ask students to complete the **Check your progress** section in the Student's Book.

Support

- Ask students for examples of items that would appear in:
  - an irrecoverable debt account
  - a provision for doubtful debts account.
- **Workbook 4.4 Support**

Consolidation

- Students prepare revision cards for the unit. They write a key term from the unit on one side of the card and the definition on the other side. Students can then work in pairs and take turns identifying a key term from the definition or providing a definition given the key term.
- **Resources**: Resource 4.4A

  Alternatively or in addition, you can use the resource provided and students can match the key terms to the definitions. You can use this matching activity as a starter activity for lessons in this unit. You may also want to include key terms from earlier units.
- **Workbook 4.4 Practice**

Stretch

- Students construct a flow chart that demonstrates how irrecoverable debts and provisions for doubtful debts are accounted for in the financial records of a business. They may require A3 paper and the chart should be planned carefully.
- **Workbook 4.4 Stretch**

4.5 Valuation of inventory

Learning objectives

By the end of this unit, students should be able to:

- understand the basis of the valuation of inventory at the lower of cost and net realisable value
- prepare simple inventory valuation statements
- recognise the importance of valuation of inventory and the effect of an incorrect valuation of inventory on gross profit, profit for the year, equity, and asset valuation.

Resources

- Student's Book pages 161–166
- Workbook pages 43–44
- Resource 4.5A
- Resource 4.5B
- Pro-forma 1
- Pro-forma 2
- Pro-forma 5
- Pro-forma 7
- Pro-forma 9

Key terms

Net realisable value (of inventory), Inventory valuation statement, Closing inventory, Gross profit, Profit for the year

STARTING POINT

Before introducing question 1, clarify what is meant by **inventory**. As a stretch task, ask students to research what is meant by: **raw materials**, **work in progress**, **finished goods**.

Question 2 follows on from question 1. As a stretch task, ask students to consider the costs of holding large quantities of inventory (for example, storage costs, insurance, damaged or outdated stock).

Suggested answers

1 Businesses need to keep stock of inventory to ensure they have goods ready to sell to their customers. Businesses need to decide how much inventory they are likely to require, to meet the needs of their customers. This may vary at different times of the year. For example, in the summer, a food retailer may increase the amount of ice cream that they hold.

2 Businesses may choose to hold large quantities of inventory in order to meet the needs of their customers. Holding large quantities will ensure that if there were a sudden surge in demand the business would be able to fulfil existing orders and meet any unexpected additional orders.

EXPLORING

These questions build on the work completed in Chapters 1, 2 and 3 and prepare students for preparation of financial statements in Chapter 5.

The two questions consider the implications of holding inventory in a business.

Suggested answers

1 Holding large quantities of inventory is very expensive. The business will need to pay for storage, security, insurance, etc. of the inventory. These costs will reduce the profit for the year. If consumer tastes change, businesses may be unable to sell the inventory that they have in stock. Businesses have started to only hold the inventory that they require to meet customer orders.

2 They may run out of goods and not be able to trade. This means customers will be forced to shop elsewhere and may not return to purchase goods in the future. The business will lose sales revenue and therefore have a decrease in gross profit and profit for the year.

DEVELOPING

Gaining an understanding of the valuation of inventory will aid students when they are preparing financial statements in chapter 5. The topic is very short, quite straightforward and could be considered either as a stand-alone topic or in conjunction with the preparation of financial statements. Business studies students may already have a working knowledge of the concepts discussed.

As a starter activity, students may consider a local business organisation such as a supermarket. Ask them to identify what inventory the supermarket may hold. They should also consider how the inventory will vary throughout the year. Clarify that opening inventory appears in the income statement as part of cost of sales, whereas closing inventory appears in the income statement as part of cost of sales as well as in the statement of financial position as a current asset.

Before they complete question 1, ensure students understand that inventory is valued at original cost or its net realisable value. Work through the worked examples in the Student Book to illustrate this principle.

Suggested answer

1 Inventory is always valued at original cost or its net realisable value, whichever is lower.

The effect of an incorrect valuation of inventory requires problem-solving skills. It may be more appropriate to consider this part of the unit after students have learnt to prepare financial statements. Question 2 requires students to have an understanding of the matching principle (see Unit 4.3 and Chapter 7).

Suggested answer

2 Closing inventory is the value of inventory held by the business at the end of the accounting period. It needs to be deducted from the purchases for the period, as this inventory will not be sold during the financial year and does not relate to that financial period. This is an application of the matching principle.

APPLYING

Use these questions to ensure students understand how closing inventory valuation affects businesses and their financial records.

Suggested answers

1 If closing inventory is overvalued, the profit for the current year will be overstated. This closing inventory will become opening inventory for the following year. Overvalued opening inventory will mean that the profit for that year will be understated.

2 When preparing the financial statements, businesses need to ensure that these represent a true and fair view of the financial position of the business performance.

If there is incorrect inventory valuation, then the current assets and therefore equity will be incorrect.

Knowledge check

- **Answers**: See pages 235–236

Check your progress

Ask students to complete the **Check your progress** section in the Student's Book.

Support

- **Resources**: Resource 4.5A

  Use the matching activity on the resource provided to review the effect of incorrect valuation of closing inventory.

- **Workbook 4.5 Support**

Consolidation

- Students prepare revision cards for the unit. They write a key term from the unit on one side of the card and the definition on the other side. Students can then work in pairs and take turns identifying a key term from the definition or providing a definition, given the key term.
- **Resources**: Resource 4.5B

  Alternatively or in addition, you can use the resource provided and students can match the key terms to the definitions. You can use this matching activity as a starter activity for lessons in this unit. You may also want to include key terms from earlier units.
- **Workbook 4.5 Practice**

Stretch

- Download a set of financial accounts for a public limited company, or ask students to do this. Alternatively, you or they could use personal contacts or write to a local business to request copies of their financial statements (although many businesses may be unwilling to release their information). If you used the stretch task Unit 1.1, you could reuse those accounts. They could also be used in later chapters. If you wish to use the stretch activity in Unit 6.3, students will also need a set of financial accounts from a second company that is similar in nature to the first.

  Students examine the accounts. They should check the notes to the accounts which usually appear after the financial statements for the year. Students answer the following questions.
  - What methods do the companies use to value inventory?
  - Does the idea of 'lower of cost' or 'net realisable value' apply to companies that publish reports?
- **Workbook 4.5 Stretch**

Chapter review

- **Resources:** Pro-forma 1, Pro-forma 2, Pro-forma 5, Pro-forma 7, Pro-forma 9
- **Answers:** See pages 236–238
- **Workbook: Chapter 4 review**

5 Preparation of financial statements

This chapter introduces students to the financial statements of a range of business organisations.

Numerical examples and tasks enable students to prepare financial statements for:

- sole traders
- partnerships
- limited companies
- clubs and societies
- manufacturing accounts
- incomplete records.

Prior knowledge

Students should already be able to:

- use the accounting equation and understand the purpose of accounting
- prepare double entry ledger accounts
- prepare a trial balance
- account for capital and revenue expenditure and receipts, depreciation, irrecoverable debts and provisions for doubtful debts
- value business inventory.

Throughout this chapter, encourage students regularly to revisit the work they completed in Chapter 4. Advise them also to have the work they completed in Chapters 1–4 readily available for making the adjustments that will be required when preparing financial statements.

Before students start work on this chapter, make sure they can confidently calculate depreciation and irrecoverable debts and understand the accounting techniques for capital and revenue expenditure and income.

Background for non-subject specialists

Due to the separation of ownership and control in businesses, managers need to provide detailed reports for business owners. In the case of financial accounting, these take the form of financial statements. Financial statements vary, depending on the type of business that is being considered.

An income statement compares business revenue with its costs and expenses to calculate the profit or loss for the financial year. This is often seen as the most important measure of financial success. A statement of financial position records the assets, liabilities and capital of the business. Based on the information contained in the financial statements, managers and owners should be able to make informed decisions about the business's future and take any remedial action that may be required.

5.1 Sole traders

Learning objectives

By the end of this unit, students should be able to:

- explain the advantages and disadvantages of operating as a sole trader
- explain the importance of preparing income statements and statements of financial position
- explain the difference between a trading business and a service business
- prepare income statements for trading businesses and for service businesses
- understand that statements of financial position record assets and liabilities on a specified date
- recognise and define the content of a statement of financial position: non-current assets, intangible assets, current assets, current liabilities, non-current liabilities and capital
- understand the interrelationship of items in a statement of financial position
- prepare statements of financial position for trading businesses and service businesses
- make adjustments for provision for depreciation using the straight line, reducing balance and revaluation methods
- make adjustments for accrued and prepaid expenses and accrued and prepaid income
- make adjustments for irrecoverable debts and provisions for doubtful debts
- make adjustments for goods taken by the owner for own use.

Resources

- Student's Book pages 172–193
- Workbook pages 48–51
- Resource 5.1A
- Resource 5.1B
- Resource 5.1C
- Resource 5.1D
- Pro-forma 8
- Pro-forma 9
- Pro-forma 10
- Pro-forma 11

Key terms

Sole trader, Unlimited liability, Income statement, Gross profit, Profit for the year, Capital, Statement of financial position

STARTING POINT

This unit is the foundation for the other units in Chapter 5. Check that students can confidently manipulate financial data so that they are ready to prepare income statements and statements of financial position.

Most students will have an understanding that profit is the main goal of most businesses. Before discussing the questions, explain that, in order to calculate annual profit, a business needs to prepare financial statements that are used to make informed business decisions.

Using their knowledge from previous chapters, elicit from students items that they would expect to be included in the financial statements.

The questions review the work studied on depreciation, accruals and prepayments and capital and revenue expenditure.

If students find the questions difficult, it can be helpful to use prompt questions, for example:

- *What is an expense?* (A revenue expenditure that has been paid during the financial year.)
- *What is meant by capital expenditure?* (See suggested answer 3 below.)
- *What is meant by revenue expenditure?* (See suggested answer 3 below.)
- *What is the difference between a prepayment and an accrual?* (See suggested answer 2 below.)

Suggested answers

1 An estimation of how the cost of an asset should be allocated over its useful life.

2 Accrued expenses are expenses relating to the current accounting period that remain unpaid at the end of the period. (Also known as 'other payables'.)

Prepaid expenses are expenses that have been paid in advance of the accounting period to which they relate. (Also known as 'other receivables'.)

3 Capital expenditure is business expenditure used to purchase or improve assets that are expected to be used in the business for more than one year. It also includes the cost of getting those assets ready for use. Capital expenditure is not classified as an expense on the income statement of a business.

Revenue expenditure is expenditure on running the business. It is clearly linked to a specific time period. Revenue expenditure is classified as an expense on the income statement of a business.

EXPLORING

Discuss why different individuals and groups may be interested in reading and analysing financial statements. Students could continue their analysis of income statements and statements of financial position by downloading a set of annual accounts for a public limited company. This will enhance their understanding and give them a practical example of what they will be producing.

The questions consider the benefits of operating as a sole trader and the items that would be included in their financial statements.

Suggested answers

1 Benefits include:
- Small businesses are easy to set up.
- There are low initial start-up costs. The owner is only required to find a small amount of capital.
- The sole trader is responsible for all business decisions.
- The sole trader can choose their own working conditions, hours and holidays to be taken.
- The sole trader does not need to share their profit with any other owner.
- A sole trader has limited legal requirements for the preparation of financial records. Sole traders do need to register to pay tax. Also, if they employ workers, they are responsible for complying with tax, employee and health and safety legislation.

2 Non-current assets include: premises, fixtures and fittings, delivery vehicles, equipment.

3 Expenses include: rent and rates, wages and salaries, carriage outwards, heat and light, insurance, advertising, increase in provision for doubtful debts, repairs and maintenance, irrecoverable debts, depreciation.

DEVELOPING

In this unit students explore the financial statements produced by a sole trader.

Simple questions may be useful as a starter exercise for lessons in this unit, for example:

- *Why would an individual choose to work alone?* (Individuals like to be in control and make all of the business decisions. When working alone, the individual will be able to take all of the profits made.)
- *What sort of businesses are operated by sole traders?* (Examples include plumbers, newsagents, gardeners.)
- *Why would a sole trader need to prepare financial statements?* (To assess the business's financial performance.)

You could use the following activity as a alternative simply to presenting the advantages and disadvantages of this form of business.

Activity: Advantages and disadvantages of operating as a sole trader

The activity is designed to enable students to consider the benefits and problems of operating as a sole trader.

Approximate time required: 30 minutes

Pair/group work: Students discuss the advantages and disadvantages of operating as a sole trader. Bring the class together and share ideas.

Answers

See the table in Unit 5.1 in the Student's Book, page 169.

Use question 1 to ensure students understand the difference between an income statement and a statement of financial position. Point out that trading *and* service businesses produce both statements at the end of each financial year.

Suggested answer

1 A financial statement shows a business's income and expenses for an accounting period and the resulting profit or loss. A business's statement of financial position lists all of the assets that are owned by a business and all of the liabilities that are owed by the business.

Question 2 ask students to give examples of expenses that would be included in income statements. Students must be able to identify expenses from a list of financial data to ensure accurate records are made in the financial statements. Common errors include the inclusion of assets in the list of expenses.

Suggested answer

2 Examples of expenses include rent and rates, electricity, advertising, depreciation, stationery, cleaning materials.

Question 3 highlights the key difference between gross profit and profit for the year. Students need to be able to distinguish between them when compiling and analysing financial statements. If students find the question difficult, it can be helpful to use prompt questions, for example:

- *How is gross profit calculated in an income statement?* (Revenue less cost of sales = gross profit)
- *What is taken away from gross profit to calculate profit for the year?* (Total expenses)
- *Where do expenses appear in an income statement?* (Expenses appear after additional income has been added to gross profit.)

Answer

3 Gross profit = sales revenue less cost of sales

Profit for the year = gross profit less expenses

Before introducing question 4, elicit from students the difference between trading and service businesses and ask them to give examples (trading businesses, such as supermarkets, clothing stores and other retail outlets buy goods with the intention of selling them to consumers and other businesses; service businesses, such as hairdressers, travel agents, garden designers, sell services rather than goods to customers). Students need to understand how the differences between trading and service businesses affect the income statements that are produced by both organisations. This will help to ensure that they can accurately prepare the financial statements for each type of business. Responses to question 4 should highlight the differences between sole traders operating in each sector.

Suggested answer

4 Unlike a trading business, a service organisation does not have a trading account. The income statements of service organisations commence with revenue received and then add additional income and deduct expenses to gain profit for the year.

Question 5 gives students practice in categorising assets and liabilities in context. Remind them to focus on the assets and liabilities of a retail store. As a stretch task, students could sub-divide their lists into non-current and current assets and liabilities.

Suggested answer

5 Assets: store premises, fixtures and fittings, bank balance, retail store inventory.
Liabilities: trade payables, bank overdraft, loan, mortgage on the store premises.

In question 6 students practise categorising assets and liabilities. This is an important skill, required to ensure the accurate completion of an income statement. For further practice, students could revisit the questions in Unit 1.2 on the accounting equation.

Answers

6 Assets: premises, motor vehicles, inventory, office equipment, fixtures and fittings, trade receivables, cash in hand.
Liabilities: bank loan, mortgage on business property, bank overdraft, trade payables.

You could continue the work on the items found in a statement of financial position by asking students for examples of the different items on the statement of financial position for a specific type of business, such as a supermarket, school or hotel.

Look at the case study with the class. It provides an example of a business that operates as a sole trader and illustrates how its financial statements may be used. Encourage students to think of local small businesses that may operate as sole traders.

Extensive practice of the preparation of financial statements is needed to ensure a good understanding of this topic. If students are not confident in the production of statements for sole trader businesses, they may find it difficult to complete the financial statements of partnership and limited companies and those from incomplete records. For extra practice, students can use the data from any of the trial balances they have produced to prepare income statements or statements of financial position.

Activity: Financial statements

This activity provides students with practice in completing financial statements.

Approximate time required: 1 hour

Resources: Resource 5.1A

Before the lesson: Print sufficient copies of the resource sheet for the class.

Pair work: Students insert numerical data into the financial statements. Remind students to ensure that the income statement and statement of financial position coincide with one another.

Support: If students lack the confidence to make up their own numerical data, tell them to use data from one of the trial balances they have prepared.

APPLYING

This task encourages reflective thinking on the difference between financial statements for a trading and for a service business. Students should identify that there is no need to produce a trading account for this business.

Answers

Cutz 4 U		
Income statement for the year ended 31 March 2018		
	$	$
Revenue received		75000
Additional income		
Decrease in provision for doubtful debts		50
		75050
***Less* expenses**		
Rent	10000	
Lighting and heating expenses	32300	
Salaries and wages	10000	
Insurance	2150	
General expenses	4450	
Depreciation: fixtures and fittings	3500	
		62400
Profit for the year		12650

Cutz 4 U			
Statement of financial position as at 31 March 2018			
	$	$	$
	Cost	**Depreciation**	**Net book value**
Non-current assets			
Fixtures and fittings	35000	10500	24500
	35000	10500	24500
Current assets			
Trade receivables	500		
Less provision for doubtful debts	50	450	
Bank		3000	
Other receivables (prepaid expenses)		550	
			4000
Total assets			28500
Capital and liabilities			
Capital			25200
Add profit for the year			12650
			37850
Less drawings			10000
			27850
Current liabilities			
Trade payables			350
Other payables (accrued expenses)			300
			650
Total liabilities			28500

Knowledge check

- **Resources**: Pro-forma 8, Pro-forma 9, Pro-forma 10, Pro-forma 11
- **Answers**: See pages 238–242

Check your progress

Ask students to complete the **Check your progress** section in the Student's Book.

Support

- **Resources**: Resource 5.1B, Resource 5.1C

  For students needing extra support, use the cards from the resources provided. Students can match the items with their definitions and/or sort the items into those appearing on an income statement and those appearing on a statement of financial position.
- **Workbook 5.1 Support**

Consolidation

- Students prepare revision cards for the unit. They write a key term from the unit on one side of the card and the definition on the other side. Students can then work in pairs and take turns identifying a key term from the definition or providing a definition, given the key term.
- **Resources**: Resource 5.1D
- Alternatively or in addition, you can use the resource provided and students can match the key terms to the definitions. You can use this matching activity as a starter activity for lessons in this unit. You may also want to include key terms from earlier units.
- **Workbook 5.1 Practice**

Stretch

- Download a set of financial accounts for a public limited company, or ask students to do this. Alternatively, you or they could use personal contacts or write to a local business to request copies of their financial statements (although many businesses may be unwilling to release their information). If you used the stretch task for Unit 1.1, you could reuse those accounts. They could also be used in later units in this chapter and in later chapters. If you wish to use the stretch activity in Unit 6.3, students will also need a set of financial accounts from a second company that is similar in nature to the first.

  Students review the format of these accounts. They compare and contrast the format of the published accounts of the public limited company with those of a sole trader. Students should highlight the key differences.
- **Workbook 5.1 Stretch**

5.2 Partnerships

Learning objectives

By the end of this unit, students should be able to:

- explain the advantages and disadvantages of forming a partnership
- outline the importance and contents of a partnership agreement
- explain the purpose of an appropriation account
- prepare income statements, appropriation accounts and statements of financial position
- record interest on partners' loans, interest on capital, interest on drawings, partners' salaries and the division of the balance of profit or loss
- make adjustments to financial statements as detailed in Unit 5.1 (sole traders)
- explain the uses of, and differences between, capital and current accounts
- draw up partners' capital and current accounts in ledger account form and as part of a statement of financial position.

RESOURCES

- Student's Book pages 194–213
- Workbook pages 52–54
- Resource 5.2A
- Resource 5.2B
- Pro-forma 11
- Pro-forma 12

Key terms

Partnership, Deed of partnership, Appropriation account, Residual profit, Goodwill

STARTING POINT

These questions recap the theory relating to sole traders.

If students find these questions difficult, it can be helpful to use prompt questions, for example:

- *What is a sole trader?* (Any business that is owned and controlled by one person.)
- *Who owns a sole trader business?* (The sole trader)
- *What financial statements does a sole trader produce?* (Income statement and Statement of financial position)

Suggested answers

1 Advantages include:

- Small businesses are easy to set up.
- There are low initial start-up costs. The owner is only required to find a small amount of capital.
- The sole trader is responsible for all business decisions.
- The sole trader can choose their own working conditions, hours and holidays to be taken.
- The sole trader does not need to share their profit with any other owner.
- A sole trader has limited legal requirements for the preparation of financial records.

2 Problems include:

- Business growth is limited by the amount of capital available from the sole trader.
- The sole trader has no one to share the responsibility of running the business with.
- The sole trader often has to work long hours and may find it difficult to take holidays or find cover when they are unwell.
- The sole trader will be liable for any debts that the business cannot pay; there is unlimited liability.

3 A financial statement shows a business's income and expenses for an accounting period and the resulting profit or loss. A business's statement of financial position lists all of the assets that are owned by a business and all of the liabilities that are owed by the business.

EXPLORING

Students should be able to produce an income statement and statement of financial position for a sole trader quite confidently. These will form the foundation of the financial statements to be produced in this unit.

These questions consider the benefits and problems of operating as a partnership. They also emphasise the importance of the income statement for a partnership, to ensure that partners receive the profit share that has been agreed.

Suggested answers

1 Benefits include:

- Greater capital and resources can be raised from the partners.
- It spreads personal risk across all of the partners, meaning that, in the case of financial difficulty, there are more people able to share the debt burden.
- Partners may bring additional skills and ideas to the business.
- Business responsibilities are shared among the partners.
- Partners can discuss issues before final decisions have to be taken.
- Partnerships may have increased public image and credibility with customers and suppliers when compared with a sole trader.

2 Problems include:

- Profits will need to be shared between the partners.
- All partners are responsible for the debts of the business.
- Partners may disagree over the direction of the business.
- The actions of one partner are binding on all of the other partners.
- Decision making can be time consuming.
- Disputes over workloads.

3 Any sensible division, for example 50% : 50%, 75% : 25%.

DEVELOPING

Students should be able to prepare financial statements (income statements and statements of financial position) for a sole trader quite confidently. Point out that they will need to use the skills they developed in Unit 5.1 to complete the work in this unit. Explain that partnership financial statements are used to make informed business decisions and enable the partners to ascertain how much profit each partner will gain.

Recap the concept of unlimited liability (owners are personally liable for the debts of the business). Highlight the difference in financial statements between a sole trader and a partnership. In particular, explain the purpose of an appropriation account.

Simple questions may be useful as a starter exercise in later lessons in this unit. For example:

- *Why would a sole trader decide to take a partner to work together with them?* (To increase capital, share decisions, for new ideas, share losses, enable holidays to be taken, etc.)
- *What sort of businesses are operated by partnerships?* (Bakers, retail stores, solicitors, accountants and estate agents)
- *Why would a partnership need to prepare financial statements?* (To show how the profit or loss will be shared between the partners)

You could use the following activity as a alternative to simply presenting the advantages and disadvantages of this form of business.

Activity: Advantages and disadvantages of operating as a partnership

This activity is designed to consider the benefits and problems of operating as a partnership.

Approximate time required: 30 minutes

Pair/group work: Students discuss the advantages and disadvantages of operating as a partnership. Bring the class together and share ideas.

Answers

See the table in Unit 5.2 in the Student's Book, page 191.

Look at the case study with the class. It provides an example of a business that was originally set up as a sole trader. The owner then decided to go into partnership. Encourage students to think of local small businesses that may operate as partnerships and discuss the advantages the partners may have brought to the business.

Alternatively or in addition, you could use the following activity as a follow-up to the case study in the Student's Book.

Activity: Business ownership

This activity is designed to allow students to investigate business ownership in practice.

Approximate time required: 1 hour

Group work: Each group chooses a business with which they are familiar and investigates:

1 the type of business ownership

2 the reasons why the form of ownership is appropriate for the business.

Bring the class together. Each group presents its findings.

As a class, consider the similarities between the businesses and ownership types that have been investigated.

Question 1 allows students to consider the importance of a deed of partnership. Point out that, to ensure their effective running, most partnership will produce a deed of partnership. Discuss the other elements of a deed of partnership. Emphasise that, in the absence of a deed of partnership, the Partnership Act (1890) will apply. Elicit from students the conditions of this Act.

Suggested answer

1 A deed of partnership will ensure that there is no confusion or conflict over the working conditions in the business. Partners will agree to items such as profit-sharing ratios, the amount of interest on capital and the partnership salaries that can be taken.

Question 2 highlights the conditions of the Partnership Act (1890). This question allows learners to see the effect on a partner's current account of not maintaining a partnership agreement.

If students find the questions difficult, it can be helpful to use prompt questions, for example

- *What applies if there is no partnership agreement?* (The conditions of the Partnership Act (1890).)
- *What is the Partnership Act (1890)?* (See Student's Book, page 192.)
- *How will profit now be shared?* (Profits and losses are shared equally.)

As a stretch task, ask students to consider the roles in the business that the three partners might have.

Suggested answer

2 Students should identify that if there was no partnership agreement:
  - interest on drawings would not be levied
  - interest on capital would not be allowed
  - partnership salaries would not be allowed
  - profits and losses would be shared equally.

3

Current Account as at 31 October 2018							
	Sabbir	**Ahnaf**	**Rubel**		**Sabbir**	**Ahnaf**	**Rubel**
	$	$	$		$	$	$
Balance b/d		930		Balance b/d	195		770
Drawings	15000	11000	17000	Interest on capital	0	0	0
Interest on drawings	0	0	0	Salaries		0	
				Share of profit	63000	63000	63000
Balance c/d	48195	51070	29770	Balance c/d			
	63195	63000	46770		63195	63000	63770
				Balance b/d	48195	51070	29770

Students need extensive practice in the preparation of financial statements, to ensure a good understanding of this topic.

APPLYING

Use the task to ensure that students are confident in preparing an appropriation account for a partnership. Encourage reflective thinking on partnerships by asking students to speculate on the nature of the partnership that would make this distribution of the loss fair or unfair and what conditions Hana and Anis could have included in a deed of partnership to make it fair.

Answers

Hana and Anis			
Appropriation account for the year ended 31 December 2017			
	$	**$**	**$**
Profit or loss for the year			(49200)
Add interest on drawings:			
Hana		0	
Anis		0	
			0
			(49200)
Less salaries		0	
Less interest on capital:			
Hana	0		
Anis	0		
		0	
			(49200)
			(49200)
Balance of profits/losses shared:			
Hana		(24600)	
Anis		(24600)	
			(49200)

Capital account as at 31 December 2017							
		Hana	Anis			Hana	Anis
		$	$			$	$
				Balance b/d		40000	50000
Balance c/d		40000	50000				
		40000	50000			40000	50000
				Balance b/d		**40000**	**50000**

Current account as at 31 December 2017							
		Hana	Anis			Hana	Anis
		$	$			$	$
Drawings		28000	23000	Balance b/d		24600	28600
Interest on drawings		0	0	Interest on capital		0	0
Share of loss		24600	24600	Salaries		0	0
				Balance c/d		28000	19000
		52600	47600			52600	47600
Balance b/d		28000	19000				

Knowledge check

- **Resources**: Pro-forma 11, Pro-forma 12
- **Answers**: See pages 242–245

Check your progress

Ask students to complete the **Check your progress** section in the Student's Book.

Support

- **Resources**: Resource 5.2A

Students complete the appropriation account in the resource provided.

- **Workbook 5.2 Support**

Answer to Support activity

Argo and Victoria			
Appropriation account for the year ended 30 June 2018			
	$	$	$
Profit or loss for the year			63000
Add interest on drawings:			
Argo		0	
Victoria		0	
			0
			63000
Less salary: Argo		18000	
Less interest on capital:			
Argo	600		
Victoria	480		

Argo and Victoria			
Appropriation account for the year ended 30 June 2018			
	$	$	$
		1080	
			19080
			43920
Balance of profits/losses shared:			
Argo (50%)		21960	
Victoria (50%)		21960	
			43920

Consolidation

- Students prepare revision cards for the unit. They write a key term and features of partnership accounts (see Resource 5.2B) from the unit on one side of the card and the definition on the other side. Students can then work in pairs and take turns identifying a term from the definition or providing a definition given the term.
- **Resources**: Resource 5.2B

  Alternatively or in addition, you can use the resource provided and students can match the key terms to the definitions. You can use this matching activity as a starter activity for lessons in this unit. You may also want to include key terms from earlier units.
- **Workbook 5.2 Practice**

Stretch

- Ask students to compare and contrast the format of published accounts of a public limited company (see stretch task for Unit 5.1) with those of a partnership.
- **Workbook 5.2 Stretch**

Answer

Argo and Victoria			
Appropriation account for the year ended 30 June 2018			
	$	$	$
Profit or loss for the year			63000
Add interest on drawings:			
Argo		0	
Victoria		0	
			0
			63000
Less salary: Argo		18000	
Less interest on capital:			
Argo	600		
Victoria	480		
		1080	
			19080
			43920
Balance of profits/losses shared:			
Argo (50%)		21960	
Victoria (50%)		21960	
			43920

5.3 Limited companies

Learning objectives

By the end of this unit, students should be able to:

- explain the advantages and disadvantages of operating as a limited company
- understand the meaning of the term limited liability
- understand the meaning of the term equity
- understand the capital structure of a limited company comprising preference share capital, ordinary share capital, general reserve and retained earnings
- understand and distinguish between issued, called-up and paid-up share capital
- understand and distinguish between share capital (preference shares and ordinary shares) and loan capital (debentures)
- prepare income statements, statements of changes in equity and statements of financial position
- make adjustments to financial statements as detailed in Unit 5.1 (sole traders).

RESOURCES

- Student's Book pages 214–231
- Workbook pages 55–57
- Resource 5.3A
- Resource 5.3B
- Resource 5.3C
- Resource 5.3D
- Pro-forma 9
- Pro-forma 10
- Pro-forma 13

Key terms

Limited company, Limited liability, Equity (of a limited company), Stock exchange, Authorised share capital, Issued share capital, Called-up share capital, Paid-up share capital, Par value, Share premium, Debenture, Retained earnings, General reserve

STARTING POINT

The questions recap the theory relating to sole traders, partnership and unlimited liability (see Units 5.1 and 5.2).

Suggested answers

1 'Sole trader' describes any business that is owned and controlled by one person. The owner, however, may decide to employ other people to work alongside them within the business. Examples include plumbers, newsagents, gardeners. Sole traders do not have a separate legal existence from their owner. This means that the owner is personally liable for the debts of the business. This is known as 'unlimited liability'.

A partnership is a business that is owned and controlled by at least two owners. The minimum number of partners that is required is two and the maximum number allowed in this type of organisation is usually 20. However, in professional partnerships, for example, solicitors, accountants and estate agents, this number can be exceeded. Like a sole trader, a partnership has unlimited liability.

2 Unlimited liability means that the owner(s) of a business are personally liable for the debts of the business if the business is unable to repay them.

3 Reasons include:

- Greater capital and resources can be raised from the partners.
- Partners can discuss issues before final decisions have to be taken.
- Partnerships may have increased public image and credibility with customers and suppliers when compared with a sole trader.
- Spreads personal risk across all of the partners meaning, in the case of financial difficulty, there are more people able to share the debt burden.
- Business responsibilities are shared among the partners.
- Partners may bring additional skills and ideas to the business.

EXPLORING

The questions focus on limited companies and the financial statements that they produce.

As a stretch task, students could continue their analysis of income statements and statement of financial position by looking at a set of annual accounts for a public limited company, which either you or they could download from the internet. This will enhance their understanding and give them a practical example of what they will be producing.

They could also discuss how interested parties will use the information in the annual report.

Suggested answers

1 The owner of a business would be personally liable for the debts of the business if the business is unable to repay them. This means that the owner may have to sell their own assets, for example, their house or car, in order to pay the business debts.

2 An investor will purchase shares in order to make a return. There are two types of return:

- capital return – the value of the shares purchased may increase over a number of years
- revenue return – the company may pay the investor a dividend as a reward for investing in company.

3 Owners of a limited company hold shares in the company. The ownership of a limited company is divided into equal parts, each part is known as a share. The individuals that own one or more shares in a limited company are known as shareholders. The total value of the shares that have been issued by the limited company is known as equity. The management in a business is responsible for its day-to-day operation. In a sole trader business, ownership and management are often one and the same. However, in a limited company, it is usual practice that the owners (shareholders) are not always part of the management team.

DEVELOPING

Most students will have an understanding that profit is the main goal of most businesses. Explain that, in order to calculate annual profit, a business needs to prepare financial statements and that these financial statements are used to make informed business decisions. Point out that limited companies have a responsibility to their shareholders. They also have a legal obligation to publish their financial statements to allow their shareholders to view the financial performance of the organisation. Potential investors make informed decisions about future investments, based on the information contained in the annual reports.

Before progressing further, ensure that students can confidently produce income statements and statements of financial position for a sole trader (see Unit 5.1).

Elicit from students the topics that they have covered that are likely to be included in the financial statements. Support students who may be having difficulties with particular topics. For example, students should be able to calculate annual and cumulative depreciation accurately, for inclusion in the financial statements. If they are unable to do this, advise individuals to recap Chapter 4.

Highlight the difference between a private limited and public limited company. Use question 1 to check that students understand the difference. The number of public limited companies is enormous, for example, McDonald's, Tesco and Twitter are all public limited companies. There are also a surprising number of private limited companies that are very large. Virgin Atlantic is one example that may be internationally known. Encourage students to think of local businesses.

It is important that students understand the concept of limited liability. Contrast this with unlimited liability that exists in sole trader and partnership businesses, previously discussed in Units 5.1 and 5.2.

Question 2 enables students to consider the benefits of limited liability. Introduce the idea by considering the disadvantages of operating as a sole trader with unlimited liability.

Suggested answer

2 The owner of the business will only lose the amount of money that they have invested in the organisation. The business has its own legal status and can therefore be sued for its own debts.

You could use the following activity as a alternative to simply presenting the advantages and disadvantages of this form of business.

Activity: Advantages and disadvantages of operating as a limited company

Use this activity to consider the advantages and disadvantages of operating as a private and public limited companies.

Approximate time required: 30 minutes

Pair/group work: One half of the class considers a private limited company, the other half considers a public limited company. Students discuss the advantages and disadvantages of operating as a limited company. Bring the class together and share ideas.

Stretch task: Students compare and contrast the responses from each half of the class.

Answers

See the tables in Unit 5.3 in the Student's Book, page 212.

Question 3 discusses the benefits to a shareholder of investing in a limited company. If students find the questions difficult, it can be helpful to use prompt questions, for example:

- *Who is a shareholder?* (An individual that owns one or more shares in a limited company)
- *What is a share?* (The ownership of a limited company is divided into equal parts, each part is known as a share.)
- *Why would an individual decide to invest in a company?* (To gain a financial return)
- *What is the risk of investing in a company?* (If the company fails, the investor would lose the money they have invested in the company.)
- *What is a dividend?* (A percentage of the face value of the shares)

Suggested answer

3 Annual profits and losses belong to the company and not to the owners. The shareholders will be paid dividends out of the profits that the company has made. A proportion of the annual profit is retained for use within the company.

The dividend due to each shareholder is often stated as a percentage of the face value of the shares.

For successful completion of this unit, students not only need to know the definitions of the key terms but must also be able to distinguish between the various different types of capital. These are presented in tabular form in the Student's Book and those tables are reproduced on the resource sheets in this unit. Also included on the resource sheets are empty tables that students could complete for themselves.

Resource 5.3A can be used to discuss the differences between ordinary shares and preference shares. Discuss also the two main types of preference shares.

Use question 4 to assess whether students understand the difference between preference shares and ordinary shares.

Suggested answers

4 See the table on page 214 of the Student's Book or on Resource 5.3A.

Present the key aspects of limited company accounts (debentures and reserves). Resource 5.3B can be used to discuss the differences between ordinary shares and debentures.

Introduce students to the financial statements of a limited company. A good starting point would be to work through the worked examples in the Student Book. Students need extensive practice of the preparation of financial statements to ensure full understanding of this topic.

Simple questions may be useful as a starter exercise for later lessons in this unit. For example:

- *What is a limited company?* (a business that has a separate legal entity from its shareholders)
- *What is the difference between a private limited company and public limited company?* (See Student's Book, page 211.)
- *Who are shareholders of a limited company?* (The owners of the limited company)
- *Why would an individual invest in a limited company?* (To gain a financial return, either with an increase in share price over time or for the revenue return in the form of dividends each year.)
- *Who would be interested in the annual reports prepared by a limited company?* (Owners, managers, trade payables, banks, investors, club members, other interested parties such as government, tax authorities)

Activity: Financial statements

Use this activity to provide additional practice in the preparation of financial statements.

Approximate time required: Approximately 1 hour

Resources: Resource 5.3C

Before the lesson: Print sufficient copies of the resource sheet for the class.

Individual work: Students add numerical data into the templates. They should ensure that the income statement and statement of financial position coincide with one another.

Stretch task: Students work in pairs. Each partly completes the financial statements and asks their partner to ascertain the missing figures.

APPLYING

Use this task to ensure students are confident in preparing a statement of financial position for a limited company.

Answers

1

Flower Power Florists Limited Statement of financial position as at 30 April 2018	
	$m
Non-current assets	
Non-current assets	482.25
Current assets	
Inventory	186.3
Trade receivables	72.7
Short-term investments	1.95
Cash at bank	119.15

Flower Power Florists Limited Statement of financial position as at 30 April 2018	
	$m
Total assets	**862.35**
Capital and reserves	
Called-up share capital	82.3
General reserves	167.65
Profit and loss account	107.95
Non-current liabilities	
Loan repayable 2021	164.4
Current liabilities	
Trade payables	327.75
Loan repayable December 2018	12.4
Total liabilities	**862.45**

2 Non-current assets for Flower Power Florists Limited may include: land and buildings, fixtures and fittings, motor vehicles, business premises, equipment.

Knowledge check

- **Resources**: Pro-forma 9, Pro-forma 10, Pro-forma 13
- **Answers**: See pages 245–247

Check your progress

Ask students to complete the **Check your progress** section in the Student's Book.

Support

- Students prepare a mind map relating to limited companies.

  The mind map could include:
  - the advantages and disadvantages of operating as a limited company
  - a definition of the term 'limited liability'
  - a definition of the term 'equity'
  - the capital structure of a limited company
  - the structure of share capital
  - examples relating to a limited company of their choice.
- **Workbook 5.3 Support**

Consolidation

- Students prepare revision cards for the unit. They write a key term from the unit on one side of the card and the definition on the other side. Students can then work in pairs and take turns identifying a key term from the definition or providing a definition, given the key term.
- **Resources**: Resource 5.3D

Alternatively or in addition, you can use the resource provided and students can match the key terms to the definitions. You can use this matching activity as a starter activity for lessons in this unit. You may also want to include key terms from earlier units.

- **Workbook 5.3 Practice**

Stretch

- Ask students to compare and contrast the format of published accounts of a public limited company (see stretch task for Unit 5.1) with those that they have produced for a private limited company.
- **Workbook 5.3 Stretch**

5.4 Clubs and societies

Learning objectives

By the end of this unit, students should be able to:

- distinguish between receipts and payments accounts and income and expenditure accounts
- prepare receipts and payments accounts
- prepare accounts for revenue-generating activities, for example, refreshments, subscriptions
- prepare income and expenditure accounts and statements of financial position
- make adjustments to financial statements as detailed in Unit 5.1 (sole traders)
- define and calculate the accumulated fund.

RESOURCES

- Student's Book pages 232–245
- Workbook pages 58–61
- Resource 5.4A
- Resource 5.4B
- Pro-forma 1
- Pro-forma 3
- Pro-forma 8
- Pro-forma 10
- Pro-forma 11

Key terms

Non-profit-making organisation, Accumulated fund

STARTING POINT

The questions recap the details of expenditure included in financial statements.

For those finding these questions difficult, prompt questions can help, for example:

- *In which financial statement of the business do expenses appear?* (Income statements)
- *What is an irrecoverable debt?* (An amount owing that is unlikely to be received)
- *What is an accrual of income?* (Incomes earned but not yet received by the business at the end of the period)

Suggested answers

1 An irrecoverable debt is treated as an expense in the period in which the business decides the debt is irrecoverable. This involves cancelling the balance on the relevant trade receivables account.

2 Expenses include: advertising, stationery, depreciation of fixtures and fittings, rent, rates, heat and light.

3 An accrual of income would be classified as a current asset in the statement of financial position.

Exploring

The questions require students to consider why some organisations exist not to make a profit.

Suggested answers

1 Some organisations exist to provide a service for their members and do not intend to make a profit. For example, a sports club may exist to provide sporting facilities for their members to use. As long as the sports club is able to cover the costs of operating the facilities, they do not need to make a profit. These organisations do not have an 'owner', they are run and managed by trustees. An owner would want a return for their investment, whereas trustees often complete the work for free.

2 The students will suggest three clubs or societies that exist in their local area. The services will relate to the club or society that has been chosen.

3 The answers will vary depending on the charity that the students have chosen. Responses may include donations, subscriptions, fund raising events, raffles.

Developing

Students should be able to prepare financial statements (income statements and statements of financial position) for trading organisations confidently. This forms the foundation of the financial statements to be produced in this unit.

This unit focuses on the financial statements of non-profit-making organisations.

Use question 1 to get students to consider non-profit-making organisations that exist in the local area. There may be work experience opportunities, if students have an interest in any of the clubs or societies.

Activity: Non-profit-making organisations

In this activity, students consider the operation of non-profit-making organisations in practice.

Approximate time required: 1 hour

Pair/group work: Each group identifies a club or society in the local area. If possible, each group should choose a different club/society. They investigate:

1 the main purpose of the club or society

2 how the club or society raises funds

3 how the club or society spends its funds.

Bring the class together. Each group presents its findings.

Question 2 allows students to consider the expenses that may be incurred by a sports club. Explain the importance of accurately identifying expenses in a receipts and payments account. If you used the activity above, it would work well if students identified the expenses that would be incurred by the organisation they investigated.

Suggested answer

2 Expenses may include: rent and rates of sports venue, for example, a football pitch; wages of sports coaches; hire of sports equipment; depreciation in value of sport equipment; depreciation in value of vehicles used to transport club members; competition prizes.

You could use simple questions, such as those below, as a starter exercise to the work on the financial statements of non-profit-making organisations.

- *What is a cash book?* (A combined cash and bank account that records all transaction involving payments and receipts of money)
- *What is the difference between a debit and a credit entry in a cash book?* (A debit entry is a receipt; a credit entry is a payment.)
- *What is meant by capital and revenue income and expenditure?* (Capital expenditure is business expenditure used to purchase or improve assets expected to be used in the business for more than one year; revenue expenditure is expenditure on running the business. Capital receipts are business income that is not part of the day-to-day operations of the business; revenue receipts are business income that comes from day-to-day operations.)

Highlight how double entry procedures are used in a receipts and payments account. Look specifically at the debit side, the credit side, debit balance and credit balance. Explain the key knowledge: what receipts and payments accounts do not do. Remind students that a receipts and payments account is a summarised cash book. If necessary, recap the theory of cash books on pages 51–55 in the Student's Book.

Take time continually to reinforce the difference in the financial statements produced by sole traders and partnerships and those of clubs and societies.

Activity: Receipts and payments accounts vs income and expenditure accounts

Use this activity to highlight the differences between receipts and payments accounts and income and expenditure accounts.

Approximate time required: 10 minutes

Discussion: Students discuss, in pairs, the differences between receipts and payments accounts and income and expenditure accounts. Bring the class together to discuss the answer.

Suggested answers

Receipts and payments accounts	Income and expenditure accounts
A summarised cash book that uses double entry procedures	A financial statement equivalent of a profit-making organisation's income statement
Does not account for accruals and prepayments	Includes adjustments in accordance with the matching principle
Does not include any non-cash transactions, for example depreciation	Includes non-cash transactions, for example, depreciation and irrecoverable debts
Does not differentiate between capital and revenue income and expenditure	Includes only revenue income and expenditure
Cash receipts are recorded on the debit side of the account and cash payments are recorded on the credit side	Expenditures are recorded on the debit side of the account and incomes are recorded on the credit side
Exists outside of the double entry system	Is part of the double entry system
Not accompanied by a statement of financial position	Accompanied by a statement of financial position

You could use simple questions, such as those below, as a starter exercise to the work on the revenue-generating activities of non-profit making organisations.

- *What is a prepayment?* (Prepaid expenses are expenses that have been paid in advance of the accounting period to which they relate; Prepaid incomes are incomes that have been received in advance of the accounting period to which they relate.)
- *What is an accrual?* (Accrued expenses are expenses relating to the current accounting period that remain unpaid at the end of a period; Accrued incomes are incomes that have been earned during the accounting period but not yet received.)
- *How is a prepayment of income treated in the financial statements?* (It is subtracted from the income received in the income statement and the prepaid amount is included as a current asset in the statement of financial position.)

Advise students to revisit Unit 4.3 and consider how to account for other payables and other receivables, if necessary.

Question 3 considers how a club or society would benefit from receiving funds in advance of their due date. Review the benefits of the club or society having extra money that they did not expect to have. They need to appreciate also that the club would be liable to return the funds if requested.

Suggested answers

3 By prepaying subscriptions, the members are allowing the non-profit-making organisation to spend this money in advance of when it was due. This will aid the cash flow of the non-profit making organisation.

Look at the case study with the class. It provides an example of a club that has introduced a life membership scheme. Students could discuss the advantages to the members of life membership to local clubs or clubs in general.

Students need extensive practice of the preparation of financial statements to ensure a good understanding of this topic.

Activity: Financial statements

Use this activity to provide students with additional practice in preparing financial statements.

Approximate time required: 1 hour

Resources: Resource 5.4A

Before the lesson: Print sufficient copies of the resource sheet for the class.

Individual work: Students complete the financial statements on the resource.

Answer

Subscriptions			
	$		$
Balance b/d (accrued)	1500	Bank/cash	121300
Income and expenditure account	118000		
Balance c/d (prepaid)	1800		
	121300		121300
		Balance b/d	1800

Western Highlands Rugby Club		
Income and expenditure account for the year ended 31 December 2018		
	$	$
Income		
Subscriptions	118000	
Competition income	11180	
		129180
Expenditure		
General expenses	25290	
Travelling expenses	21660	
Rent	24900	
Loss on sale of motor van	2500	
Depreciation of motor van	15000	
		89350
Surplus for the year		39830

Applying

Use this task to ensure students are confident in preparing financial statements for non-profit-making organisations.

Answers

1 Subscriptions workings:

Subscriptions			
	$		$
Balance b/d (accrued)	2000	Bank/cash	2000
Income and expenditure account	4000	Bank/cash	4000
Balance c/d (prepaid)	800	Bank/cash	800
	6800		6800
		Balance b/d	800

Northern Theatre Group		
Income and expenditure account for the year ended 28 February 2018		
	$	$
Income		
Subscriptions	4000	
Proceeds of sale of theatre props and equipment	1400	
Profit from theatre performances (3800 – 2500)	1300	
		6700
Expenditure		
General expenses	430	
Insurance	650	
Rent (2 800 + 560)	3360	
		4440
Surplus for the year		**2260**

2 Statement of financial position

Northern Theatre Group			
Statement of financial position as at 28 February 2018			
	$	$	$
	Cost	Depreciation	Net book value
Non-current assets			
Theatre props and equipment (2400 + 6700 – 1400)			2400
			2400
Current assets			
Bank		2500	

Northern Theatre Group			
Statement of financial position as at 28 February 2018			
	$	$	$
	Cost	Depreciation	Net book value
Other receivables (rent)		840	
			3340
Total assets			**5740**
Accumulated fund			2680
Add surplus for the year			2260
			4940
Current liabilities			
Subscriptions prepaid			800
			800
Total liabilities			**5740**

Knowledge check

- **Resources**: Pro-forma 1, Pro-forma 3, Pro-forma 8, Pro-forma 10, Pro-forma 11
- **Answers**: See pages 247–249

Check your progress

Ask students to complete the **Check your progress** section in the Student's Book.

Support

- **Resources**: Resource 5.4A

  Students complete the financial statements in the resource provided.
- **Workbook Unit 5.4 Support**

Consolidation

- Students prepare revision cards for the unit. They write a term relating to clubs and societies from the unit (see Resource 5.4B) on one side of the card and the definition on the other side. Students can then work in pairs and take turns identifying a term from the definition or providing a definition, given the term.
- **Resources**: Resource 5.4B

  Alternatively or in addition, you can use the resource provided and students can match the key terms to the definitions. You can use this matching activity as a starter activity for lessons in this unit. You may also want to include key terms from earlier units.
- **Workbook Unit 5.4 Practice**

Stretch

- Students use the internet to research a national charity. Alternatively, they could use personal contacts or write to a local club, society or charity to request copies of their financial statements (although many organisations may be unwilling to release their information).

  Students review the format of any accounts they are able to obtain and examine how their chosen organisation raises money.
- **Workbook Unit 5.4 Stretch**

5.5 Manufacturing accounts

Learning objectives

By the end of this unit, students should be able to:

- distinguish between direct and indirect costs
- understand direct material, direct labour, prime cost and factory overheads
- understand and make adjustments for work in progress
- calculate factory cost of production
- prepare manufacturing accounts: income statements and statements of financial position
- make adjustments to financial statements as detailed in Unit 5.1 (sole traders).

Resources

- Student's Book pages 246–257
- Workbook pages 62–64
- Resource 5.5A
- Resource 5.5B
- Pro-forma 10
- Pro-forma 11

Key terms

Manufacturing account, Prime cost, Royalties, Direct costs, Indirect costs

STARTING POINT

The questions recap the work covered on irrecoverable debts and the sale of non-current assets.

If students find these questions difficult, it may be helpful to use prompt questions, for example:

- *What is an irrecoverable debt?* (An amount owing that is unlikely to be received)
- *What is a non-current asset?* (An asset that is not likely to be turned into cash)
- *List three examples of non-current assets.* (For example, premises, equipment, fixtures and fittings, motor vehicles, machinery)
- *What is the general journal?* (The book of prime entry used to record transactions not found in any other journal)
- *What are loose tools?* (Small items of equipment, such as hammers, spanners, screwdrivers, that are used in a business)

Suggested answers

1 An irrecoverable debt written off may be recovered in the future. This means that the business is paid an amount it had already written off as an irrecoverable debt. The recovery of debts written off is also known as bad debts recovered.

There are two approaches to accounting for the recovery of debts written off.

1. Amounts received are debited to the bank and credited to the income statement as a revenue receipt.
2. Amounts received are debited to the bank and credited to the income statement as a revenue receipt and the original amount owing is reinstated as a trade receivable. The personal account of the credit customer in the sales ledger is credited with the amount received on recovery of the debt.

2 • A sale of a non-current asset is classified as a capital receipt because the money received from the sale does not belong to a particular period of time.

• A sale of non-current assets is referred to as an asset disposal. Asset disposal also applies to the situation of a business scrapping a non-current asset before the end of its useful life.

• The profit or loss on asset disposal is based on how much the asset is sold for compared with the net book value of the asset at the time of sale.

• When an asset is sold, an asset disposal account is opened to record the transactions connected to the sale. The entries needed in the asset disposal account are:

Entries in asset disposal account	
Debit entries	**Credit entries**
Original cost value of asset being sold/scrapped	Accumulated depreciation of asset sold/scrapped
Profit on disposal*	Proceeds from sale (or trade receivables if on credit)
	Loss on disposal

These entries would be replicated in the journal.

Once these entries have been made, the account is closed. If the asset is sold for the same amount as its net book value, there will be no profit or loss made on its disposal. The account would balance without any entry to transfer amounts to the income statement.

3 In this method of depreciation, the amount of depreciation charged each year is the change in the asset's estimated value between the start and the end of the year.

The revaluation method of depreciation involves the business deciding each year on a fair value for the asset. The value of the asset can be increased or decreased, based on an estimate of its value. The revaluation method is most likely to be used when a business owns lots of small-value items that are held by the business for more than one year, such as loose tools.

Using the revaluation method, the yearly depreciation is based on the change in the estimated value of the asset between the start and the end of the year. Adjustments are also made for any purchases of non-current assets during the year.

EXPLORING

These questions encourage students to think about businesses that produce the goods they sell. Develop the discussion by asking students to think about how the differences between this type of business and a trading business will affect the financial statements that they produce. (The financial statements of these organisations vary from those of a trading business, as a manufacturer will have no 'purchases' figure, since the business will have made the goods for resale and not purchased them to sell on to their customers.)

Suggested answers

1 Students' own answer, for example, a bakery.

2 Appropriate components may include, for example, mirror, door, headlight, engine.

3 If the business is unable to make the products, its shop will not be able to make any revenue. A business that buys goods to sell could change suppliers to ensure continuity of supply.

DEVELOPING

Again, the work in this unit builds on the work on income statements and statements of financial position for a sole trader covered in Unit 5.1.

Elicit from students other topics that they have covered that are likely to be included in the financial statements. Support students who may be having difficulties with particular topics. For example, students should be able to calculate annual and cumulative depreciation accurately for inclusion in the manufacturing accounts. If they are unable to do this, advise individuals to recap Chapter 4.

Most students will have an understanding that some businesses manufacture or make the products that they sell. Elicit the difference between a manufacturing and a trading business. Consider that manufacturing businesses can be sole traders, partnerships or limited companies. Explain that the purchases figure in the trading account is replaced by the production cost of goods completed.

Use question 1 as a plenary to the work on prime cost.

Suggested answer

1 Direct labour refers to the money paid to workers that are directly involved in the production of the goods being sold. For example, in the car manufacturing industry, a worker who works on the production line would be classed as direct labour. Indirect labour refers to the costs incurred to pay employees who are not directly involved in the production process, for example, canteen staff, management.

Before introducing question 2, clarify that in a manufacturing business there will be no 'purchases' figure to include in the trading section of the income statement. This is because the business is not buying in goods to sell to the public – they are making the products to sell.

Suggested answer

2 A manufacturing account is required to calculate the cost of manufacturing the products made in the business. This is the total of the prime cost and the overhead cost added together. This total cost of production is then transferred to the trading section of an income statement, where it will appear instead of the purchases figure in the accounts you have seen so far.

Question 3 ask students to identify how inventory will differ for a manufacturing business compared to a trading business. They should be able to speculate, based on their knowledge of what a manufacturing business is. For those having difficulty with the question, prompt questions can help, for example:

- *What is inventory for a sole trader?* (Goods for resale)
- *Think about a manufacturing business. What does it produce?* (Examples could include cars, televisions, lamps.)
- *What does it need to make these products?* (Raw materials)
- *How long do you think it takes to make a car? What about for a carpenter to produce a table?*

Suggested answer

3 As well as finished goods for resale it will also include partly finished goods and raw materials.

Question 4 asks students to identify three examples of finished goods for a manufacturing business. There is no definitive answer here, but answers could include loaves of bread, cars, machines, etc.

Introduce the financial statements of a manufacturing account and work through the worked examples in the Student's Book.

You could use questions such as those below as starter exercises for later lessons in this unit.

- *What is a manufacturing business?* (One that takes raw materials and turns them into finished goods that can be sold to customers. For example, a bakery may take flour, eggs, butter, etc and make bread and cakes.)
- *What is the difference between direct and indirect costs? Give me an example of each.* (Direct costs are costs that can be traced to the product being manufactured and are related to the level of output, for example, wages of workers on a production line, raw materials, royalties; indirect costs are costs that cannot be traced to the product being manufactured yet are still a cost of the factory, for example, factory rent, factory electricity, depreciation of machinery.)
- *What is a royalty? Is this a direct cost or an indirect cost?* (A fee that is paid to the individual who originally invented the product being manufactured. It is a direct cost.)

Students need extensive practice of the preparation of financial statements to ensure a good understanding of this topic.

Activity: Financial statements

This activity provides additional practice in the preparation of a manufacturing account.

Approximate time required: 1 hour

Resources: Resource 5.5A

Before the lesson: Print sufficient copies of the resource sheet for the class.

Individual work: Students add numerical data to complete the manufacturing account.

Stretch task: Students work in pairs. Each partly completes the manufacturing account and asks their partner to ascertain the missing figures

APPLYING

Use this task to ensure students are confident preparing financial statements for manufacturing businesses.

Answers

Morella Bakery Equipment Manufacturers			
Manufacturing account for the year ending 31 December 2018			
	$	$	$
Raw materials			
Opening inventory		25000	
Purchases		120000	
		145000	
Less closing inventory		21000	
Cost of raw materials consumed			124000
Direct wages			63000
Royalties paid			2500
PRIME COST			**189500**
Add factory overheads			
Supervisor's wages		15000	
Factory electricity		7250	
Insurance		7500	
			29750
			219250
opening work in progress			5500
			224750
Less closing work in progress			7650
Manufacturing cost of goods completed			**217100**

Morella Bakery Equipment Manufacturers			
Statement of financial position (Extract) as at 31 December 2018			
	$	$	$
Current assets			
Inventory:			
Raw materials		21000	
Work in progress		7650	28650

Knowledge check

- **Resources**: Pro-forma 10, Pro-forma 11
- **Answers**: See pages 249–251

Check your progress

Ask students to complete the **Check your progress** section in the Student's Book.

Support

- Students identify and research a local manufacturing company. They create a list of costs incurred by the manufacturing company. They prepare a table that states whether these costs are:
  - direct material
  - direct labour
  - direct costs
  - indirect costs
  - factory overheads**[/Sub BL]**
- **Workbook Unit 5.5 Support**

Consolidation

- Students prepare revision cards for the unit. They write a term relating to manufacturing accounts (see Resource 5.5B) from the unit on one side of the card and the definition on the other side. Students can then work in pairs and take turns identifying a term from the definition or providing a definition, given the term.
- **Resources**: Resource 5.5B
- Alternatively or in addition, you can use the resource provided and students can match the terms to the definitions. You can use this matching activity as a starter activity for lessons in this unit. You may also want to include key terms from earlier units.
- **Workbook Unit 5.5 Practice**

Stretch

- Students choose a manufacturing business with which they are familiar. They prepare a presentation that explains the different types of inventory held by the business. Encourage students to consider raw materials, work in progress and finished goods.
- **Workbook Unit 5.5 Stretch**

5.6 Incomplete records

LEARNING OBJECTIVES

By the end of this unit, students should be able to:

- explain the disadvantages of not maintaining a full set of accounting records
- prepare opening and closing statements of affairs
- calculate profit for the year from changes in capital over time
- calculate sales, purchases, gross profit, trade receivables and trade payables and other figures from incomplete information
- prepare income statements and statements of financial position from incomplete records
- make adjustments to financial statements as detailed in Unit 5.1 (sole traders)
- apply the techniques of mark-up, margin and inventory turnover to arrive at missing figures.

RESOURCES

- Student's Book pages 258–272
- Workbook pages 65–67
- Resource 5.6A page 000
- Resource 5.6B page 000
- Pro-forma 1
- Pro-forma 8
- Pro-forma 10
- Pro-forma 11

KEY TERMS

Statement of affairs

STARTING POINT

The questions recap the purpose of an income statement and statement of financial position.

If students find the questions difficult, it may be helpful to use prompt questions, for example:

- *What is a sole trader?* (Any business that is owned and controlled by one person)
- *What is a statement of financial position?* (A financial statement showing the assets of the business and the financing for these assets, either from owner's equity or liabilities)
- *What is an income statement?* (A financial statement showing a business's income and expenses for an accounting period and the resulting profit or loss)
- *What is inventory?* (Trading businesses: goods available for sale; manufacturing businesses: finished goods, partly finished goods and raw materials)

Continue the discussion by asking where a business records inventory appears in the financial statements. (Opening and closing inventory is recorded in the cost of sales section of the income statement. Closing inventory is also recorded in the current assets section of the statement of financial position.)

Suggested answers

1 A statement of financial position is a formal way of representing the accounting equation. A business's statement of financial position lists all of the assets that are owned by a business and all of the liabilities that are owed by the business.

2 An income statement shows the business's income and expenses for an accounting period and the resulting profit or loss. The resulting profit or loss is transferred to the business's statement of financial position.

3 Inventory is valued at original cost or its net realisable value, whichever is lower. The net realisable value (of inventory) is the selling price *less* any costs incurred getting the inventory into saleable condition. The original cost is how much the business paid for the inventory when it was purchased. The net realisable value is the expected selling price *less* any costs incurred getting the inventory ready for sale. For example, inventory may be damaged and need repairing before it can be sold. Normally, the original cost is lower than the net realisable value as it is expected a business will sell inventory for more than its original cost.

EXPLORING

The questions require students to consider the importance of maintaining financial records. Develop the discussion by asking students to speculate on what might happen if the records are incomplete.

Suggested answers

1 A sole trader needs to maintain a full set of double entry accounting records to ensure financial statements can be produced at the year end. This will ensure that the sole trader will pay the correct amount of tax, as the profit for the year will have been accurately calculated.

2 When calculating profit, only revenue expenditure is subtracted from the income earned by the business. Therefore, profit will be lower if an item of capital expenditure is included. Some expenditure might include portions of both capital and revenue expenditure. It is important to separate the two wherever possible. (See Student's Book, Unit 4.1, page 122 for definitions.)

DEVELOPING

This topic is the most complex of those covered in Chapter 5. The principles involved require students to have good numerical dexterity, in order to calculate the missing totals from incomplete accounting data. Before commencing work on incomplete records, students must be able confidently to produce financial statements for a sole trader. Without this basic understanding, it will be virtually impossible for them to complete the tasks in this unit.

Introduce the topic. Use question 1 to initiate a discussion on the types of record that a small business may keep and which records it is unlikely to keep. For those having difficulty with the question, prompt questions can help, for example:

- *What is an accounting record?* (Accounting records begin with a business transaction that generates a business document. The next stage of the process is to transfer the details from the business document into the appropriate book of prime entry. Once the information has been transferred, the details of the transaction can then be posted to the double entry accounts in the various ledgers of the business. To produce the financial statements of the business, the accountant balances these accounts and transfers the balances to the financial statements.)
- *What is a business document or a source document?* (A document received or issued by businesses. These documents contain vital information about the transactions made between businesses and are used to make entries in the accounting records of businesses.)
- *What are ledger accounts?* (Ledger accounts are used to record business transactions by making two entries – one debit entry and one credit entry.)

Suggested answers

1 Answers may include receipts, invoices, ledger accounts.

Discuss how incomplete records could be turned into financial statements. Emphasise that it is not a legal requirement to keep comprehensive double entry accounting records. However, businesses are required to have accounts to ascertain the amount of tax that needs to be paid. Discuss the principles of single entry accounts.

Use question 2 as a plenary to the work on calculation of profit from changes in profit or as a starter to the work on statements of affairs.

Suggested answers

2 A sole trader will use the profit for the year figure to decide how many drawings can be taken. The sole trader will also use the profit figure to calculate the amount of tax that needs to be paid for the year.

Use question 3 as a plenary to the work on statements of affairs or as a starter to the work on calculation of financial figures from incomplete information.

Suggested answers

3 The sole trader may not able to keep the accounting records as he has not been educated to do so. Alternatively, the sole trader may not have time to keep accurate records.

You will need to decide when to teach the topic, using ratios to calculate missing figures. It may be more appropriate to revisit this section of the unit once students have studied Chapter 6, where the ratios that are used to calculate missing figures are studied in detail, along with the formulae. A thorough knowledge of the ratio formulae will aid students when deciding which ratio to use.

Students often confuse mark-up and margin, so ensure you clarify the difference.

The diagram gives a visual representation of mark-up. It may help students to understand how they can deduce the cost of an item or cost of sales from a selling price or sales revenue by deducting mark-up.

Selling price = cost + mark-up

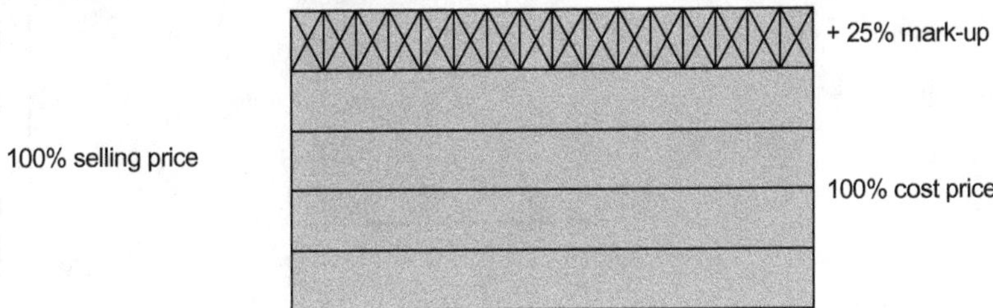

APPLYING

Use this task to ensure students are confident in preparing financial statements from incomplete records. It can be completed without having studied the section on ratios.

Answers

(a)

Anita			
Statement of affairs as at 31 October 2017			
	$	**$**	**$**
	Cost	**Depreciation**	**Net book value**
Non-current assets			
Motor vehicles	9000	0	9000
Office equipment	3200	0	3200
Fixtures and fittings	2500	0	2500
	14700	0	14700
Current assets			
Other receivables		800	
Cash at bank		4860	
Cash in hand		240	
			5900
Total assets			20600
Capital			**14600**
Current liabilities			
Bank loan			6000
			6000
Total liabilities			20600

(b)

Anita			
Statement of affairs as at 1 November 2018			
	$	**$**	**$**
	Cost	**Depreciation**	**Net book value**
Non-current assets			
Motor vehicles	10000	0	10000
Office equipment	4000	0	4000
Fixtures and fittings	300	0	300
	14300	0	14300
Current assets			
Other receivables		700	
Cash at bank		1340	
Cash in hand		300	
			2340
Total assets			16640
Capital			**6640**
Current liabilities			
Bank loan			10000
			10000
Total liabilities			16640

(c) Profit = closing capital – opening capital – capital introduced + drawings

Profit = 6640 – 14600 – 0 + 11000 = **$3040**

Knowledge check

Note that questions 2, 3, 8 and 9 relate to the work on calculating missing figures from ratios.

- **Resources**: Pro-forma 1, Pro-forma 8, Pro-forma 10, Pro-forma 11
- **Answers**: See pages 251–252

Check your progress

Ask students to complete the **Check your progress** section in the Student's Book.

Support

- **Resources**: Resource 5.6A, Resource 5.6B

Resource 5.6A: For students who need extra practice calculating missing figures

Resource 5.6B: To give students practice deciding whether items belong on the income statement or the statement of financial position and in deciding whether items are current or non-current assets or liabilities

- **Workbook Unit 5.6 Support**

Mixed ability

- Students work in small mixed-ability groups. They choose a sole trader business with which they are familiar. Students prepare a presentation for the business owner that provides information about the records that they need to maintain throughout the year. The students could be encouraged to consider records of sales and purchases, control accounts, journals, etc. The presentation could be enhanced with the inclusion of numerical examples based on actual or simulated data.

- **Workbook Unit 5.6 Practice**
- **Workbook Unit 5.6 Stretch**

Chapter review

Note that question 7 relates to the work on calculating missing figures from ratios.

- **Resources**: Pro-forma 8, Pro-forma 10, Pro-forma 11
- **Answers:** See pages 252–260
- **Workbook: Chapter 5 review**

Answer to Support activity

Resource 5.6A

	$	$	$	$	$
Opening capital	20000	50000	100000	70000	250000
Add capital introduced	10000	20000	50000	30000	50000
Add profit for the year	10000	10000	20000	20000	30000
Less drawings	5000	20000	90000	30000	50000
Equals closing capital	35000	60000	80000	90000	280000

Resource 5.6B

1 Income statement: revenue, purchases, heat and light, carriage inwards, closing inventory.

Statement of financial position: premises, motor vehicles, office equipment, fixtures and fittings, trade receivables, cash in hand, short term bank loan , mortgage on business property, bank overdraft, trade payables.

2 Current assets: trade receivables; cash in hand

Current liabilities: short-term bank loan; bank overdraft; trade payables

Non-current assets: premises; motor vehicles; office equipment; fixtures and fittings

Non-current liabilities: mortgage on business property

6 Analysis and interpretation

This chapter explains the basics of ratio analysis. It will provide the ratio formulae required to make an analysis of a business's performance.

Numerical examples and tasks enable students to practise ratio calculations and explain the importance of ratio analysis in business organisations.

Prior knowledge

Students should already be able to:

- use the accounting equation and understand the purpose of accounting
- prepare double entry ledger accounts
- prepare a trial balance
- account for capital and revenue expenditure and receipts, depreciation, irrecoverable debts and provisions for doubtful debts
- value business inventory
- prepare financial statements for:
  - sole traders
  - partnerships
  - limited companies
  - clubs and societies
  - manufacturing accounts
  - incomplete records.

Background for non-subject specialists

Analysis and interpretation of financial and accounting information and data can be completed in a number of ways. Businesses tend to use ratio analysis as one method.

Ratio analysis involves the calculation and interpretation of various ratios to provide key performance indicators. In particular, ratio analysis aids businesses to assess profitability, liquidity and efficiency. Individuals and groups who have an interest in the financial affairs of a business may seek to find out:

1. how well the business is operating
2. how strong the financial position of the business is
3. what the future prospects for the business are.

6.1 Calculation and understanding of ratios

Learning objectives

By the end of this unit, students should be able to:

- calculate and explain the importance of the following ratios:
  - gross margin
  - profit margin
  - return on capital employed (ROCE)
  - current ratio
  - liquid (acid test) ratio
  - rate of inventory turnover (times)
  - trade receivables turnover (days)
  - trade payables turnover (days).

Resources

- Student's Book pages 284–295
- Workbook pages 75–77
- Resource 6.1A

Key terms

Gross margin, Profit margin, Return on capital employed, Rate of inventory turnover, Trade receivables turnover, Trade payables turnover, Liquidity (of a business), Current ratio, Liquid (acid test) ratio

STARTING POINT

The questions identify key components of financial statements. Most students will be able to identify these and understand how they can be used by users of financial records. Business studies students may have covered the topic of ratio analysis in their studies.

When considering the answers to questions 2 and 3, advise students that they may find it helpful to review the financial statements they produced in Chapter 5.

Encourage students to consider why different individuals and groups of people (interested parties) may need to analyse financial data and financial statements. Ask students to identify items in financial statements that may be of interest to readers of the financial records.

If students find the questions difficult, it may be helpful to use prompt questions, for example:

- *What is a sole trader?* (Any business that is owned and controlled by one person)
- *What does a sole trader aim to achieve?* (A profit for the year)
- *What items does an income statement contain?* (Revenue, cost of sales, gross profit, expenses, profit for the year)
- *How may a business try to pay its short-term debts, for example, trade payables?* (They may try to pay cash or within the deadline of their contract. In general, businesses wish to pay their debts after they have received payment from their customers.)

Suggested answers

1 Sole traders analyse their accounts to assess their profitability and consider how many drawings they can take. The accounts will also inform them of whether the business is likely to be able to expand in the future, whether they are able to take out a loan, and assess what remedial action may need to be taken. 'Remedial action' refers to the action a business owner may need to take to ensure their business can continue to operate in the future – for example, obtaining a short-term bank loan or chasing their trade receivables.

2 The income statement of a business calculates both the gross profit and profit for the financial year.

3 Liquidity is a measure of the ability of a business to pay its short-term debts.

EXPLORING

The questions consider how financial statements can be used by users of financial records.

Suggested answers

1 The local bakery should compare itself against other bakeries of a similar size in the local area. They should not compare themselves against large national or international businesses.

2 Business owners will compare their income statement and statement of financial position data over several years, to see whether key indicators have increased or decreased. Examples would include gross profit, profit for the year, non-current assets and bank balance.

3 Current bank balance, other business debts, non-current assets that could be used by the bank as security in the unlikely event that the loan cannot be repaid.

DEVELOPING

This unit reviews and analyses financial statements through ratio analysis. Advise students of the importance of learning the formula for each ratio. To reinforce this, you could start each lesson with a quiz on the ratio formulae.

Students also need to know what the ratios say about a business and how they are used. The in-text questions help students to understand the purpose of the ratios. Ratio analysis is further developed in the subsequent units.

Look at the case study with the class. It provides an example of how important it is to look at numerical data in context.

Students must be able to differentiate between the three categories of ratio that they will study at this level. By considering each set of ratios in turn, they will gain an understanding of their functions and learn to calculate them. Ensure students are confident with one set of ratios before moving on to the next.

Also, ensure that students know that:

- the information used to calculate the profitability ratios is found in the income statement
- the information used to calculate the activity or efficiency ratios comes from both the income statement and the statement of financial position
- the liquidity or solvency ratios use information from the statement of financial position.

Use question 1 to reinforce that not all sales revenue is generated in cash. Many customers will expect to be given a certain number of days to pay for the goods they have received. Discuss why big businesses usually expect to be given longer to pay (big businesses are generally expected to order in large quantities and may be less likely not to pay).

Suggested answer

1 By offering 90 days' credit to customers, a business may attract the custom of large businesses.

Question 2 builds on question 1 and leads into the work on liquidity or solvency ratios. Students need to appreciate that businesses are not able to pay their debts until their customers pay for the goods they have sold. The business requires the cash received to pay its own debts rather than converting other assets to cash, to pay.

Suggested answer

2 Businesses need to collect their debts quickly in order for them to earn interest on the money they receive. They do this by placing it into an interest-bearing bank account. In addition, they need the money collected to be able to pay the debts that they have to pay. If they pay the money they owe as slowly as possible, they have the money available for their own use and to gain interest when the money is in the bank account.

Students often need extensive practice in the calculation of the various ratios to ensure a good understanding of ratio analysis.

If you did not cover the work in Unit 5.6 on using ratios to calculate missing figures, this is a good time for students to study it.

APPLYING

Use this task to ensure students are confident calculating the ratios.

Answers

Where appropriate, ratios are expressed correct to 2 decimal places (2 dp).

$$\text{Gross margin} = \frac{\text{gross profit}}{\text{revenue}} \times 100 = \frac{235\,862}{407\,256} \times 100 = 57.91\%\ \text{(to 2 dp)}$$

$$\text{Profit margin} = \frac{\text{profit for the year}}{\text{revenue}} \times 100 = \frac{32\,411}{407\,256} \times 100 = 7.96\%\ \text{(to 2 dp)}$$

$$\text{Return on capital employed} = \frac{\text{profit for the year}}{\text{capital employed}} \times 100 = \frac{32\,411}{118\,889} \times 100 = 27.26\%\ \text{(to 2 dp)}$$

$$\text{Rate of inventory turnover} = \frac{\text{cost of sales}}{\text{average inventory}}$$

$$\text{Average inventory} = \frac{\text{opening inventory + closing inventory}}{2} = \frac{21\,442 + 23\,004}{2} = 22\,223$$

$$\text{Rate of inventory turnover} = \frac{171\,394}{22\,223} = 7.71\ \text{times (to 2 dp)}$$

$$\text{Trade receivables turnover} = \frac{\text{trade receivables}}{\text{credit sales}} \times 365$$

$$= \frac{33\,398}{414\,640} \times 365 = 29.40\ \text{days (to 2 dp)}$$

$$\text{Trade payables turnover} = \frac{\text{trade payables}}{\text{credit purchases}} \times 365 = \frac{29\,110}{192\,552} \times 365 = 55.18\ \text{days (to 2 dp)}$$

$$\text{Current ratio} = \frac{\text{current assets}}{\text{current liabilities}} = \frac{61\,372}{38\,908} = 1.58 : 1\ \text{(to 2 dp)}$$

$$\text{Liquid (acid test) ratio} = \frac{\text{current assets – closing inventory}}{\text{current liabilities}} = \frac{61\,372 - 23\,004}{38\,908} = 0.99 : 1\ \text{(to 2 dp)}$$

Knowledge check

- **Answers**: See page 260

Check your progress

Ask students to complete the **Check your progress** section in the Student's Book.

Support

- **Resources:** Resource 6.1A

Students match the ratios with their formulae and with their definitions and purposes.

- **Workbook Unit 6.1 Support**

Consolidation

- Students prepare a poster about the ratios they have studied in this unit. They should include:
  - the formula
  - the definition and purpose

- the name of the financial statement that will provide the required data for each item in the formulae, for example, the figure for trade receivables is found in the statement of financial position.

- **Workbook Unit 6.1 Practice**

Stretch

- Ask students to use the information in the published accounts of a public limited company (see stretch task for Unit 5.1) to calculate each of the ratios studied in this unit. If you wish to use the stretch activity in Unit 6.3, students will also need a set of financial accounts from a second company that is similar in nature to the first.

Students can keep the ratios they calculate to analyse the business's performance when they have studied Unit 6.2.

- **Workbook Unit 6.1 Stretch**

6.2 Interpretation of accounting ratios

Learning objectives

By the end of this unit, students should be able to:

- prepare and comment on simple statements showing comparison of results for different years
- make recommendations and suggestions for improving profitability and working capital
- understand the significance of the difference between the gross margin and the profit margin as an indicator of a business's efficiency
- explain the relationship of gross profit and profit for the year to the valuation of inventory, rate of inventory turnover, revenue, expenses, and equity.

Resources

- Student's Book pages 296–312
- Workbook pages 78–79
- Resource 6.2A

Key terms

Economy, Competitor, Financial analyst, Trend analysis, Interpretation (of financial ratios), Working capital, Debt factoring

STARTING POINT

Revisit the discussion from earlier units: why different individuals and groups of people (interested parties) may need to analyse financial data and financial statements. The questions recap the use of ratio analysis in a business.

If students find the questions difficult, it may help to use prompt questions, for example:

- *What is liquidity?* (The ability of a business to meet its short-term debts)
- *Why does a business need to pay their debts on time?* (To ensure suppliers will continue to supply them in the future)
- *What is the relationship between current assets and current liabilities?* (Current assets – current liabilities = working capital (a measure of liquidity))
- *What does a business subtract from gross profit to calculate profit for the year?* (Expenses)
- *What are the formulae for the current ratio and the liquid (acid test) ratio?* (Current ratio = current ratio ÷ current liabilities; liquid (acid test) ratio = (current assets – closing inventory) ÷ current liabilities)

Suggested answers

1 Working capital is the capital of a business that is used in its day-to-day trading operations. It is calculated as current assets less current liabilities.

2 Gross profit is the revenue received from sales minus the cost of the goods sold. Profit for the year is calculated as gross profit minus all expenses incurred by the business during the financial year.

3 The current ratio is a measure of the liquidity of a business, which compares current assets to current liabilities. The liquid (acid test) ratio also measures the liquidity of a business. It compares current assets (excluding closing inventory) to current liabilities. This ratio is a more severe test of a business's liquidity and its ability to pay short-term debts. The ratio assumes that inventory may be perishable, go out of date or become obsolete (due to changes in fashion or technology). This would mean that the business will be left with inventory that it cannot sell and therefore would not be able to be use to pay its short-term debts.

EXPLORING

The questions consider how ratio data can be analysed by users.

If students find the questions difficult, it may help to use prompt questions, for example:

- *What happens to profit for the year if the expenses of a business increase?* (It will decrease.)
- *What could a business do to reduce its cost of sales?* (Reduce opening inventory, reduce purchases or increase closing inventory.)
- *What happens to gross profit if a business increases the selling price of its goods but the number of sales remains the same?* (Gross profit will increase.)
- *What does the return on capital employed ratio measure?* (Profitability)
- *Name the liquidity ratios.* (Current ratio, Liquid (acid test) ratio)

Suggested answers

1 It could increase the selling price per unit, reduce the cost of the goods that it purchases for resale, reduce its expenses, for example, staff wages, heat and lighting expenses.

2 The business will be pleased with its performance. The ROCE is 4% higher than the current base rate. Therefore, investors are getting a higher return than they would by keeping their money in an interest-bearing bank account. However, investors must take into account the potential risks when investing in a business.

3 Adi should use ratio analysis. He should calculate and review the current ratio and liquid (acid test) ratio. He could compare his results with those of previous years, with other businesses or against a benchmark.

DEVELOPING

This unit builds on the work of the previous unit. By this point, students should be able to calculate the ratios confidently and understand their purpose. In this unit, students interpret what the ratios they have calculated mean for a business and its stakeholders. Emphasise to students that ratios can only be interpreted fully when compared with other ratios. Individually, they are meaningless.

Question 1 invites students to consider how financial statements can be used for trend analysis. Ask students to identify the key components of an income statement and statement of financial position that could be reviewed by a business.

Suggested answer

1 An income statement will provide information about revenue received, cost of sales, expenses, gross profit and profit for the year.

The statement of financial position highlights the non-current assets, current assets, current liabilities, non-current liabilities and equity.

The business could review whether the figures contained in the financial statements have increased or decreased over a period of time. The financial statements will also allow businesses to calculate a range of ratios. These can also be compared from one year to the next.

Look at the case study with the class. It provides an example of how financial ratios may be used. It also emphasises the need to look at financial information in context.

You could use prompt questions as a plenary exercise after the introductory section or as a starter exercise before moving on to discuss the profitability ratios.

- *Suggest what type of business a local clothing retailer could use to compare their ratio results.* (Another clothing retailer of a similar size in a similar location)
- *What is meant by trend analysis?* (Comparing one year's data or ratios with previous year's results to identify any trends)
- *How would a business use an industry average when reviewing their financial performance?* (It would compare its performance against an industry average to decide if it was doing well.)

As the content of this unit is based on analysis, students are required to use higher-order skills. Emphasise that simple statements such as 'the current ratio is 1 : 1', is not interpretation. Give students practice in reviewing ratio results and making analytical statements, for example:

- The liquid ratio has increased by *x*.
- The liquid ratio has decreased by *x*.
- The current ratio is considerably higher than that of the competitor.
- The gross margin has decreased over the last three years.

Question 2 builds on the work completed in Unit 6.1. Students consider how the gross margin ratio is calculated. You could use prompt questions as necessary, for example:

- *What is the formula for gross margin?* $\left(\frac{\text{gross profit}}{\text{revenue}} \times 100\right)$
- *What is meant by the gross margin?* (The gross profit of a business expressed as a percentage of revenue generated by sales)
- *Identify the potential causes of a fall in gross margin for a business.* (Failing to pass on cost increases to customers; reduction in selling prices; offering a higher rate of trade discount)

Suggested answer

2 Suggestions may include:

- Increase its selling prices to ensure that any increase in costs incurred in purchasing the goods for resale is covered.
- Reduce the amount of trade discount offered to other businesses.
- Ask suppliers for an increase in trade discount.

Question 3 encourages students to consider the implications of a shortage of working capital. Facilitate an initial discussion about how to improve the working capital position of a business.

If students find this question difficult, it may help to use prompt questions, for example:

- *What is working capital?* (The amount of money a business has to operate on a day to day basis)
- *How is working capital calculated?* (Current assets *less* current liabilities)
- *Why is working capital important to a business?* (Without sufficient working capital, a business would not be able to pay its day to day expenses.)

Suggested answer

3 A business will have difficulty in securing finance, such as a loan or overdraft.

It will limit amount of drawings that an owner will be able to take from the business.

Suppliers may stop offering credit terms to the business.

Students will need extensive practice of both the calculation and the analysis of the various ratios to ensure a good understanding of ratio analysis.

APPLYING

Use this task to ensure students are confident not only calculating the ratios but also making analytical comments on the financial performance of the business, by comparing two years' financial results.

Answers

Where appropriate, ratios are expressed correct to 2 decimal places (2 dp).

1 Gross margin = $\frac{\text{gross profit}}{\text{revenue}} \times 100$

2017: $\frac{11680}{12900} \times 100 = 90.54\%$ (to 2 dp)

2018: $\frac{10\,390}{13\,250} \times 100 = 78.42\%$ (to 2 dp)

Profit margin = $\frac{\text{profit for the year}}{\text{revenue}} \times 100$

2017: $\frac{10\,910}{12\,900} \times 100 = 84.57\%$ (to 2 dp)

2018: $\frac{9400}{13\,250} \times 100 = 70\ 94\%$ (to 2 dp)

Return on capital employed = $\frac{\text{profit for the year}}{\text{capital employed}} \times 100$

2017: $\frac{10\,910}{3050} \times 100 = 357.70\%$ (to 2 dp)

2018: $\frac{9400}{2950} \times 100 = 318.64\%$ (to 2 dp)

Rate of inventory turnover = $\frac{\text{cost of sales}}{\text{average inventory}}$

Average inventory = $\frac{\text{opening inventory + closing inventory}}{2}$

2017: $\frac{650 + 980}{2} = 815$

2018: $\frac{980 + 870}{2} = 925$

2017: $\frac{1220}{815} = 1.50$ times (to 2 dp)

2018: $\frac{2860}{925} = 3.09$ times (to 2 dp)

Trade receivables turnover = $\frac{\text{trade receivables}}{\text{credit sales}} \times 365$

2017: $\frac{810}{12\,900} \times 365 = 22.92$ days (to 2 dp)

2018: $\frac{930}{13\,250} \times 365 = 25.62$ days (to 2 dp)

Trade payables turnover = $\frac{\text{trade payables}}{\text{credit purchases}} \times 365$

2017: $\frac{570}{1550} \times 365 = 134.23$ days (to 2 dp)

2018: $\frac{710}{2750} \times 365 = 94.24$ days (to 2 dp)

Current ratio = $\frac{\text{current assets}}{\text{current liabilities}}$

2017: $\frac{1843}{570} = 3.23 : 1$ (to 2 dp)

2018: $\frac{2035}{710} = 2.87 : 1$ (to 2 dp)

Liquid (acid test) ratio = $\frac{\text{current assets – closing inventory}}{\text{current liabilities}}$ current assets – $\frac{\text{closing inventory}}{\text{current liabilities}}$

2017: $\dfrac{1843 - 980}{570}$ = 1.51 : 1 (to 2 dp)

2018: $\dfrac{2035 - 870}{710}$ = 1.64 : 1 (to 2 dp)

2 Comments may include:

- The gross margin has decreased from 2017 to 2018. This is also the case for the profit margin. Business expenses have increased from 770000 to 990000 during the year.
- The current ratio is marginally higher in 2017 than in 2018; however, both are considerably above the generally accepted level. The business should consider paying off their debts.
- The trade receivables turnover has increased from 2017 to 2018. Dover and Sole need to ensure that they chase their trader receivables to ensure that they pay on time.

Knowledge check

- **Answers**: See pages 260–262

Check your progress

Ask students to complete the **Check your progress** section in the Student's Book.

Support

- Ask students needing extra support to work in pairs or small groups to produce a mind map for the topic. They should include actions that could improve the various ratios. These actions can be used as recommendations when analysing business financial performance.
- **Workbook Unit 6.2 Support**

Consolidation

- Students prepare revision cards for the unit. They produce one card for each ratio, summarising the analytical points relating to it.
- **Resources**: Resource 6.2A

  In addition, the cards on the resource provided can added to a matching activity on key terms and definitions from the course.
- **Workbook Unit 6.2 Practice**

Stretch

- Use the ratios calculated in the stretch task for Unit 6.1.
- Ask students to prepare a presentation to the management, analysing the business's financial performance based on the ratio analysis.
- **Workbook Unit 6.2 Stretch**

6.3 Inter-firm comparison

Learning objectives

By the end of this unit, students should be able to:

- understand the problems of inter-firm comparison
- apply accounting ratios to inter-firm comparison.

Resources

- Student's Book pages 313–325
- Workbook pages 80–81
- Resource 6.3A

Key terms

Inter-firm comparison, Accounting principles

STARTING POINT

The questions recap the work completed in Units 6.1 and 6.2 on ratios and financial statements. Most students will be able to identify key components of financial statements and how they can be used by users of financial records. If necessary, they should review the work of Units 6.1 and 6.2.

Suggested answers

1 Trade receivables turnover, trade payables turnover, rate of inventory turnover

2 A business can review whether its profitability, liquidity and efficiency have improved or deteriorated over a period of time. Once a pattern has been identified, the business can review the reasons for the changes and then modify its actions to ensure future success. For example, if a business has improved over the last year and it has been identified that higher-quality goods have caused an increase in sales revenue, this can be continued in the future.

3 Items include:
   - non-current assets, for example, premises, fixtures and fittings, motor vehicles
   - current assets, for example, inventory, bank balance, cash in hand
   - current liabilities, for example, trade payables, bank overdraft.

EXPLORING

The questions consider how ratio analysis can be used to compare business performance. The students are able to apply theory to practice. You may wish to continue the discussion by asking students to think about the differences in the financial statements produced by different types of business – for example, a sole trader and a partnership. Highlight the problems of comparing financial statements and accompanying ratios for different business structures.

Suggested answers

1
   - It allows the business to identify their areas of strength and weakness.
   - It highlights and identifies issues in a business's performance. For example, a business may have a current ratio of 1.5:1 and consider it satisfactory but if a competitor's current ratio is 1.75:1 they may need to consider ways to improve this ratio.
   - Competitors' data can act as a target for the future, which may be motivational to the workforce.

2 Students may suggest 'real' examples from the local area. A generic answer would be another butcher's store of a similar size in the local area.

DEVELOPING

This unit is a development of the analysis completed in Unit 6.2. Explain to students that the analysis required to make inter-firm comparisons uses the same principles as the analysis they completed in Unit 6.2. The same knowledge and skills should be applied throughout this unit. Emphasise the importance of comparing similar types of business. It is also essential that students understand the limitations of completing an inter-firm comparison.

When making inter-firm comparisons, students need to understand that different accounting methods will affect the final profit figures for a business: question 1 draws out one aspect of this.

If students find the question difficult, it may help to use prompt questions, for example:

- *What is depreciation?* (An estimation of how the cost of an asset should be allocated over its useful life)
- *What are the three main methods of depreciation?* (Straight line, reducing balance, revaluation)
- *Where is depreciation included in the financial statements?* (Annual depreciation is included in the expenses section of the income statement and cumulative depreciation is used to calculate the net book value of non-current assets in the statement of financial position.)

Suggested answer

1 Straight line depreciation is calculated as (cost *less* residual value) *divided by* number of years owned. This depreciation method charges the same amount of depreciation to the income statement each year during the life of the asset. It is frequently used for office equipment. Using the straight line depreciation method, if all other expenses remain constant, profit for the year would remain constant from one year to the next.

Reducing balance depreciation calculates depreciation based on the net book value of an asset. This means that the depreciation charge included in the income statement reduces each year. It is frequently used for motor vehicles to offset the increasing cost of maintenance. Using the reducing balance depreciation method, if all other expenses remain constant, profit for the year would increase from one year to the next as the expenses would decrease.

Revaluation depreciation is a method of depreciation in which the amount of depreciation charged each year is the change in the asset's estimated value from the start to the end of the year. It requires the business to decide each year on a fair value for the asset. The value of the asset can be increased or decreased, based on an estimate of its value. Using the revaluation method, the yearly depreciation is based on the change in the estimated value of the asset from the start to the end of the year. Adjustments are also made for any purchases of the non-current asset during the year.

Question 2 enables students to consider business situations that occur. These are likely to be one-off events that affect the financial statements of the business. Discuss why big businesses are most likely to survive during adverse business situations. Business studies students may identify economies of scale and the effect these will have on larger business organisations.

Suggested answer

2 Examples include:

- seasonal activities, for example, the increase of ice-cream sales during a heat wave
- national recession, meaning that members of the public have considerably reduced spending power to purchase goods or services
- natural disaster, for example, a flood, meaning a business cannot operate for a number of weeks
- sudden increase in demand, for example, the introduction of a new computer game would increase sales in computing stores
- situation, for example, if a world-wide tournament, such as the Football World Cup or Olympics, takes place in a particular area, the businesses will have a significant increase in customers.

Look at the case study with the class. It provides an example of inter-firm comparison. Encourage students to think of supermarket chains in their country. They could decide which of the chains target the low-, medium- and high-cost segments of the market and research which chain has the biggest market share.

You could use prompt questions as a plenary exercise after the introductory section or as a starter exercise before moving on to discuss the profitability ratios, for example:

- *What is meant by 'inter-firm comparison'?* (Comparing the financial data or ratio results of one business with those of another similar business)
- *What are the benefits of using inter-firm comparisons?* (It allows a business to analyse how successful it is and how it could improve in the future; it enables a business to identify areas of strength and weakness.)
- *What are the limitations of using inter-firm comparisons?* (Results of the comparison may be inaccurate; non-financial factors, for example, staff motivation or goodwill will not be considered; may not be clear which accounting principles have been used, leading to inaccurate comparisons.)
- *Suggest what type of business a national supermarket chain could use to compare its ratio results.* (Another national supermarket business in the same area)

As the content of this unit is based on comparison, students are required to use higher-order skills. Emphasise that simple statement of facts such as: 'The current ratio for company A is 1 : 1 and for company B is 2 : 1,' is not comparison. Give students practice comparing ratio results and making analytical statements, for example:

- The liquid ratio of company A is 0.3 higher than that of company B.
- The liquid ratio of company A is 0.1 lower than that of company B.
- The gross margin for company A is considerably lower than that of company B.

Question 3 reinforces the importance of comparing businesses that are similar. Regularly remind students that unless they are comparing similar businesses the information is meaningless. If any students find the question difficult, it may help to use prompt questions, for example:

- *What is meant by similar businesses?* (Organisations of a similar size, operating within the same industry)
- *Think about businesses in your local area. Identify two businesses that could compare their financial results.*

Suggested answer

3 Comparing one business organisation's performance with that of another is a meaningless activity, unless they are similar. For example, it would be inappropriate to compare a local take-away with a large national business such as McDonald's. Ideally the business organisations should be of a similar size and operating in the same industry, in order to give meaningful information that could be used for analysis and evaluation. Business size can be measured in terms of sales revenue or capital employed. This form of comparison and industry analysis allows a business organisation to assess how other business organisations are dealing with external factors that also affect them. For example, a Premier League Football Club could compare itself against another club competing in the same league. They could then review how both clubs are managing changes in television rights and funding.

Question 4 considers the types of issue that a business needs to take into account when making a comparison. Accounting policies used and seasonality are key factors when comparing business accounts. Facilitate a discussion about different seasonal businesses and how this will affect the financial statements that are produced. The holiday industry is one example. You may wish to elicit or suggest appropriate local and national examples to aid understanding.

Suggested answer

4 Accounting policies used, for example, different methods of inventory valuation, depreciation, irrecoverable debts.

A limited company should consider that the information provided is historical data. Historic data may not predict the future.

Financial year ends. Different business organisations have different financial year ends. Depending on the type of business organisation, inventory levels may be lower at certain times of the year and this would be reflected in the final accounts. This is particularly relevant for seasonal business organisations. For example, an ice-cream business will have considerably more inventory during the summer months than during the winter period.

Activity: Causes of differences in profitability ratios

Use this activity at the end of the unit to ensure there is a good understanding of the causes of differences in profitability ratios.

Approximate time required: 15 minutes

Resources: Resource 6.3A

Before the lesson: Print one resource sheet per pair. Cut out and shuffle the cards.

Pair work: Students separate the cards into:

1 causes of differences between two businesses' gross margins
2 causes of differences between two businesses' profit margins.

Stretch task: Students produce similar cards for the liquidity and efficiency ratios.

APPLYING

Use this task to ensure students are confident in interpreting the differences in the ratios of two businesses.

Answers

- The current ratio of White Cliffs Outdoor Supplies is marginally higher than the result for Glencoe Mountain Warehouse.
- The liquid (acid test) ratio of Glencoe Mountain Warehouse is considerable below the result of White Cliffs Outdoor Supplies. This could be caused by a high level of inventory. It could lead to problems if they are unable to pay their trade payables in a timely manner.
- The gross margin of Glencoe Mountain Warehouse is 25% lower than that of the competitor. This could have been caused by a reduction in selling price or mark up in an attempt to attract more customers. Alternatively, Glencoe Mountain Warehouse could have paid a higher purchase price for their goods for resale.
- The inventory turnover rate of White Cliffs Outdoor Supplies is higher than that of the competitor. This would imply that the White Cliffs Outdoor Supplies has reduced its selling price in order to increase sales.
- The profit margin of Glencoe Mountain Warehouse is considerable lower than that of White Cliffs Outdoor Supplies. This would imply that expenses are very high and need to be controlled. A review of marketing or selling costs should be undertaken.
- The return on capital employed of Glencoe Mountain Warehouse is considerably lower than that of White Cliffs Outdoor Supplies. The current rate does not provide investors with an adequate return. There are alternative investments available that would have higher returns with less risk.

Knowledge check

- **Answers**: See pages 262–263

Check your progress

Ask students to complete the **Check your progress** section in the Student's Book.

Support

- Ask students to work in pairs to prepare example comparison statements for each ratio. For example:

  current ratio – company A has a **higher** current ratio than company B.

  Students then highlight the comparison words in each statement.
- **Workbook Unit 6.3 Support**

Consolidation

- Students prepare revision cards for the unit. They produce one card for each ratio, listing the causes of differences in the ratio for two businesses.
- **Workbook Unit 6.3 Practice**

Stretch

- Put students in pairs or groups to compare the ratios they calculated in the stretch task for Unit 6.1 for two companies in the same industry. Students provide an inter-firm comparison to advise an investor as to which business they should invest in.
- **Workbook Unit 6.3 Stretch**

6.4 Interested parties

Learning objectives

By the end of this unit, students should be able to:

- explain the uses of accounting information by the following interested parties for decision making:
  - owners
  - managers
  - trade payables
  - banks
  - investors
  - club members
  - other interested parties such as governments and tax authorities.

Resources

- Student's Book pages 326–335
- Workbook page 82
- Resource 6.4A

Key terms

Stakeholder, Internal stakeholder, External stakeholder, Collateral

STARTING POINT

The questions recap the ratio calculations and analysis studied in earlier units of this chapter.

If students find these questions difficult, it may be helpful to use prompt questions, for example:

- *What are ratios used for?* (Ratio analysis is an accounting technique that allows financial accounts to be analysed.)
- *Name the ratios we have been studying.* (gross margin, profit margin, ROCE, current ratio, liquid (acid test) ratio, rate of inventory turnover, trade receivables, trade payables turnover)
- *What would a business compare its ratio results with?* (With other similar businesses (interfirm comparisons), against a benchmark or against previous years' results)
- *What is the formula for the current ratio?* $\left(\frac{\text{current assets}}{\text{current liabilities}}\right)$
- *What does the current ratio show?* (Measures the liquidity of a business; compares current assets to current liabilities; assesses a business's ability to meet its short-term debts.)

Suggested answers

1 Rate of inventory turnover, trade receivables turnover and trade payables turnover.

2 To undertake trend analysis and interpret the financial statements of the business, in order to assess its performance and progress. The business manager will be able to review profitability, efficiency and liquidity.

3 The current ratio measures the liquidity of the sole trader's business and compares current assets to current liabilities. The ratio assesses a business's ability to meet its short-term debts. For most businesses a ratio in excess of 2:1 is generally considered to be acceptable. A lower ratio, for example 1:1, means that a business may not be able to pay its debts if required to do so. A higher ratio, for example 5:1, may mean that a business is inefficient and has too much money tied up in inventory.

EXPLORING

The questions encourage students to consider how interested parties use accounting information to make informed business decisions. Encourage students to identify key items in financial statements that would be important to a range of business stakeholders.

Suggested answers

1 Sole traders will analyse their income statement to assess their profitability and consider how many drawings they can take. The income statement of a business calculates both the gross profit and profit for the year for a financial period of time. The sole trader will be able to consider trends over time by comparing one year's income statement with another year's. The sole trader will be able to assess whether the business has made sufficient profit to enable them to expand.

2 The potential shareholder will review the financial information of a public limited company to assess whether:
   - the company is profitable
   - it has sufficient liquidity to pay its debts
   - the company is likely to continue in the future
   - the company has paid dividends to its shareholders in the past
   - the company is likely to have sufficient funds to pay dividends in the future.

3 Both are measures of profitability. A partner can compare their gross margin with their profit margin to assess how well they are managing their expenses. The profit margin is lower than the gross margin, as all business expenses are deducted from the gross profit.

DEVELOPING

Most students will be able to identify key components of financial statements and how they can be used by users of financial records. Business studies students may have already covered the topic of stakeholders (interested parties) in their course.

The purpose of this unit is to explain the uses of accounting information and to consider how this information will be used by various groups for making decisions. You may wish to consider Unit 7.2 alongside this topic. International accounting standards have ensured that financial statements meet the needs of both internal and external stakeholders.

Ensure students consider each of the interested parties in turn. Elicit from students the items in financial statements that may be of interest each group.

Question 1 requires students to consider stakeholders in practice, in the context of a hotel. If students find the question difficult, it may be helpful to use prompt questions, for example:

- *What is a stakeholder?* (An individual or group that has an interest in a business.)
- *Who uses a hotel?* (Guests, employees, managers, members, for example leisure centre, one-off visitors, for example, for a wedding)
- *Who would have an interest in the financial affairs of a hotel?* (The owners, guests, suppliers, government, local hotels, etc.)

Suggested answer

1 Internal stakeholders may include, for example, managers, employees, owners.

External stakeholders may include, for example, hotel guests, hotel spa/leisure club members, banks, government, regulators/inspectors, investors.

Question 2 builds on work in previous units and considers how stakeholders may use financial information and ratio analysis. You could extend the discussion by asking students to explain why their choice of ratios would be of interest to a potential partner thinking of joining an existing partnership.

Suggested answer

2 Ratios include gross margin, profit margin, current ratio, liquid (acid test) ratio, return on capital employed.

Question 3 focuses on external stakeholders, in particular, potential investors. If students find the question difficult, it may be useful to ask prompt questions, for example:

- *What is an investor?* (An individual or group that invests money in a business with the aim of a financial return)
- *Why does an individual invest in a company?* (Usually for financial gain)
- *What does an investor want to gain from investing in a company?* (Dividends each year and/or benefit if the share price of the company increases)

Suggested answer

3 Answers could include: gross profit, profit for the year, dividends, liquidity based on current assets and current liabilities, trends over a period of time.

When considering government and tax authorities as stakeholders, discuss with students how businesses are taxed in their country.

Look at the case study with the class. It provides an example of how tax authorities have used the financial information published by companies. Ask students if they were aware of this issue and if there have been similar issues in their country. Use question 4 as a follow-up to the case study.

Suggested answer

4 The company may get bad publicity and gain a poor reputation. This may lead to low sales and therefore less profit. The government will have less income, thus reducing the money available to invest in the country's economy.

Use some straightforward questions as a starter exercise, for example:

- *Who would be interested in a sole trader's financial statements?* (sole trader, customers, suppliers, government, competitors, etc.)
- *Why would a public limited company's annual report be of interest to a local government?* (The government would need to ensure the business has paid the correct amount of tax.)
- *If a bank is going to lend money to a business, what part of a business's financial statements would be of interest to the bank?* (Income statement and statement of financial position – the bank would be interested in the profit levels and the liquidity (current assets and current liabilities) of the business.)

Activity: Stakeholders

Use this activity to provide students with the opportunity to consider stakeholder interests in practice.

Approximate time required: 30 minutes

Pair/group work: Ask students about the most recent product they purchased, for example, coffee in a café, food from a supermarket, stationery from a retail store. Ask them to choose one item and compile a list of all of the people or businesses (stakeholders) that may have an interest in the business from which the item was purchased. Finally, students consider what accounting information may be of interest to these individuals or businesses.

Applying

Use this task to ensure students are confident in identifying how financial statements will be used by stakeholders.

Suggested answers

1 Profitability: $\frac{\text{gross profit}}{\text{profit for the year}}$

Potential returns

2 Salaries and wages

Profitability: $\frac{\text{gross profit}}{\text{profit for the year}}$

Liquidity: $\frac{\text{current assets}}{\text{current liabilities}}$

3 Salaries and wages

Profitability: $\frac{\text{gross profit}}{\text{profit for the year}}$

Liquidity: $\frac{\text{current assets}}{\text{current liabilities}}$

4 Profitability: $\frac{\text{gross profit}}{\text{profit for the year}}$

Liquidity: $\frac{\text{current assets}}{\text{current liabilities}}$

Non-current assets available as security

5 Profitability: $\frac{\text{gross profit}}{\text{profit for the year}}$

Potential returns

6 Profitability: $\frac{\text{gross profit}}{\text{profit for the year}}$

Tax liabilities: ability to pay tax when due

7 Liquidity: $\frac{\text{current assets}}{\text{current liabilities}}$

Ability to repay debts on time

Knowledge check

- **Answers**: See pages 263–264

Check your progress

Ask students to complete the **Check your progress** section in the Student's Book.

Support

- Ask students who need extra support to revisit the financial statements they produced in Chapter 5 and highlight who would be interested in each of the sections of the financial statements.
- **Workbook Unit 6.4 Support**

Consolidation

- Students prepare revision cards for the unit. They write a stakeholder on one side of the cards and the items in the financial statements that would be of interest to them on the other side. They then take turns providing information of interest for the stakeholders.
- **Resources**: Resource 6.4A

  In addition, the cards on the resource provided can added to a matching activity on key terms and definitions from the course.
- **Workbook Unit 6.4 Practice**

Stretch

- Put students into groups to investigate a situation in which the aims of shareholders and other stakeholders in a company were in conflict. Groups could prepare short presentations about the company, explaining who the stakeholders are and why their aims are different.
- **Workbook Unit 6.4 Stretch**

6.5 Limitations of accounting statements

Learning objectives

By the end of this unit, students should be able to:

- recognise the limitations of accounting statements due to such factors as:
  - historic cost
  - difficulties of definition
  - non-financial aspects.

RESOURCES

- Student's Book pages 336–341
- Workbook pages 83–84
- Resource 6.5A

Key terms

Historic data, Quantitative information, Qualitative information

STARTING POINT

The questions recap the ratio analysis work completed in earlier units of this chapter. If students find these questions difficult, it can be helpful to ask prompt questions, for example:

- *What is ratio analysis?* (An accounting technique that allows financial accounts to be analysed)
- *How are ratios used?* (By different stakeholders to analyse and evaluate financial data. They form the basis of informed decision making.)
- *How are ratios used to compare financial information?* (Ratio results can be compared against previous years' results, against a benchmark or industry averages or against another business's results (inter-firm comparison).)
- *What is meant by 'gross profit' and 'profit for the year'?* (Gross profit is the sales revenue *less* the cost of sales, whereas, profit for the year is the gross profit *plus* additional income less expenses.)

Suggested answers

1 This occurs when a business compares its ratio results against benchmarks or industry averages and previous years' results.

2 Profitability assesses whether a business has met its objectives in relation to profits.

3 Limitations include:
- Ratios only show the results of businesses that will continue for the foreseeable future.
- The accuracy of the ratio analysis depends upon the quality of the information from which they are calculated.
- Ratios can only be used to compare like with like.
- Ratios tend to ignore the time factor in seasonal businesses.
- They can be misleading if accounts are not adjusted for inflation.

EXPLORING

The limitations of ratio analysis were discussed in Unit 6.3 and reviewed in Starting point question 3, so students should be able to speculate on the limitations of the financial statements.

Suggested answers

1 Problems include:
- Different businesses may apply different accounting principles when preparing their financial statements, for example, for inventory valuation and depreciation.

- Accounting statements do not account for the effects of inflation.
- Non-monetary items, such as goodwill and the skills of the workforce, do not appear in the accounting records of a business.
- The information available for the other business may not be typical.
- Different businesses may apply different operating policies. This may include renting premises in preference to purchasing premises and obtaining long-term finance from business owners only, rather than equity from business owners and long-term loans.
- The information available for the other business may not be sufficient for a comprehensive comparison. For example, a statement of financial position provides a net book value for non-current assets. It does not inform the reader when they were purchased, how old each asset is or when it is planned to sell these assets.

2 Non-financial factors include:

- customer service
- reputation
- goodwill
- qualification of workforce
- management expertise.

DEVELOPING

This unit consider the limitations of accounting statements. Encourage students to consider different types of business and different financial statements.

Use question 1 to highlight how the principle of historic cost affects the valuation of assets in a business.

Suggested answer

1 Non-current assets are valued at their net book value when recorded in the statement of financial position. This is calculated as original cost less cumulative depreciation.

Question 2 builds on question 1. Discuss why it is difficult to value certain assets in a business. Point out the difference between quantitative and qualitative information, using practical examples to aid students' understanding.

- Only quantitative information is included in accounting statements and is expressed in monetary terms. Examples include revenue, inventory, purchases, expenses, non-current assets, current assets, current liabilities, non-current liabilities and equity.
- Qualitative information cannot be expressed in monetary terms and is therefore omitted from accounting statements. Examples include customer satisfaction, management skills, location of the business organisation, customer loyalty and the motivation of the workforce.

Suggested answers

2 Valuation is subjective. One person's view of the value may not be the same as another person's view.

Look at the case study with the class. It provides an example of some non-financial aspects of a hotel. Point out to students that, even though location and luxury features cannot be included in the financial statements, this does not mean they don't have an effect on them. Ask students to consider how these features affect revenue, assets and expenditure in comparison to a hotel in a less desirable location, with fewer or no luxury features. They could research local examples.

The following questions can be used as a plenary exercise.

- *How are non-current assets valued in a statement of financial position?* (Non-current assets are valued at their net book value – calculated as original cost less cumulative depreciation.)

- *What is meant by 'historic cost'?* (The only accepted way to record financial transactions is to use the original cost price. Financial statements are produced using data from the past.)
- *Identify accounting terms that may have different definitions.* (For example, profit, provisions, loan interest, depreciation, inventory valuation)

APPLYING

Use this task to ensure students understand the limitations of financial statements. Encourage students to use their imaginations, to add detail to the scenario and give practical examples of the limitations.

Suggested answers

Amala Confectionery Ltd prepares an income statement and statement of financial position each year. These provide useful information for anyone interested in how well the business is doing.

All of the company's stakeholders use this data to make informed judgements. However, the data that Amala Confectionery Ltd has produced have a number of limitations. These include:

- Historic cost – the only accepted way to record financial transactions is to use the original cost price. Financial statements are produced using data from the past.
- Non-financial aspects – only numerical data may be included in the financial records of a business. Non-financial aspects are ignored.
- Difficulties of definition – different businesses define accounting terms in different ways. Comparisons are only meaningful if like for like comparisons are made.

Knowledge check

- **Answers**: See page 264

Check your progress

Ask students to complete the **Check your progress** section in the Student's Book.

Support

- Put students needing extra support into groups and ask them to discuss practical limitations of accounting statements. For example, the valuation of a property may vary depending on the person valuing the property. Ask them to categorise their ideas under the headings 'historic cost', 'difficulties of definition' and 'non-financial aspects'.
- **Workbook Unit 6.5 Support**

Consolidation

- Students prepare revision cards for the unit, summarising the limitations of financial information.
- **Resources**: Resource 6.5A

  In addition, the cards on the resource provided can be added to a matching activity on key terms and definitions from the course.
- **Workbook Unit 6.5 Practice**

Stretch

- Ask students to look at the information in the published accounts of two public limited companies (see stretch task for Unit 6.1) and identify similarities and differences between them. For example, they could consider the dates the companies use for their year end and the method of depreciation they use.
- **Workbook Unit 6.5 Stretch**

Chapter review

- **Resources:** Resource Ch6 review
- **Answers:** See pages 264–266
- **Workbook: Chapter 6 review**

7 Accounting principles and policies

This chapter introduces the various accounting rules that exist around the world. Students have the opportunity to review how accounting principles and policies can be applied to businesses, accounting procedures and financial transactions.

It may be studied as a stand-alone topic after students have completed all of the other chapters. However, you may find it more practical to cover the content alongside other units. This would help students to understand how the accounting principles and policies are applied in practice rather than as a purely theoretical topic.

Prior knowledge

Students should already be able to:

- use the accounting equation and understand the purpose of accounting
- prepare double entry ledger accounts
- prepare a trial balance
- account for capital and revenue expenditure and receipts, depreciation, irrecoverable debts and provisions for doubtful debts
- value business inventory
- prepare financial statements for:
  - sole traders
  - partnerships
  - limited companies
  - clubs and societies
  - manufacturing accounts
  - incomplete records
- analyse and interpret financial information for a range of organisations.

Background for non-subject specialists

Businesses use accounting techniques to provide information about their financial performance. This information is reviewed by internal and external users to enable informed decisions to be made. In order for the information to be understandable and meaningful, it must be reliable and allow comparisons to be made. To ensure a level of uniformity, businesses produce financial statements, following a set of accepted accounting rules. These are studied in Chapter 7 and are known as 'accounting principles and policies'.

7.1 Accounting principles

Learning objectives

By the end of this unit, students should be able to:

- explain and recognise the application of the following accounting principles:
  - matching
  - business entity
  - consistency
  - duality
  - going concern
  - historic cost
  - materiality
  - money measurement
  - prudence
  - realisation.

Resources

- Student's Book pages 348–358
- Workbook pages 88–89
- Pro-forma 2
- Resource 7.1A
- Resource 7.1B

Key terms

True and fair view, Accounting principles, Prudence principle, Matching principle, Consistency principle, Going concern principle, Historic cost principle, Materiality principle, Business entity principle, Duality principle, Money measurement principle, Realisation principle

STARTING POINT

The questions recap three of the main accounting theories and concepts that have been studied during the course.

If students find these questions difficult, it may be helpful to ask prompt questions, for example:

- *What is depreciation?* (An estimation of how the cost of an asset should be allocated over its useful life)
- *What type of assets are depreciated?* (Non-current assets)
- *When do businesses prepare financial statements?* (At the end of a financial year)

Suggested answers

1 Two from: straight line method of depreciation, reducing balance method of depreciation, revaluation method of depreciation.

2 An accounting period is a time period, usually one year, into which a business's life is arbitrarily divided for financial reporting purposes. The year may or may not coincide with the calendar year.

3 Accrued expenses are expenses relating to the current accounting period that remain unpaid at the end of the period, and are also known as 'other payables'. Accrued incomes are incomes earned but not yet received by the business at the end of the period.

   Prepaid expenses are expenses that have been paid in advance of the accounting period to which they relate, and are also known as 'other receivables. Prepaid incomes are incomes received in advance of the period in which they were earned by the business.

EXPLORING

The questions consider the need for and use of accounting principles in businesses.

Suggested answers

1 The financial accounts of any business need to reflect a true and fair view of its current financial position. If every business and accountant applied their own rules to the production of financial records, they would become meaningless and make inter-firm comparisons impossible.

2 If a different method was used, it would be very difficult to complete trend analyses and compare one year's financial statements with that of another. Also, a change in method can distort the value of the profit for the year; for example, an increase in depreciation would increase expenses and therefore reduce the profit for the year.

3 Double entry book-keeping is based on the fact that a business transaction always has two effects on the business and requires two entries, one debit and one credit, to be made in the accounts.

DEVELOPING

Explain that there are a number of rules, known as accounting principles, that must be applied when preparing accounting records and financial statements. As a stretch task, students could consider what would happen if the accounting world had no rules and the effect this would have on how financial statements are understood.

Encourage students to review the work they have covered in Chapters 1 to 5. In each of these topics, they will have applied various accounting principles; for example, in Chapter 1 students studied the accounting equation and learnt to apply the duality concept.

Activity: Principles in practice

This activity is designed to enable students to consider how accounting principles may be used in practice

Approximate time required: 30 minutes

Group work: Each group makes a list of all of the topics covered in the course, and then identifies which accounting principles apply to them. Bring the class together for a discussion.

Consider each of the accounting principles with students. To ensure they have a working knowledge of the principles, it would be advisable to link each principle to a topic they have already studied, for example:

- duality – double entry book-keeping
- historic cost – calculation of non-current asset net book values in a statement of financial position
- money measurement – exclusion of non-cash items from financial statements
- prudence – the inclusion of irrecoverable debts as expenses.

To help students make links, it may be useful to ask simple questions, for example:

- *What is a debit and what is a credit?* (The duality principle states that a business transaction always has two effects on the business and requires two entries, one debit and one credit, to be made in the accounts; this is also known as 'double entry'.)
- *What is the accounting equation?* $\left(\text{Assets} - \text{liabilities} = \frac{\text{capital}}{\text{equity}}\right)$
- *What is an irrecoverable debt?* (An amount owing to a business that is unlikely to be received.)

Question 1 invites students to consider why accounting principles are important for a public limited company. If students are having difficulty with the question, it can be helpful to ask prompt questions, for example:

- *What is a public limited company?* (A limited company is a business that has a separate legal identity from its shareholders. A public limited company issues shares which are traded on the stock exchange.)
- *Why do you need accounting rules?* (If every business and accountant applied their own rules to the production of financial records, they would become meaningless and make inter-firm comparisons impossible.)
- *What does 'a true and fair view' mean?* (This describes financial records that are free from misinformation and accurately represent the financial position of a business.)

Suggested answer

1 To enable investors and other interested parties to understand their financial statements. Accounting principles ensure that the financial statements are understandable and comparable with those of other limited companies. Investors can make informed decisions about which company they should invest their money in.

The accounting principles will ensure that the company's financial statements will show a true and fair view. They will ensure that financial records are free from misinformation and accurately represent the financial position of the company.

Look at the case study with the class. It provides an example of how accounting policies and principles affect the preparation of a business's accounts and the information it reports. Lego's annual report is available online and you might like students to look at it and find the information given in the case study.

With the duality principle, emphasise that every transaction has two aspects and requires two entries in the accounts. Question 2 ask students to apply this in practice. For students having difficulty with the question, advise them to revisit the work they completed in Chapters 1 and 2.

Suggested answers

2 (a)

Insurance					
Dr					Cr
	Cash	$ 300			$

Cash					
Dr					Cr
		$		Insurance	$ 300

(b)

Equipment					
Dr					Cr
	Bryn Equipment Supplies	$ 2500			$

Bryn Equipment Supplies					
Dr					Cr
		$		Equipment	$ 2500

Students often find the realisation principle difficult to understand. Explain that revenue should be recognised when the exchange of goods or services takes place. Use the practical example given in the Student's Book to reinforce this. Ensure students understand that profits should not be recorded until they have been earned.

APPLYING

- **Resources**: Resource 7.1A

Use this task to ensure students are confident in identifying the application of accounting principles.

Answers

1 matching
2 prudence
3 business entity
4 realisation
5 money measurement
6 consistency
7 duality
8 materiality
9 going concern
10 historic cost

Knowledge check

- **Answers**: See pages 266–267

Check your progress

Ask students to complete the **Check your progress** section in the Student's Book.

Support

- Students prepare revision cards for the unit. They write a key term from the unit on one side of the card and the definition on the other side. Students can then work in pairs and take turns identifying a key term from the definition or providing a definition, given the key term.
- **Resources**: Resource 7.1B

  Alternatively or in addition, you can use the resource provided and students can match the key terms to the definitions. You can use this matching activity as a starter activity for lessons in this unit. You may also want to include key terms from earlier units.
- **Workbook Unit 7.1 Support**

Mixed ability

- Divide the class into ten small groups. Allocate each group one of the twelve principles covered in this unit. Each group prepares three or four presentation slides on how a business organisation applies the principle. Encourage students to include numerical examples to support their explanations. Students can also examine the annual reports of public limited companies. These have a section that states the accounting principles that the company has used when preparing its financial statements. They can include information about how the companies have used the principle in their presentation.

  Allow time for the groups to give their presentations to the rest of the class.
- **Workbook Unit 7.1 Practice**
- **Workbook Unit 7.1 Stretch**

7.2 Accounting policies

Learning objectives

By the end of this unit, students should be able to:

- recognise the influence of international accounting standards and understand the following objectives in selecting accounting policies:
  - comparability
  - relevance
  - reliability
  - understandability.

Resources

- Student's Book pages 359–363
- Workbook page 90
- Resource 7.2A

Key terms

International accounting standards (IASs), Comparability, Relevance, Reliability, Bias, Understandability

STARTING POINT

If students find these questions difficult, it may be helpful to use prompt questions, for example:

- *What is the consistency principle?* (This principle states that, when faced with a choice between different accounting techniques, an accountant should not change accounting policies without good reason.)
- *What is the business entity principle?* (This principle states that the financial affairs of a business must be maintained separately from those of the owner.)

Suggested answers

1 A business is able to obtain important information by comparing its accounting ratios with those of another business.

2 Without consistent use of accounting methods and policies, it would be very difficult to complete trend analyses and compare one year's financial statements with those of another.

3 The financial records of a business only relate to the transactions of the business – for example, rent of business premises, purchases of goods and sales revenue. The personal assets and liabilities of a business's owner(s) do not appear in the accounting records of their business.

EXPLORING

The questions help students consider the need for and use of accounting policies.

Suggested answers

1 Methods to assess efficiency include the preparation of financial statements and calculation of appropriate ratios; performing trend analysis and review of coffee shop results over a number of years; the comparison of data against another business or industry benchmarks.

2 A new partner would be interested in the long-term future of the partnership. They would need to ensure that they will receive a return for their investment. The partner may review the profitability and liquidity ratios of the business.

3 A supplier will need to ensure that any business it supplies will be able to pay its debts on time. The supplier will need to ensure that the business it is supplying has sufficient liquidity and working capital to pay for the goods supplied. Comparing two businesses may allow the supplier to make a better assessment.

DEVELOPING

This unit covers an overarching topic that demonstrates how objectives in selecting accounting policies have impacted on the production of financial information. You may wish to consider this topic alongside Unit 6.4 on interested parties.

If necessary, expand on the starting point questions to recap the other accounting principles in Unit 7.1.

Ensure students understand the practical aspects of each of the accounting policies as well as the theory based definitions. They will find it helpful to revisit the work they completed in Chapters 1 to 6. All of the accounting practices they have considered must be completed in accordance with the accounting policies. Students should consider how they have applied the principles from Unit 7.1 and the policies from Unit 7.2.

Activity: Accounting policies

This activity highlights the importance of accounting policies and principles.

Approximate time required: 30 minutes

Group work: Students make a list of accounting policies and principles that they have applied when producing financial statements. Bring the groups together to share their solutions with the rest of the class.

Look at the case study with the class. It provides some additional information about International Accounting Standards.

Discuss the accounting policies and procedures that students have applied for sole traders, partnerships, limited companies and clubs and societies. Elicit from students that using accounting policies and principles avoids confusion, inconsistency and bias. Bias is a difficult concept for students to understand and may need further explanation. Elicit examples from the class of bias to help clarify understanding. Point out that the main aim is to present financial information that is 'true and fair' and to ensure that none of the information is misleading.

Question 1 allows students to consider the comparability of accounting information.

Suggested answers

1 Other International Fast Food restaurants such as KFC, Burger King

The following questions can be used as a plenary exercise.

- *What is a policy?*
- *Why do we need accounting policies and procedures?*

  As a stretch activity, students could discuss how accounting principles and policies may affect the usability of the information that has been prepared.

APPLYING

Use this task to ensure students understand the objectives that a business needs to consider when selecting the accounting policies and principles to be applied. Encourage students to use their imagination to add detail to the scenario and give practical examples.

Suggested answers

Edfu Motors needs to consider:

- Comparability: financial information is comparable when accounting principles and policies are consistently applied from one accounting period to the next and from one business to another.
- Relevance: a non-numerical characteristic in accounting, associated with accounting information that is timely, useful and will make a difference to an interested party when they are making a decision.
- Reliability: relates to the trustworthiness of a business's financial statements.
- Understandability: an accounting policy that states that a business's financial information should be presented in a way that an individual with a reasonable knowledge of business and finance and a willingness to study the information provided should be able to understand it.

Knowledge check

- **Answers**: See page 267

Check your progress

Ask students to complete the **Check your progress** section in the Student's Book.

Support

- Students prepare revision cards for the unit. They write a key term from the unit on one side of the card and the definition on the other side. Students can then work in pairs and take turns identifying a key term from the definition or providing a definition, given the key term.
- **Resources**: Resource 7.2A

Alternatively or in addition, you can use the resource provided and students can match the key terms to the definitions. You can use this matching activity as a starter activity for lessons in this unit. You may also want to include key terms from earlier units.

- **Workbook Unit 7.2 Support**

Consolidation

- Divide the class into five or ten small groups. Allocate each group one of these types of business organisation: sole trader, partnership, limited company, club or society, manufacturing business. Each group prepares an information sheet on how the business type applies the accounting policies of comparability, relevance, reliability and understandability.

  Allow time for the groups to share their information sheets with the rest of the class. Facilitate a discussion comparing how different business types apply the four accounting policies.
- **Workbook Unit 7.2 Practice**

Stretch

- Ask students to research the International Accounting Standards. Students should select three International Accounting Standards and prepare a short presentation on how these standards are used when preparing financial statements.
- **Workbook Unit 7.2 Stretch**

Chapter review

- **Answers:** See pages 267–269
- **Workbook: Chapter 7 review**

Pro-forma 1

Double entry accounts 1

		$			$

		$			$

		$			$

Pro-forma 2

Double entry accounts 2

		$			$

		$			$

		$			$

		$			$

		$			$

Pro-forma 3

Double entry accounts 3

		$			$

Pro-forma 4

Journals

....		
Date	**Details**	**Total**
		$

....		
Date	**Details**	**Total**
		$

....		
Date	**Details**	**Total**
		$

Pro-forma 5

General journal

General journal			
Date	Details	Dr	Cr
		$	$

General journal			
Date	Details	Dr	Cr
		$	$

General journal			
Date	Details	Dr	Cr
		$	$

Pro-forma 6

Cash book

Cash book									
		Discount	Cash	Bank			Discount	Cash	Bank
		$	$	$			$	$	$

Cash book									
		Discount	Cash	Bank			Discount	Cash	Bank
		$	$	$			$	$	$

Cash book									
		Discount	Cash	Bank			Discount	Cash	Bank
		$	$	$			$	$	$

Pro-forma 7

Trial balance

....		
	Dr	**Cr**
	$	**$**

....		
	Dr	**Cr**
	$	**$**

Pro-forma 8

Financial statement 1

....		
	Dr	**Cr**
	$	**$**

....		
	Dr	**Cr**
	$	**$**

Pro-forma 9

Financial statement 2

....	
	$

Pro-forma 10

Financial statement 3

....

....

	Dr	Cr
	$	**$**

Pro-forma 11

Financial statement 4

....

....

	$	$	$

Pro-forma 12

Partnership accounts

....							
....							
	$	$	$		$	$	$

....							
....							
	$	$	$		$	$	$

Pro-forma 13

Statement of changes in equity

.... Statement of changes in equity for the year ended					
	Ordinary share capital	**Preference share capital**	**General reserve**	**Retained earnings**	**Total**
	$	**$**	**$**	**$**	**$**
Opening balance					
Profit for the year					
Dividend paid					
Transfer to general reserve					
Share issue					
Closing balance					

....					
	Ordinary share capital	**Preference share capital**	**General reserve**	**Retained earnings**	**Total**
	$	**$**	**$**	**$**	**$**
Opening balance					
Profit for the year					
Dividend paid					
Transfer to general reserve					
Share issue					
Closing balance					

....					
	Ordinary share capital	**Preference share capital**	**General reserve**	**Retained earnings**	**Total**
	$	**$**	**$**	**$**	**$**
Opening balance					
Profit for the year					
Dividend paid					
Transfer to general reserve					
Share issue					
Closing balance					

Resource 1.1A

Activity: Calculation of profit

A business earns $45 000 from sales and has expenses of $23 500 for the same period.	Profit of $21 500
A business sells goods for $109 000. It has expenses of $67 250.	Profit of $41 750
A business sells 18 000 units for $5 each. Total expenses for period are $54 000.	Profit of $36 000
A business sells 4500 units for $25 each. Total expenses for period are $76 000.	Profit of $36 500
Sales revenue for a business is $28 000. Total expenses for same period are $47 500.	Loss of $19 500
A business sells output for $11 for each unit. It sells 5500 units. Total expenses are $85 000.	Loss of $24 500
A business sells output for $8.50 for each unit. It sells 24 000 units. Total expenses are $125 000.	Profit of $79 000
A business sells 18 800 units for $10.75 each. Total costs are $97 500.	Profit of $104 600

Resource 1.1B

Activity: Key terms

Book-keeping	The process of recording the financial transactions of a business.
Accounting	The process of recording financial transactions, producing financial statements and analysing financial performance of a business.
Financial statements	Statements produced for an **accounting period** summarising business performance. They include an **income statement** and a statement of financial position.
Profit maximisation	Aiming to earn as high a level of profit as is possible.
Profit	Total income less total expenses for a period of time.
Accounting period	The time period for which financial statements are prepared.
Income statement	A financial statement showing income and expenses for the period and the resulting profit or loss.
Management accounting	Using financial information to make business decisions concerning costs, revenues and output.

Resource 1.2A

Activity: Classification of assets, liabilities and owner's equity

Assets	Liabilities	Owner's equity
Business premises	Trade payables	Owner's car introduced to business
Bank balance	Bank overdraft	Money placed in business by owner
Trade receivables	Bank loan	Profit
Computer	Mortgage	Loss
Cash in till	Amount owing to a supplier	
Fixtures		
Inventory		
Amount owed by customer		
Office equipment		

Resource 1.2B

Activity: Using the accounting equation

Use the accounting equation to find the missing figures in this table.

Assets ($)	Liabilities ($)	Owner's equity ($)
4324	3212	
5654		4343
15280	7840	
	9945	16825
12311		8170
21010		13150
	9999	6671
89793	23123	
124500		89950
	23677	56823

Activity: Using the accounting equation

Use the accounting equation to find the missing figures in this table.

Assets ($)	Liabilities ($)	Owner's equity ($)
4324	3212	
5654		4343
15280	7840	
	9945	16825
12311		8170
21010		13150
	9999	6671
89793	23123	
124500		89950
	23677	56823

Resource 1.2C

Activity: Key terms

Duality principle	Principle that states that a business transaction always has two effects on the business and requires two entries, one debit and one credit, to be made in the accounts; also known as 'double entry'.
Assets	Resources used within the business for its activities.
Liabilities	Amounts borrowed to fund business activity.
Owner's equity	Business resources supplied by the owner of the business.
Statement of financial position	A financial statement showing the assets of the business and the financing for these assets, either from owner's equity or liabilities.
Liquidity	A measure of how easy it is to convert an asset into cash without it losing its value.
Inventory	Goods held by a business for resale – they may be in the form of finished goods, partly finished goods or raw materials.
Trade payable	The amount that a business owes to a supplier for goods or services supplied on credit. The supplier may also be known as a 'trade payable' or a c'reditor'.
Trade payables	The sum of the amounts that a business owes to its suppliers for goods or services supplied on credit. All the suppliers of a business may also be referred to collectively as 'trade payables'.
Trade receivable	The amount that a business is owed by a customer for goods or services supplied on credit. The customer may also be known as a 'trade receivable' or a 'debtor'.
Trade receivables	The sum of the amounts that a business is owed by its suppliers for goods or services supplied on credit. All the customers of a business may also be referred to collectively as 'trade receivables'.

Resource 2.1A

Activity: Applying the rules of double entry book-keeping for asset, liability and owner's equity accounts

For each of the following transactions, state which accounts should be debited and which should be credited.

	Account to be debited	Account to be credited
1 Owner introduces cash into business bank account.		
2 Cash is deposited in the business bank account.		
3 Equipment is purchased on credit from Hunter.		
4 Motor vehicle sold – payment received by cheque.		
5 Amount owing to Faisal paid in cash.		
6 Owner brings own computer into business use.		
7 A customer – Maria – pays amount owing in cash.		
8 Fixtures and fittings purchased on credit from Usman.		
9 Office equipment bought on credit from Rashmi – returned due to unsuitability.		
10 Van sold on credit to Herbert returned to us due to it being unsafe.		
11 Shanays – a credit supplier – is paid by cheque.		
12 Ester – a credit customer – pays in cash.		
13 Bank loan obtained from Nanchester Bank.		
14 Cash borrowed from Alex.		
15 Loan from Leyla repaid in cash.		
16 Car sold on credit to Kalim.		
17 Machinery sold for cash.		
18 Van purchased and payment made by cheque.		

Resource 2.1B

Activity: Applying the rules of double entry book-keeping for inventory, expense and income transactions

For each of the following transactions, state which accounts should be debited and credited.

	Account to be debited	Account to be credited
1 Goods sold on credit to Oliver.		
2 Equipment sold on credit to Irena.		
3 Goods sold on credit to George are returned to business.		
4 Inventory purchased on credit from Janine.		
5 Goods sold for cash.		
6 Purchases paid by cheque.		
7 Purchases returned to credit supplier – Reynarsh.		
8 Motor vehicle purchased for resale paid by cheque.		
9 Purchases on credit from Beatriz.		
10 Machinery sold as inventory on credit to Lau.		
11 Amount owing to Loukas – a credit supplier – paid in cash.		
12 Sundry expenses paid in cash.		
13 Rent paid by cheque.		
14 Commission received by cheque.		
15 Wages paid in cash.		
16 Money taken from bank by owner for private use.		
17 Rent received by cheque.		
18 Owner takes furniture out of business for own use.		

Resource 2.1C

Activity: The rules of double entry book-keeping

Complete the tables to show the rules of double entry book-keeping.

Asset accounts	
Debit	Credit
____________ entered on this side	____________ entered on this side

Liability accounts	
Debit	Credit
____________ entered on this side	____________ entered on this side

Owner's equity accounts	
Debit	Credit
____________ entered on this side	____________ entered on this side

Accounting for inventory	
Increases in inventory	**Decreases in inventory**
Account to be debited	Account to be credited
____________ or ____________	____________ or ____________

Accounting for expenses	
Account to be debited	Account to be credited
____________	____________ or ____________

Resource 2.1C (Continued)

Accounting for income	
Account to be debited	Account to be credited
______________________ or ______________________	______________________

Accounting for drawings	
Account to be debited	Account to be credited
______________________	______________________ e.g. ______________________

Resource 2.1D

Activity: Key terms

Double entry book-keeping	A system of recording business transactions by making two entries (one debit entry and one credit entry) for each transaction.
Trader	A business organisation that aims to make profit from the buying and selling of goods – no production takes place.
Purchases	Inventory bought by the business either for immediate payment or on credit.
Sales	Inventory sold by the business either for immediate payment or on credit.
Purchases returns	Inventory previously bought by the business, returned to the original supplier due to some problem with the inventory (also known as 'returns outwards').
Sales returns	Inventory previously sold by the business, returned by the customer due to some problem with the inventory (also known as 'returns inwards').
Drawings	Assets (money or other resources) that the owner withdraws from the business for personal use.
Balance (of an account)	The overall difference between the total on the debit side and the total on the credit side of an account, at a point in time.
Sales ledger	Book recording trade receivables – it contains the personal accounts of all the credit customers of the business.
Purchases ledger	Book recording trade payables – it contains the personal accounts of all the credit suppliers of the business.
Nominal ledger	Book containing all other accounts not found in sales or purchases ledger.
Personal accounts	Accounts of other businesses or people that the business has a financial relationship with.

Resource 2.2A

Activity: Producing documents for a set of transactions

<table>
<tr><td colspan="4" align="center">................................
....
................................</td></tr>
<tr><td colspan="4" align="center">INVOICE</td></tr>
<tr><td colspan="2">To: ....
....
....
.....................................</td><td colspan="2">Invoice no: ....
Date: ....</td></tr>
<tr><td>Quantity</td><td>Description</td><td>Unit price ($)</b></td><td><b>Total ($)</td></tr>
<tr><td></td><td></td><td></td><td></td></tr>
<tr><td></td><td></td><td></td><td></td></tr>
<tr><td></td><td></td><td></td><td></td></tr>
<tr><td></td><td></td><td></td><td></td></tr>
<tr><td></td><td></td><td></td><td></td></tr>
</table>

<table>
<tr><td colspan="4" align="center">................................
....
................................</td></tr>
<tr><td colspan="4" align="center">DEBIT NOTE</td></tr>
<tr><td colspan="2">To: ....
....
....
....
The following goods are to be returned:</td><td colspan="2">Debit note no: ....
Date: ....</td></tr>
<tr><td>Quantity</td><td>Description</td><td>Unit price ($)</b></td><td><b>Total ($)</td></tr>
<tr><td></td><td></td><td></td><td></td></tr>
<tr><td></td><td></td><td></td><td></td></tr>
<tr><td></td><td></td><td></td><td></td></tr>
<tr><td></td><td></td><td></td><td></td></tr>
<tr><td></td><td></td><td></td><td></td></tr>
</table>

Resource 2.2A (Continued)

……………………………

……………………………

……………………………

CREDIT NOTE

To: …………………………… Credit note no: ……………………………

………………………………… Date: ……………………………

…………………………………

…………………………………

Quantity	Description	Unit price ($)	Total ($)

……………………………

……………………………

……………………………

STATEMENT OF ACCOUNT

To: …………………………… Account no: ……………………………

………………………………… Date: ……………………………

…………………………………

…………………………………

Date	Details	Debit ($)	Credit ($)	Balance ($)

Resource 2.2A (Continued)

Bank statement				
Account name:				
Sort code:				
Account number:				
Date	**Details**	**Debit ($)**	**Credit ($)**	**Balance ($)**
	Opening balance			

Date:

$100 notes		
$50 notes		
$20 notes		
$10 notes		
$5 notes		
$1 notes		
Coins		
Cheques		
TOTAL ($)		

Date:

Cashier's stamp

ACCOUNT HOLDER'S NAME

....

No. of cheques

Sort code

\- - -

....

Account number

....

$100 notes		
$50 notes		
$20 notes		
$10 notes		
$5 notes		
$1 notes		
Coins		
Cheques		
TOTAL ($)		

Date:

/ /

Payee

Amount:

$

Pay

Date:

/ /

$

Cheque number

Branch sort code

Account number

Resource 2.2B

Activity: Knowledge check

4

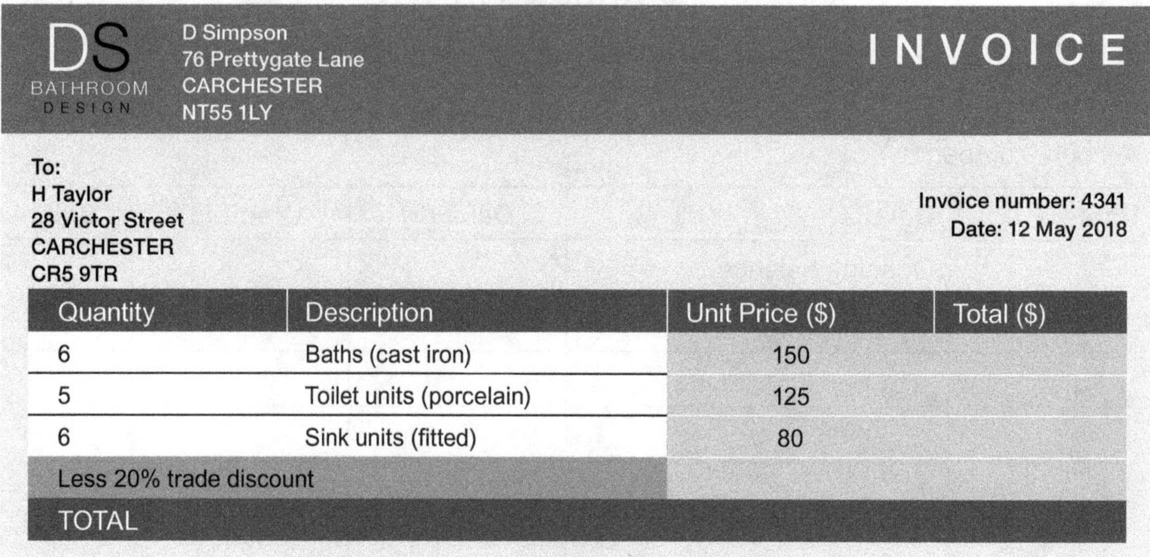

DS BATHROOM DESIGN

D Simpson
76 Prettygate Lane
CARCHESTER
NT55 1LY

INVOICE

To:
H Taylor
28 Victor Street
CARCHESTER
CR5 9TR

Invoice number: 4341
Date: 12 May 2018

Quantity	Description	Unit Price ($)	Total ($)
6	Baths (cast iron)	150	
5	Toilet units (porcelain)	125	
6	Sink units (fitted)	80	
Less 20% trade discount			
TOTAL			

5

Date: / /

Payee

Amount:

$

Pay

Date: / /

$

Cheque number

Branch sort code

Account number

Resource 2.2B (Continued)

6 (a)

PARTYFOOD SUPPLIES LTD
12 Oakholme Street
OLDTOWN
OT1 9DR

INVOICE

To: .... Invoice no: ....

.... Date: ....

....

....

Quantity	**Description**	**Unit price ($)**	**Total ($)**

(b)

PARTYFOOD SUPPLIES LTD
12 Oakholme Street
OLDTOWN
OT1 9DR

CREDIT NOTE

To: .... Credit note no: ....

.... Date: ....

....

....

Quantity	**Description**	**Unit price ($)**	**Total ($)**

Resource 2.2B (Continued)

7

DEX SYSTEMS SOLUTIONS
Unit 5, Business Park
NEWTOWN
NT55 1LY

STATEMENT OF ACCOUNT

To: .... Account no: ....

.... Date: ....

....

....

Date	**Details**	**Debit ($)**	**Credit ($)**	**Balance ($)**

Resource 2.2C

Activity: Business documents and double-entry bookkeeping

Place the cards under the correct headings in the table.

Business document	Account to be debited	Account to be credited

(Sales) invoice	Debtor	Sales
(Purchases) invoice	Purchases	Creditor
Cheque counterfoil	Account related to payment	Bank
Cheque received	Bank	Debtor
Credit note	Sales returns	Debtor
Receipt	Bank or cash	Account related to receipt
Bank statement	Bank (depends on movement)	Bank (depends on movement)

Resource 2.2D

Activity: Key terms

Business document	A document received or issued by a business when a transaction takes place. It contains information relevant to the transaction.
Invoice	A document issued by a business when making a credit sale.
Trade discount	A discount given by one business to another business. It is calculated as a percentage reduction in the invoice quantity.
Debit note	A document issued by a business to the supplier when the goods received are unsuitable.
Credit note	Document issued by a business to a customer when goods are returned to the business because they are unsuitable.
Statement of account	A document issued to all customers still owing money to the business. It contains details relating to the transactions taking place between the business and the customer.
Cheque	A written document authorising payment from the bank account of a business to another person or business.
Cheque counterfoil	Part of the cheque which is kept by the business as a record of the payment made by cheque. It may also be referred to as a 'cheque stub'.
Payer	The person or business making a payment to another. The payer may also be called the drawer.
Payee	The person or business receiving payment from the business. The payee may also be called the drawee.
Paying-in slip	A document used to deposit funds (cheques or notes and coins) into a bank account.
Receipt	A written document issued by a business when it receives a payment, as proof of receiving money.
Bank statement	A document issued by the bank of the business, showing all bank transactions for a period of time.

Resource 2.3A

Activity: Which book of prime entry?

Place the cards under the correct headings in the table.

Cash book	**Sales journal**	**Purchases journal**	**Sales returns journal**	**Purchases returns journal**	**General journal**

Wages paid in cash	Sales of cars by a car retailer	Credit purchases	Goods sold but returned by customer	Supplier agrees to received goods purchased back from us	Owner contributes own car to business
Owner contributes money into business bank account	Sales of goods on credit	Purchase of vegetables on credit by a grocer	Car retailer receives cars back from customers	Inventory purchased on credit returned to supplier	Owner takes computer out of business for own use
Machinery purchased by cheque	Sales of items purchased for resale on credit	Purchase on credit of inventory			Fixtures and fittings purchased on credit
Cash sales	Sale of computer by computer retailer	Inventory purchased but payment not yet made			Equipment used in business sold on credit

Resource 2.3B

Activity: Linking books of prime entry to double-entry accounts

For each of the following transactions, state which book of prime entry the transaction belongs in and which double entry accounts should be debited and credited.

Transaction	Book of prime entry	Account to be debited	Account to be credited
1 Owner contributes money in bank for business use.			
2 Goods purchased on credit returned to Gabriel.			
3 Motor expenses paid in cash.			
4 Owner takes equipment out of business for personal use.			
5 Sale of printer used in business, on credit to Lewis.			
6 Rent received by cheque.			
7 Discount received, given by Leyla.			
8 Purchase of office furniture on credit, for business use, from Mariam.			
9 Cash held in business deposited into bank account.			
10 Goods sold on credit to Jon are returned to business.			
11 Machinery given to Nathan in return for debt owed to this credit supplier.			
12 Purchase of cash till by a baker, paid by cheque.			

Resource 2.3C

Unit 2.3: Knowledge check

5

Petty cash book							
Receipts	**Date**	**Details**	**Voucher**	**Total**	**Cleaning**	**Travel expenses**	**Stationery**
$				$	$	$	$

6

General journal			
Date	**Details**	**Dr**	**Cr**
		$	$

Resource 2.3D

Activity: Key terms

Book of prime entry	A book, or journal, in which transactions are first recorded before being posted to the double entry accounts.
Posting	The process of transferring information from books of prime entry to the correct double entry account.
Cash book	A combined cash and bank account which records all transactions involving payments and receipts of money.
Cash discount	A reduction in the amount owing on a credit transaction, to encourage prompt payment.
Discount allowed	A reduction in the invoice total offered by a business to its credit customers to encourage early settlement of invoices.
Discount received	A reduction in the amount a business owes to the credit supplier of the business, to encourage early settlement.
Petty cash book	A book of prime entry used for small items of payment by cash.
Imprest system	A system of maintaining a petty cash book by always ensuring the opening balance of the petty cash book is the same amount for each time period.
Float	The amount of petty cash available at the start of each month.
Sales journal	The book of prime entry used to record credit sales.
Purchases journal	The book of prime entry used to record credit purchases.
Sales returns journal	The book of prime entry used to record sales returns.
Purchases returns journal	The book of prime entry used to record purchases returns.
The general journal	The book of prime entry used to record transactions not found in any other journal, sometimes referred to as the journal.
Narrative	A description of a transaction entered in the general journal.

Resource Ch2 review

Chapter 2: Chapter review

13

Petty cash book						
Receipts	Date	Details	Total	Cleaning	Petrol	General expenses
$	2018		$	$	$	$

Resource 3.1A

Activity: Trial balance – debit or credit?

Debit	Credit

Resource 3.1B

Activity: Preparing a trial balance

Is each item a debit or credit entry in the trial balance? Tick the correct column.

Item	Debit	Credit
Revenue		
Purchases		
Bank overdraft		
Land and buildings		
Wages and salaries		
Trade receivables		
Trade payables		
Owner's equity		
Drawings		
Rent received		
Sales returns		
Purchases returns		
Bank loan		
Opening inventory		

Resource 3.1C

Activity: Key terms

Trial balance	A list of all balances from the double entry accounts.
Revenue	Income generated by a business from its normal business activities, usually the sale of goods or services. May also be referred to as 'sales', 'sales revenue' or 'turnover'.
Stocktake	A physical count and valuation of inventory held by a business.
Error of commission	An error caused by a transaction being entered into the wrong personal account.
Compensating error	Two or more errors are made that affect the debit and credit columns of the trial balance by exactly the same amount. The totals of the debit and credit columns of the trial balance are the same but the totals are incorrect.
Error of complete reversal	A transaction is entered in the correct accounts and with the correct amount but the entries are on the wrong side of both double entry accounts. The totals of the debit and credit columns of the trial balance are the same but the totals are incorrect.
Error of omission	The entries needed for a transaction are not entered in the accounts. The totals of the debit and credit columns of the trial balance are the same but the totals are incorrect.
Error of original entry	Entries are made in the correct accounts on the correct sides of each account but the amounts entered are not correct, although they are the same for the debit and credit entry. The totals of the debit and credit columns of the trial balance are the same but the totals are incorrect.
Error of Principle	The correct amounts are entered for a transaction but they are entered in the wrong type or class of account.

Resource 3.2A

Activity: Key terms

Undercasting	The amount recorded in the accounts is lower than the correct figure.
Overcasting	The amount recorded in the accounts is higher than the correct figure.
Transposition	Numbers (or parts of a larger number) are mixed up or reversed, for example, $142 is written as $241.
Suspense account	A temporary account used when the trial balance totals differ. It is used to ensure that the totals of the trial balance are the same.

Resource 3.3A

Activity: Debit or credit?

Cash book Debit	Cash book Credit
Bank statement Debit	Bank statement Credit

Resource 3.3B

Activity: Terms related to bank reconciliation

Bank reconciliation	The process of checking why the cash book bank balance and the bank statement balance are different from each other (as they should be the same in theory).
Credit transfer	An automated payment of money into a bank account.
Direct debit	A regular automated payment of varying amounts made from a bank account (usually for utility bills).
Standing order	A regular automated payment of a fixed amount made from a bank account.
Updated cash book	A cash book brought up to date by the business, by the addition of automated transactions and other transactions the business has yet to enter into the cash book.
Bank reconciliation statement	A statement explaining the differences between the cash book bank balance and the balance on the bank statement.
Unpresented cheque	A cheque that has been issued but the payment has not yet appeared on the bank statement. The payment will have been credited to the business cash book when the cheque was issued.
Uncredited deposit	An amount that has been received but the receipt has not yet appeared on the bank statement. The receipt will have been debited to the business cash book when the payment was received.
Stale cheque	A cheque that a bank will not process because it is more than six months old.
Dishonoured cheque	A cheque presented to the bank, for which the payer has insufficient funds in their account for the bank to transfer money to make payment.
Automated transaction	Payment of an amount into or out of a bank account without the payee or payer having to take direct action.
Timing difference	One reason why there may be a difference between the balances in the cash book and on the bank statement – when payments and receipts entered in the cash book have not yet been paid into or out of the bank account.
Fraud	Deliberate deception by a person to gain money or other advantage.
Embezzlement	Theft of money from a company or organisation by an employee.
Bank charges	Amounts paid by an account holder to the bank for the services it provides.
Interest paid	An amount paid to borrow money. It is based on the interest rate and is calculated as a percentage of the amount borrowed.
Interest received	An amount received for lending money or having money in a bank account. It is based on the interest rate and is calculated as a percentage of the amount lent or the balance of the bank account.
Dividend	An amount paid to the holder of shares in companies.

Resource 3.4A

Activity: Books of prime entry

Complete the table by writing the transactions that are recorded in each of the books of prime entry.

Book of prime entry	Transactions recorded
Cash book	
Petty cash book	
Sales journal	
Purchases journal	
Sales returns journal	
Purchases returns journal	
General journal	

Activity: Books of prime entry

Complete the table by writing the transactions that are recorded in each of the books of prime entry.

Book of prime entry	Transactions recorded
Cash book	
Petty cash book	
Sales journal	
Purchases journal	
Sales returns journal	
Purchases returns journal	
General journal	

Resource 3.4B

Activity: Control accounts

Complete these tables.

Information used in the sales ledger control account	
Item in the sales ledger control account	**Location of information**
Opening balance	
Credit sales	
Payments received	
Discounts allowed	
Sales returns	
Closing balance	

Information used in the purchases ledger control account	
Item in the purchases ledger control account	**Location of information**
Opening balance	
Credit purchases	
Payments made to suppliers	
Discounts received	
Purchases returns	
Interest due on overdue accounts owing to suppliers	
Closing balance	

Resource 3.4C

Activity: Key terms

Sales ledger control account	A memorandum account used to check the accuracy of the sales ledger.
Purchases ledger control account	A memorandum account used to check the accuracy of the purchases ledger.
Memorandum account	An account that is not part of the double entry system.
Irrecoverable debt	An amount owed to a business by a credit customer that cannot pay or will not pay the money that is owed. The amount is written off.
Written off	Cancelling a debt owed to the business due to the failure to collect the amount owing.
Contra entry	A double entry where both the debit and credit entries are in the same account.

Resource 4.1A

Activity: Capital vs Revenue expenditure

Complete the table with examples of capital and revenue expenditure relating to the assets.

Asset	Capital expenditure	Revenue expenditure
Delivery van		
Machinery		

Activity: Capital vs Revenue expenditure

Complete the table with examples of capital and revenue expenditure relating to the assets.

Asset	Capital expenditure	Revenue expenditure
Delivery van		
Machinery		

Resource 4.1B

Activity: Capital and revenue expenditure and receipts

Capital expenditure	**Revenue expenditure**
Capital receipts	**Revenue receipts**

Resource 4.1C

Activity: The effect of incorrect treatment of expenditure

Revenue expenditure treated as capital expenditure	Revenue expenditure undervalued Capital expenditure overvalued	Profit overvalued Assets overvalued
Capital expenditure treated as revenue expenditure	Revenue expenditure overvalued Capital expenditure undervalued	Profit undervalued Assets undervalued

Resource 4.1D

Activity: Key terms

Capital expenditure	Business expenditure used to purchase or improve assets that are expected to be used in the business for more than one year. It also includes the cost of getting those assets ready for use. Capital expenditure is not classed as an expense on the income statement of a business.
Revenue expenditure	Expenditure on running the business. It is clearly linked to a specific time period. Revenue expenditure is classed as an expense on the income statement of a business.
Capital receipts	Business income that is not part of the day-to-day operations of the business. Capital receipts are not classed as income on the income statement of the business.
Revenue receipts	Business income that comes from the day-to-day business operations. Revenue receipts are classed as income on the income statement of the business.

Resource 4.2A

Activity: Which depreciation method is best?

Complete the table.

The advantages of each method of depreciation		
Straight line method	Reducing balance method	Revaluation method

Activity: Which depreciation method is best?

Complete the table.

The advantages of each method of depreciation		
Straight line method	Reducing balance method	Revaluation method

Activity: Which depreciation method is best?

Complete the table.

The advantages of each method of depreciation		
Straight line method	Reducing balance method	Revaluation method

Resource 4.2B

Activity: Key terms

Non-current asset	An asset bought for use within the business and normally kept for more than one year.
Depreciation	An estimation of how the cost of an asset should be allocated over its useful life.
Provision	An amount set aside. A charge made against profit by transferring part of the cost of the asset. It does not involve any movement of cash.
Straight line method of depreciation	A method of depreciation in which the amount of depreciation charged each year remains constant throughout the asset's life.
Residual value	The estimated value of a non-current asset at the end of its life.
Reducing balance method of depreciation	A method of depreciation in which the amount of depreciation charged is greater in the earlier years and reduces with every successive year of the asset's life.
Net book value	Original cost of a non-current asset less accumulated depreciation.
Revaluation method of depreciation	A method of depreciation in which the amount of depreciation charged each year is the change in the asset's estimated value between the start and the end of the year.
Asset disposal	The selling or scrapping of a non-current asset.
Asset disposal account	The ledger account used to record asset disposal and to calculate the profit or loss on the disposal.

Resource 4.3A

Activity: Principles of accrued and prepaid expenses and income

Complete the summary.

EXPENSES	
Definition	**Description**
Accrued expense / Accrual / Other (1)....................................... An amount due in an accounting period that remains unpaid at the end of that period, for example, a gas bill.	Accruals are **(2)**....................................... to the relevant expense in the income statement and shown as **(3)**....................................... in the statement of financial position.
Prepaid expense / Prepayment / Other (4)....................................... A payment made in advance of the accounting period to which it relates, for example, insurance.	Prepayments are **(5)**....................................... from the relevant expense in the income statement and shown as **(6)**.............................. in the statement of financial position.
INCOME	
Prepaid income / deferred income Income received in advance of the period to which it relates, for example, rent received.	Prepayments are **(7)**....................................... from the relevant additional income in the Income statement and shown as a **(8)**....................................... in the statement of financial position.
Accrued income Income due in the period but not yet received, for example, rent receivable.	Accruals are **(9)**....................................... to the relevant additional income in the income statement and shown as **(10)**....................................... in the statement of financial position.

Activity: Principles of accrued and prepaid expenses and income

Complete the summary.

Resource 4.3B

Activity: Key terms

Matching principle	This principle ensures that incomes are matched to expenses in a particular accounting period. Incomes and expenses need to be entered into a business's financial statements as they are earned or incurred, not when the money is received or paid.
In arrears	An expense paid in arrears is one that is paid for after having been received, for example, electricity is often paid for in arrears – the amount owing is calculated after the electricity has been used.
Accrued expenses	Expenses relating to the current accounting period that remain unpaid at the end of the period. Also known as 'other payables'.
Prepaid expenses	Expenses that have been paid in advance of the accounting period to which they relate. Also known as 'other receivables'.
Accrued incomes	Incomes earned but not yet received by the business at the end of the period.
Prepaid incomes	Incomes received in advance of the period in which they were earned by the business.

Resource 4.4A

Activity: Key terms

Irrecoverable debt	An amount owed to a business by a credit customer that cannot pay or will not pay the money that is owed. The amount is written off.
Recovery of debts	When money is received in payment of a debt that had been previously written off.
Credit control	The monitoring of credit sales and the collection of payments from credit customers.
Provision for doubtful debts	An adjustment made to trade receivables based on an estimate of future irrecoverable debts.

Resource 4.5A

Activity: The effect of incorrect valuation of inventory

Closing inventory is overstated	Profit is overstated	Assets and equity on the statement of financial position are overstated
Closing inventory is understated	Profit is understated	Assets and equity on the statement of financial position are understated

Resource 4.5B

Activity: Key terms

Inventory	Goods held by a business for resale. They may be in the form of finished goods, partly finished goods or raw materials.
Net realisable value (of inventory)	The selling price *less* any costs incurred getting the inventory into saleable condition.
Inventory valuation statement	A report including the different valuations for each type of inventory held by a business.
Closing inventory	Value of inventory held by the business at the end of the accounting period.
Gross profit	Sales revenue less cost of sales.
Profit for the year	Gross profit *less* expenses.

Resource 5.1A

Activity: Financial statements

Make up numbers to complete these financial statements. Remember that the information on the financial statements must match.

Income statement for the year ended					
			$	$	$
Revenue				☐	
Less	Sales returns			(☐)	
					☐
	Opening inventory		☐		
Add	Purchases		☐		
Add	Carriage inwards		☐		
Less	Purchases returns		(☐)		
				☐	
Less	Closing inventory			(☐)	
Cost of sales					(☐)
Gross profit (or loss)					☐
Additional income:					
Decrease in provision for doubtful debts				☐	
Rent received				☐	
					☐
Expenses:					
Rent and rates				☐	
Wages and salaries				☐	
Carriage outwards				☐	
Heat and light				☐	
Insurance				☐	
Advertising				☐	
Repairs and maintenance				☐	
Irrecoverable debts				☐	
Depreciation				☐	
					(☐)
Profit (or loss) for the year					☐

Resource 5.1A (Continued)

Statement of financial position as at			
	$	**$**	**$**
	Cost	**Depreciation**	**Net Book Value**
Non-current assets			
Premises	☐	☐	☐
Fixtures & Fittings	☐	☐	☐
Motor Van	☐	☐	☐
	☐	☐	☐
Current assets			
Inventory		☐	
Trade receivables	☐		
Less provision for doubtful debts	☐	☐	
Cash		☐	
Accrued income		☐	
Other receivables (prepaid expenses)		☐	
			☐
Total assets			☐
Capital and liabilities			
Capital			☐
Add Profit for the year			☐
			☐
Less Drawings			(☐)
			☐

Non-current liabilities			
Mortgage			☐
			☐
Current liabilities			
Trade payables			☐
Bank overdraft			☐
Other payables (accrued expenses)			☐
Prepaid income			☐
			☐
Total liabilities			☐

Resource 5.1B

Activity: Items on an income statement

Trading account	Calculates the gross profit that a business has made by buying and selling its goods during a particular period of time.
Revenue	Earned when goods have been sold to customers. These are goods in which the business normally deals and that were bought with the primary intention of resale.
Sales returns	The cost of the goods that have been returned by customers to the business.
Purchases	The cost of the goods bought for resale.
Purchase returns	The cost of the goods that the business has sent back to suppliers.
Carriage inwards	Delivery costs of transporting the goods purchased to the business.
Cost of sales	Total purchases made during a financial year adjusted for inventory held.
Gross profit	Sales revenue less the cost of those same sales.
Additional income	Any income the business has earned from sources other than their normal trading activities.

Resource 5.1C

Activity: Items on a statement of financial position

Non-current assets	Resources that are acquired by a business and are likely to be used for a considerable amount of time (more than one year).
Intangible assets	Assets of a business that do not have a physical existence. Any valuation is subjective.
Current assets	Resources of a business that are likely to be converted into cash within one year.
Current liabilities	Liabilities that occur through day-to-day business activities. These debts are likely to be repaid within one year.
Non-current liabilities	Long-term borrowing that is not likely to be repaid within the next year. These liabilities will appear in a number of consecutive statements of financial position.
Capital	Describes how much a business is worth. The capital of a business represents how much the owner(s) of the business have invested.

Resource 5.1D

Activity: Key terms

Sole trader	A business that is owned and controlled by one individual.
Unlimited liability	The owner(s) of a business are personally liable for the debts of the business if the business is unable to repay them.
Income statement	A financial statement showing a business's income and expenses for an accounting period and the resulting profit or loss.
Gross profit	Sales revenue less cost of sales.
Profit for the year	Gross profit less expenses.
Capital	Resources invested into a business. It is calculated as capital = assets – liabilities. Also known as owner's equity.
Statement of financial position	A financial statement showing the assets of the business and the financing for these assets, either from owner's equity or liabilities.

Resource 5.2A

Activity: Partnership Financial statements

Fill in the boxes to complete the appropriation account.

Argo and Victoria			
Appropriation account for the year ended 30 June 2018			
	$	**$**	**$**
Profit or loss for the year			63 000
Argo		0	
Victoria		0	
			0
Less Salary: Argo			
Less Interest on capital:			
	600		
Victoria			
		1 080	
			19 080
			43 920
Balance of profits / losses shared:			
Argo (50%)			
Victoria (50%)			
			43 920

Resource 5.2B

Activity: Key terms and features of partnership accounts

Partnership	A business that is owned and controlled by a minimum of two owners.
Deed of partnership	An agreement that outlines the conditions that partners have consented to. It may also be referred to as a 'partnership agreement'.
Appropriation account	An account that shows how a partnership's profit or loss for the year is shared out between the partners.
Residual profit	The profit for the year for a partnership + interest on drawings – salaries and interest on capital.
Goodwill	An intangible non-current asset that represents the value of a business in excess of the assets that physically exist.
Interest on capital	A reward for contributing capital.
Interest on drawings	A deterrent to partners from taking excessive drawings.
Partnership salaries	Wages and salaries recorded in the appropriation account.
Profit sharing ratio	The profit for the year of a partnership is allocated in the appropriation account prepared by the partnership.

Resource 5.3A

Activity: Preference shares vs ordinary shares

Shareholders of preference shares	Shareholders of ordinary (equity) shares
receive a fixed percentage rate of dividend	receive a variable dividend each year or may not receive one at all
are not entitled to vote at a limited company's annual general meeting	are entitled to vote at shareholder meetings – one vote per share
receive their dividends before ordinary shareholders receive their dividends	receive their dividend payment after the preference shareholders have received their dividend payment
receive capital before ordinary shareholders in the event of the limited company going bankrupt	are the last people to receive their share capital in the event of the limited company going bankrupt

Shareholders of preference shares	Shareholders of ordinary (equity) shares

Resource 5.3B

Activity: Ordinary shares vs Debentures

Ordinary shares	Debentures
Owners	Liability (loan)
More speculative	Less speculative
Right to vote	No voting rights
No guaranteed dividend	Fixed rate of interest
Can be held long term	Redemption date

Ordinary shares	Debentures

Resource 5.3C

Activity: Financial statements of limited companies

Make up numbers to complete these financial statements. Remember that the information on the financial statements must match.

Pointer Ltd

Income statement for the year ended 30 April 2018

	$
Revenue	☐
Cost of sales	(☐)
Gross profit	☐
Distribution costs	(☐)
Administrative expenses	(☐)
Profit from operations	☐
Finance income	☐
Finance costs	(☐)
Profit before tax	☐
Taxation	(☐)
Profit for the year	☐

Pointer Ltd

Statement of changes in equity for the year ended 30 April 2018

	Ordinary Share Capital	Preference Share Capital	General Reserve	Retained Earnings	Total
	$	$	$	$	$
Opening Balance	☐	☐	☐	☐	☐
Profit for the year				☐	☐
Dividend paid				(☐)	(☐)
Transfer to general reserves			☐	(☐)	–
Share issue	☐	☐			☐
Closing Balance	☐	☐	☐	☐	☐

Resource 5.3C (Continued)

Pointer Ltd			
Statement of financial position as at 30 April 2018			
			$
			Net book value
Non-current assets			
Premises			☐
Fixtures & Fittings			☐
Equipment			☐
Motor Van			☐
			☐
Current assets			
Inventory		☐	
Trade receivables		☐	
Cash and cash equivalents		☐	
Accrued income		☐	
Other receivables (Prepaid expenses)		☐	
			☐
Total assets			☐
Capital and reserves			
Ordinary share capital			☐
% Non-redeemable preference share capital			☐
General reserve			☐
Retained earnings			☐
			☐
Non-current liabilities			
% Debentures (year)			☐
% Redeemable preference share capital			☐
			☐
Current liabilities			
Trade payables			☐
Bank overdraft and loans			☐
Other payables (Accrued expenses)			☐
Prepaid income			☐
			☐
Total liabilities			☐

Resource 5.3D

Activity: Key terms

Limited company	A business that has a separate legal identity from its shareholders.
Limited liability	Shareholders of limited companies are not personally liable for the debts of the business.
Equity	The value of the shares issued by a limited company.
Stock exchange	A market where shares are bought and sold.
Authorised Share Capital	The maximum amount of share capital that can be issued by a limited company. It is stated in the Memorandum of Association.
Issued Share Capital	The amount of share capital that has actually been raised by the company by the sale of shares.
Called-up share capital	The total amount of money that will be due to a limited company from the issue of shares.
Paid-up share capital	The amount of money that has actually been received by a limited company from the issue of shares.
Par Value	The issue price of the shares. This is also called the nominal value of the shares.
Share Premium	The difference between the par value and the sale price of the share.
Debenture	A legal document that is given to an individual who has loaned money to a limited company.
Retained earnings	This is the profit that is not appropriated (used) to pay shareholder dividends and forms part of the company's share capital and reserves.
General reserve	A reserve created for general purposes in the future. It forms part of the capital of the company.

Resource 5.4A

Activity: Financial statements of clubs and societies

Fill in the boxes to complete the financial statements.

Subscriptions			
	$		$
Balance b/d (Accrued)			
	118 000		
Balance c/d (Prepaid)			
	121 300		121 300
		Balance b/d	1 800

Western Highlands Rugby Club					
Income and Expenditure Account for the year ended 31 December 2018					
		$		$	
Income					
Subscriptions					
Competition income		11 180			
				129 180	
Expenditure					
General expenses		25 290			
Travelling expenses					
Rent		24 900			
Loss on sale of motor van		2 500			
Depreciation of motor van		15 000			
				89 350	
___________ for the year					

Resource 5.4B

Activity: Terms relating to clubs and societies

Non-profit -making organisation	An organisation formed by groups of individuals to pursue a common not-for-profit goal. They exist with the intention of distributing their revenue to achieve their purpose or mission.
Accumulated fund	The difference in value between the assets and liabilities of the organisation.
Receipts and payments account	Summarised cash book.
Income and expenditure account	A financial statement equivalent to a profit-making organisation's income statement.
Matching principle	Incomes are matched to expenses in a particular accounting period.
Subscriptions account	Allows the club or society to adjust the amount received for prepayments and accruals at both the start and end of the financial period.
Life membership scheme	A system that allows a new member to pay a substantial one-off fee for use of all of the organisation's facilities for the remainder of their life.
Donations	A means of increasing annual income for a club or society.

Resource 5.5A

Activity: Manufacturing accounts

Make up numbers to complete the manufacturing account.

Robot Manufacturing					
Manufacturing account for the year ending 30 April 2017					
	$		$		$
Raw materials					
Opening inventory			☐		
Purchases			☐		
Carriage inwards			☐		
Less returns			(☐)		
			☐		
Less Closing inventory			(☐)		
Cost of raw materials consumed					☐
Direct wages/labour					☐
Direct expenses					☐
PRIME COST					☐
Add: Factory overheads					
Rent and insurance			☐		
Salaries			☐		
Machinery repairs			☐		
Indirect wages			☐		
Light and power			☐		
Depreciation of machinery			☐		
					☐
					☐
Add: Opening work in progress					☐
					☐
Less: Closing work in progress					(☐)
Manufacturing cost of goods completed					☐

Resource 5.5B

Activity: Terms relating to manufacturing accounts

Term	Definition
Manufacturing account	An account in which it is calculated how much it has cost a business to manufacture the goods produced in a financial year.
Prime cost	The total of direct costs of goods produced in terms of material, labour and expenses involved in its production.
Royalties	A fee that is paid to the individual who originally invented the product being manufactured.
Direct costs	The costs incurred in physically making the products; they are related to the level of output.
Direct material	Materials required to make finished goods.
Direct labour	The cost of the wages that are paid to individuals who are employed to make the goods being produced.
Direct expenses	Costs that a manufacturer can link directly to the goods that are being produced. Examples include, royalties and packaging costs.
Indirect costs	The costs involved in the operation of a factory, that cannot be directly linked to the goods that are being produced.

Resource 5.6A

Activity: Calculating changes in capital

Calculate the missing figures.

	$	$	$	$	$
Opening capital	20 000	50 000	100 000	70 000	
Add Capital introduced	10 000	20 000		30 000	50 000
Add Profit for the year		10 000	20 000	20 000	30 000
Less Drawings	5 000	20 000		30 000	50 000
Equals Closing capital	35 000	60 000	80 000		280 000

Activity: Calculating changes in capital

Calculate the missing figures.

	$	$	$	$	$
Opening capital	20 000	50 000	100 000	70 000	
Add Capital introduced	10 000	20 000		30 000	50 000
Add Profit for the year		10 000	20 000	20 000	30 000
Less Drawings	5 000	20 000		30 000	50 000
Equals Closing capital	35 000	60 000	80 000		280 000

Activity: Calculating changes in capital

Calculate the missing figures.

	$	$	$	$	$
Opening capital	20 000	50 000	100 000	70 000	
Add Capital introduced	10 000	20 000		30 000	50 000
Add Profit for the year		10 000	20 000	20 000	30 000
Less Drawings	5 000	20 000		30 000	50 000
Equals Closing capital	35 000	60 000	80 000		280 000

Resource 5.6B

Activity: Income statement or statement of financial position?

1 Should each item be included in the income statement or the statement of financial position? Tick the correct column.

2 For the items to be included in the statement of financial position, state whether they are current assets, current liabilities, non-current assets or non-current liabilities.

	Income statement	Statement of financial position	Current asset, current liability, non-current asset or non-current liability?
Premises			
Revenue			
Motor vehicles			
Purchases			
Heat and light			
Carriage inwards			
Closing Inventory			
Office equipment			
Fixtures and fittings			
Trade receivables			
Cash in hand			
Short-term bank loan			
Mortgage on business property			
Bank overdraft			
Trade payables			

Resource 6.1A

Activity: Ratio formulae, definitions and purposes

Gross margin	$\frac{\text{gross profit}}{\text{revenue}} \times 100$	The gross profit of a business organisation expressed as a percentage of sales revenue – a measure of profitability.
Profit margin	$\frac{\text{profit for the year}}{\text{revenue}} \times 100$	The profit for the year of a business organisation expressed as a percentage of sales revenue – a measure of profitability.
Rate of inventory turnover (times)	$\frac{\text{cost of sales}}{\text{average inventory}}$	A measure of how quickly a business organisation uses or sells its inventory.
Return on capital employed (ROCE)	$\frac{\text{profit for the year}}{\text{capital employed}} \times 100$	The profit for the year expressed as a percentage of the capital employed. It informs a business organisation of the profits that have been made, based on the resources made available to them.
Trade receivables turnover (days)	$\frac{\text{trade receivables}}{\text{credit sales}} \times 365$	The average number of days that it takes a business organisation to collect its debts from its customers (trade receivables).
Trade payables turnover (days)	$\frac{\text{trade payables}}{\text{credit purchases}} \times 365$	The average number of days that it takes a business organisation to pay its debts to its suppliers (trade payables).
Current ratio	$\frac{\text{current assets}}{\text{current liabilities}}$	A measure of the liquidity of a business organisation which compares current assets to current liabilities.
Liquid (acid test) ratio	$\frac{\text{current assets} - \text{closing inventory}}{\text{current liabilities}}$	A measure of the liquidity of a business organisation which compares current assets excluding closing inventory to current liabilities.

Resource 6.2A

Activity: Key terms

Economy	The system by which goods and services are produced, sold and purchased in a particular area.
Competitor	A business that is engaged in commercial competition with other businesses.
Financial analyst	An individual whose job is to review the financial performance of a business to assess whether it is a sound investment.
Trend analysis	This is where a business compares its ratio results against benchmarks or industry averages and previous years' results.
Interpretation (of financial ratios)	Comparing financial results with benchmarks or targets, previous years or similar businesses.
Working capital	The difference between current assets and current liabilities. It is sometimes referred to as 'net current assets' and is the amount of money available to fund the day-to-day operations of a business.
Debt factoring	Occurs when a business sells its outstanding customer accounts to a debt factoring company. The factoring company pays the business a set percentage of the value of the debts (80–90%) and then collects the full amount of the debts. Once debts are collected the business receives the remaining amount less a charge.

Resource 6.3A

Activity: Causes of differences in profitability ratios

Causes of differences between two businesses' gross margin	Causes of differences between two businesses' profit margin
Selling prices	Cost of sales
Organisational advertising and sales promotions	Gross margin
Supplier costs	Expenses
Rate of trade discounts	Accounting principles
Sales revenue	Sales revenue

Resource 6.4A

Activity: Key terms

Stakeholder	An individual or group who has an interest in a business and may be directly affected by the activities of the business.
Internal stakeholder	Any individual or group that is directly involved with the business; for example, employees, managers, owners.
External stakeholder	Any individual or group who has an interest in a business but may not be directly involved with the business; for example, a local resident.
Collateral	An asset that is pledged as security for the repayment of a debt. In the event that the debt cannot be repaid, the asset will be taken by the lender.

Resource 6.5A

Activity: Key terms

Historic data	This is financial data or information from the past. In an income statement, this is traditionally the last year.
Quantitative information	Factual information and data that is not based on opinions.
Qualitative information	Information collected based on an individual's opinions and views.

Resource Ch6 review

Chapter 6: Chapter review

11

Vedhika Engineering			
Statement of financial position as at 30 April 2018			
	Cost	Depreciation	Net book value
	$	$	$
Non-current assets			
Premises	93 000	7 460	**(i)**
Equipment	29 000	11 180	17 820
	122 000	18 640	103 360
Current assets			
Inventory		16 300	
Trade receivables		**(ii)**	
General expenses prepaid		550	
			39 684
Total assets			143 044
Capital			
Capital			110 000
(iii)________________			(3 556)
			106 444
Drawings			**(iv)**
			104 644
Current (v)________________			
Trade payables			26 200
Salaries outstanding			3 400
Bank charges owing			**(vi)**
Bank **(vii)**________________			8 200
			38 400
Total liabilities			143 044

Resource 7.1A

Applying

Complete the sentences with the names of appropriate accounting principles.

1 The ______________________ principle states that income and expenses should be entered in the financial records when they are earned or incurred and not when the money is received.

2 A business thinks that a number of their credit customers may not pay the debts that they owe. The business needs to account for all potential losses in accordance with the ______________________ principle.

3 An accountant has informed a business owner that they only need to know the value of their drawings and not that the owner purchased a holiday with this money. This is in accordance with ______________________ principle.

4 A business has taken an order for goods but the goods have not left the warehouse. According to the ______________________ principle, the business should not record the revenue from the sale.

5 The management of QNet are exceptionally well qualified. However, the skills cannot be recorded in the statement of financial position due to the ______________________ principle.

6 A business always uses the FIFO method to value their closing inventory. This meets the requirements of the ______________________ principle.

7 The ______________________ principle describes the concept of double entry book keeping.

8 An accounting clerk is considering accounting for every sheet of paper that they use in the office. According to the ______________________ principle items of a low value should not be accounted for.

9 Financial statements are prepared on the basis that the business is going to continue for the foreseeable future. This is in accordance with the ______________________ principle.

10 In the statement of financial position, a business needs to include their motor vehicles at their net book value. This meets the ______________________ principle.

Resource 7.1B

Activity: Accounting principles – key terms

True and fair view	Describes financial records that are free from misinformation and accurately represent the financial position of a business.
Accounting principles	Rules that accountants use when preparing financial records.
Prudence principle	Revenue and profit should only be recognised when they are achieved.
Matching principle	Ensures incomes are matched to expenses in a particular accounting period.
Consistency principle	When faced with a choice between different accounting techniques, an accountant should not change accounting policies without good reason.
Going concern principle	A business's financial statements should be prepared on the assumption that the business will continue to trade for the foreseeable future.
Historic cost principle	An asset should be recorded in the financial accounts at the cost for which it was purchased, not its current value.
Materiality principle	Accountants should not spend time trying to record items that are immaterial accurately.
Business entity principle	The financial affairs of a business must be maintained separately from those of the owner.
Duality principle	A business transaction always has two effects on the business and requires two entries, one debit and one credit, to be made in the accounts.
Money measurement principle	Only transactions that can be expressed in monetary terms should be recorded in a business's accounts.
Realisation principle	Revenue should be recognised when the exchange of goods or services takes place.

Resource 7.2A

Activity: Key terms

International Accounting Standards (IASs)	A set of internationally agreed principles and procedures that inform businesses how to present their accounts.
Comparability	Financial information is comparable when accounting principles and policies are consistency applied from one accounting period to the next and from one business to another.
Relevance	A non-numerical characteristic in accounting. Relevance is associated with accounting information that is timely, useful and will make a difference to an interested party when making a decision.
Reliability	Relates to the trustworthiness of a business's financial statements.
Bias	Prejudice in favour of or against one thing, usually in a way that would be considered as unfair.
Understandability	An accounting policy that states that a business's financial information should be presented in a way that an individual with a reasonable knowledge of business and finance and a willingness to study the information provided should be able to understand it.

Student's Book answers

1 THE FUNDAMENTALS OF ACCOUNTING

1.1 The purpose of accounting

Answers to knowledge check questions

1 D

2 C

3 D

4 Suggested answers:

- **(i)** Shareholders will be interested in profit and sales. This is because most shareholders are interested in the dividends paid to shareholders from the profits earned by the business.
- **(ii)** The people to whom the business owes money will be interested in profit and cash flow. The main concern will be whether the business can keep up with the repayment of any debts they owe.
- **(iii)** Customers may be interested in profits. For example, regular customers or customers holding long-term contacts with a business (such as a mobile phone network provider) will be interested in the survival of the business. Customers may also look for excessive profit to see if there is a case for lobbying for price reductions.
- **(iv)** Owners will be interested in profits and expenses. They will be interested in profit because it shows how much money they may be able to take out of the business and also because profit is a sign of success. They will monitor expenses because they will be keen to ensure expenses are not higher than they need to be.
- **(v)** Managers will be interested in sales revenue and profit. Many managers are paid according to the revenue they achieve. Profit is also a sign of the manager's success.

5 Book-keeping involves the recording of financial transactions generated by business activity. Accounting includes book-keeping but also includes additional activities, such as the preparation of financial statements and assessing the financial performance of the business.

6 Possible answers include:

- **A** Book-keeping records and financial statements can provide information as to how a business is performing and allow the business to monitor, for example, whether or not it has sufficient cash to pay its debts or profits to pay its owners.
- **B** Book-keeping records and financial statements can provide information for making decisions, such as whether or not to expand the business, acquire finance or launch new products (which would require adequate financing).

1.2 The accounting equation

Answers to knowledge check questions

1 D

2 A

3 Assets: A, C, D. Liabilities: B, E

4

Statement of financial position as at 31 October			
	$		$
Property	230000	Bank loan	85000
Vehicles	38750	Trade payables	8927
Inventory	11900	Owner's equity	191258
Bank	4535		
	285185		285185

Answers to chapter review

1 A

2 B

3 C

4 B

5 C

6 C

7 D

2 SOURCES AND RECORDING OF DATA

2.1 The double entry system of book-keeping

Answers to knowledge check questions

1 C

2 A

3 B

4

	Account to be debited	Account to be credited
(a)	Computer	Bank
(b)	Delivery van	Peng
(c)	Bank	Owner's equity
(d)	Li	Fixtures and fittings
(e)	Bank	Li
(f)	Cash	Equipment

5

	Account to be debited	Account to be credited
(a)	Purchases	Bank
(b)	Hania	Purchases returns
(c)	Rachid	Sales
(d)	Sunita	Bank
(e)	Sales returns	Martin

6

	Account to be debited	Account to be credited
(a)	Rent	Bank
(b)	Wages	Cash
(c)	Bank	Commission received
(d)	Drawings	Computer equipment
(e)	Purchases	Somchi

7

Bank

		$			$
1 Aug	Owner's equity	2000	2 Aug	Computer equipment	900
7 Aug	Western Bank	1000			

Cash

		$			$
1 Aug	Owner's equity	400			

Computer equipment					
		$			$
2 Aug	Bank	900	4 Aug	123 Computers	200

Owner's equity					
		$			$
			1 Aug	Cash	400
			1 Aug	Bank	2000

123 Computers					
		$			$
4 Aug	Computer equipment	200			

Western Bank					
		$			$
			7 Aug	Bank	1000

8

Bank					
		$			$
1 May	Owner's equity	3000	2 May	Cash	500
			16 May	ABC Supplies	1400
			20 May	Car	1000

Owner's equity					
		$			$
			1 May	Bank	3000

Cash					
		$			$
2 May	Bank	500			

ABC Supplies					
		$			$
16 May	Bank	1400	8 May	Equipment	900
			12 May	Equipment	500

Equipment					
		$			$
8 May	ABC Supplies	900			
12 May	ABC Supplies	500			

Car					
		$			$
20 May	Bank	1000			

9

Owner's equity					
		$			$
30 Sep	Balance c/d	6500	1 Sep	Bank	6500
			1 Oct	Balance b/d	6500

Equipment					
		$			$
4 Sep	Bank	1900	30 Sep	Balance c/d	1900
1 Oct	Balance b/d	1900			

Bank					
		$			$
1 Sep	Capital	6500	4 Sep	Equipment	1900
18 Sep	Maria	380	6 Sep	Insurance	55
			21 Sep	Janine	21
			30 Sep	Balance c/d	4904
		6880			6800
1 Oct	Balance b/d	4904			

Insurance					
		$			$
6 Sep	Bank	55	30 Sep	Balance c/d	55
1 Oct	Balance b/d	55			

Purchases					
		$			$
7 Sep	Santiago	65	30 Sep	Balance c/d	86
7 Sep	Janine	21			
		86			86
1 Oct	Balance b/d	86			

Santiago					
		$			$
16 Sep	Purchases returns	34	7 Sep	Purchases	65
30 Sep	Balance c/d	31			
		65			65
			1 Oct	Balance b/d	31

Purchases returns					
		$			$
30 Sep	Balance c/d	34	16 Sep	Santiago	34
			1 Oct	Balance b/d	34

Janine					
		$			$
21 Sep	Bank	21	7 Sep	Purchases	21

Vehicle					
		$			$
10 Sep	Oliver	6000	30 Sep	Balance c/d	6000
1 Oct	Balance b/d	6000			

Oliver					
		$			$
30 Sep	Balance c/d	6000	10 Sep	Vehicle	6000
			1 Oct	Balance b/d	6000

Sales					
		$			$
30 Sep	Balance c/d	380	14 Sep	Maria	380
			1 Oct	Balance b/d	380

Maria					
		$			$
14 Sep	Sales	380	18 Sep	Bank	380

10

Purchases					
2018		$	**2018**		$
31 Dec	Balance b/d	48 900	31 Dec	Income statement	48 900

Commission received					
2018		$	**2018**		$
31 Dec	Income statement	289	31 Dec	Balance b/d	289

11 **(a)** Nominal

(b) Sales

(c) Sales

(d) Nominal

(e) Nominal

(f) Purchases

2.2 Business documents

Answers to knowledge check questions

1 C

2 B

3 D

4

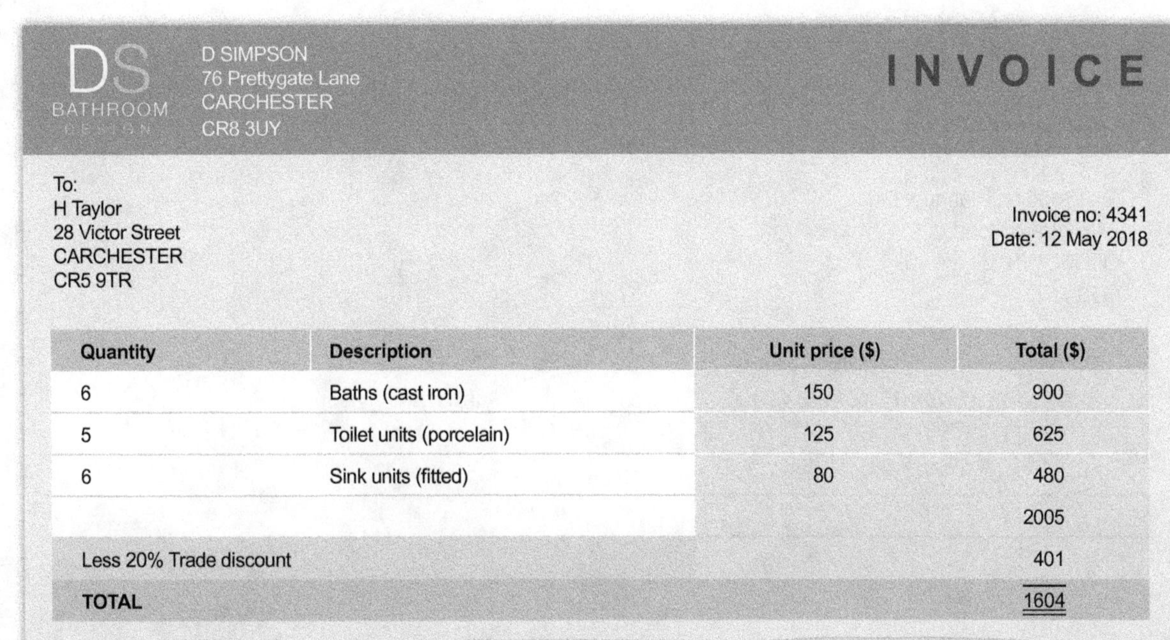

DS BATHROOM DESIGN

D SIMPSON
76 Prettygate Lane
CARCHESTER
CR8 3UY

INVOICE

To:
H Taylor
28 Victor Street
CARCHESTER
CR5 9TR

Invoice no: 4341
Date: 12 May 2018

Quantity	Description	Unit price ($)	Total ($)
6	Baths (cast iron)	150	900
5	Toilet units (porcelain)	125	625
6	Sink units (fitted)	80	480
			2005
Less 20% Trade discount			401
TOTAL			1604

5

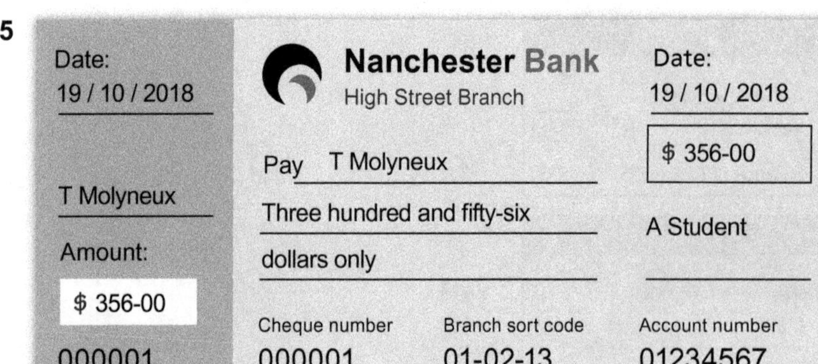

Date:
19 / 10 / 2018

T Molyneux

Amount:
$ 356-00

000001

Nanchester Bank
High Street Branch

Date:
19 / 10 / 2018

$ 356-00

Pay T Molyneux

Three hundred and fifty-six

dollars only

A Student

Cheque number	Branch sort code	Account number
000001	01-02-13	01234567

6 (a)

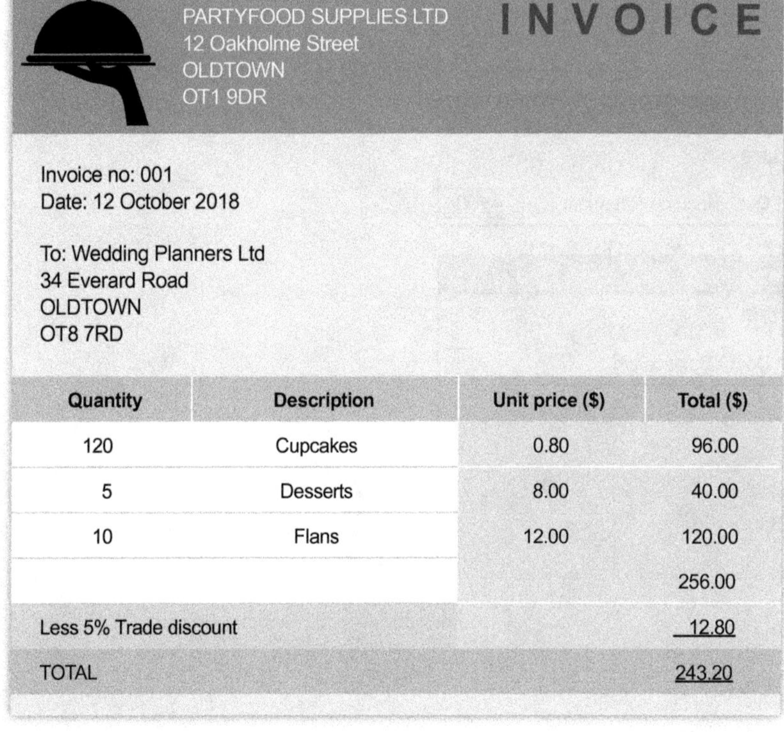

PARTYFOOD SUPPLIES LTD
12 Oakholme Street
OLDTOWN
OT1 9DR

INVOICE

Invoice no: 001
Date: 12 October 2018

To: Wedding Planners Ltd
34 Everard Road
OLDTOWN
OT8 7RD

Quantity	Description	Unit price ($)	Total ($)
120	Cupcakes	0.80	96.00
5	Desserts	8.00	40.00
10	Flans	12.00	120.00
			256.00
Less 5% Trade discount			12.80
TOTAL			243.20

6 (b)

PARTYFOOD
SUPPLIES LTD

CREDIT NOTE

12 Oakholme Street
OLDTOWN
OT1 9DR

Credit note no: 2018-5
Date: 13 October 2018

To: Wedding Planners Ltd
34 Everard Road
OLDTOWN
OT8 7RD

Quantity	Description	Unit price ($)	Total ($)
20	Cupcakes – damaged on arrival	0.80	16.00
	TOTAL		16.00

7

DEX SYSTEMS SOLUTIONS
Unit 5, Business Park
NEWTOWN
NT55 1LY

STATEMENT OF ACCOUNT

Account no: 7280
Date: 30 April 2018
To: G Hill
78 Hartope Road
NEWTOWN
NT4 5UN

Date	Details	Debit ($)	Credit ($)	Balance ($)
5 Apr	Invoice number 1045	540		540
19 Apr	Invoice Number 1047	310		850
23 Apr	Credit note Number 05/18		105	745
27 Apr	Bank		500	245
30 Apr	**Balance owing**			**245**

2.3 Books of prime entry

Answers to knowledge check questions

1 A

2 B

3 D

4 **(a)** Sales journal
(b) Sales returns journal
(c) General journal
(d) Cash book
(e) Cash book
(f) Purchases journal

5

Petty cash book							
Receipts	Date	Details	Voucher	Total	Cleaning	Travel expenses	Stationery
$				$	$	$	$
100	1 May	Cash					
	2 May	Rail fares	1	17		17	
	4 May	Petrol	2	8		8	
	8 May	Stationery	3	4			4
	10 May	Cleaning	4	11	11		
	18 May	Petrol	5	16		16	
	21 May	Cleaning	6	15	15		
	22 May	Bus fares	7	4		4	
	25 May	Cleaning	8	2	2		
				77	28	45	4
77	31 May	Cash					
	31 May	Balance c/d		100			
177				177			
100	1 Jun	Balance b/d					

6

		Dr.	Cr.
		$	$
1 July	Equipment	900	
	Tau		900
8 July	Manuel	280	
	Sohar		280
13 July	Drawings	490	
	Equipment		490
19 July	Car	2900	
	Quality Cars Ltd		2900
25 July	Computer	325	
	Wei		325

7

Cash book							
2018		Cash	Bank	2018		Cash	Bank
		$	$			$	$
1 July	Balance b/d	42		1 July	Balance b/d		860
4 July	Machinery		320	7 July	Cash		250
7 July	Bank	250		11 July	Purchases		100
14 July	M Zhang		84	18 July	Wages		530
26 July	Sales	230		22 July	Advertising	51	
29 July	Cash		431	29 July	Bank	431	
31 July	Balance c/d		905	31 July	Balance c/d	40	
		522	1740			522	1740
1 Aug	Balance b/d	40		1 Aug	Balance c/d		905

Answers to chapter review

1 C

2 D

3 D

4 C

5 B

6 A

7 A

8 C

9 B

10 C

11 (a)

Cash book									
		Discount	Cash	Bank			Discount	Cash	Bank
2018		£	£	£	2018		£	£	£
1 June	Balance b/d **(1 mark for both)**		218	5642	Jun 05	Office furniture			2300 **(1)**
17 June	Nathan	15 **(1)**		585 **(1)**	Jun 15	Thalia	30 **(1)**		890 **(1)**
21 June	Sales			680 **(1)**	Jun 24	Office expenses		150 **(1)**	
					Jun 30	Balances c/d		68 **(1)**	3717 **(1)**
		15 **(1)**	218	6907			30	218	6907
30 June	Balances b/d		68	3717					

11 (b)

Nathan					
2018		$	2018		$
2 June	Sales	900 **(1)**	June 9	Sales returns	300 **(1)**
			June 17	Discounts allowed	15 **(1)**
			June 17	Bank	585 **(1)**
		900 **(1)**			900 **(1)**

11 (c) (i) The sales ledger **(1)**

(ii) The sales journal **(1)**

12 (a)

General journal			
2018		Dr.	Cr.
		$	$
5 Aug	Van	900 **(1)**	
	Motorcycle		900 **(1)**
8 Aug	Bank	50 **(1)**	
	Irrecoverable debt	250 **(1)**	
	Alysha		300 **(1)**
13 Aug	Office equipment	810 **(1)**	
	Sulaiman		810 **(1)**
25 Aug	Drawings	120 **(1)**	
	Purchases		120 **(1)**
30 Aug	Uma	50 **(1)**	
	Fen		50 **(1)**

(1 mark for correct layout of general journal – i.e. debit entries first, dates, etc.)

12 (b)

Denys					
		$			$
Sep 1	Balance b/d	75 **(1)**	Sep 18	Sales returns	114 **(1)**
Sep 4	Sales	855 **(1)**	Sep 27	Bank	340 **(1)**
			Sep 27	Discounts allowed	15 **(1)**
			Sep 30	Balance c/d	461 **(1)**
		930			930
Oct 1	Balance b/d	461			

12 (c) (i) The cash book **(1)**

(ii) The purchases returns journal **(1)**

13 (a)

Petty cash book						
Receipts	**Date**	**Details**	**Total**	**Cleaning**	**Petrol**	**General expenses**
$	**2018**		**$**	**$**	**$**	**$**
200 **(1)**	2 Mar	Newspapers	3			3 **(1)**
	4 Mar	Petrol	5		5 **(1)**	
	8 Mar	Magazines	12			12 **(1)**
	10 Mar	Cleaning costs	14	14 **(1)**		
	20 Mar	Petrol	22		22 **(1)**	
	21 Mar	Cleaning costs	24	24 **(1)**		
	22 Mar	Petrol	18		18 **(1)**	
	25 Mar	Newspapers	7			7 **(1)**
			105 **(1)**			
105 **(1)**	31 Mar	Cash				
	31 Mar	Balance c/d	200 **(1)**			
305			305	38	45	22
200	1 April	Balance b/d				

13 (b) (i) Restoring the petty cash paid out each period **(1)** so as to start the next period with the same amount of petty cash as the start of the previous period **(1)**.

(ii) The amount of petty cash available **(1)** at the start of each period **(1)**.

(c)
- Stops the main cash book containing too many items of small amounts **(1)** as monthly totals can be transferred from the petty cash book to the main cash book **(1)**.
- Allows specialisation between workers **(1)** – a different worker can work on the petty cash book from that of the main cash book **(1)**.

3 VERIFICATION OF ACCOUNTING RECORDS

3.1 The trial balance

Answers to knowledge check questions

1 B

2 C

3 D

4 A

5

Sara Trial balance as at 31 December 2018		
	Dr.	Cr.
	$	$
Revenue		45808
Sales returns	113	
Purchases	32341	
Purchases returns		242
Inventory as at 1 Jan 2018	2910	
General expenses	6306	
Drawings	980	
Owner's equity		18600
Assets	22000	
	64650	64650

Additional information:

Inventory as at 31 December 2018 is valued at $4150.

6

- **(a)** Original entry
- **(b)** Principle
- **(c)** Commission
- **(d)** Complete reversal

3.2 Correction of errors

Answers to knowledge check questions

1 B

2 D

3 D

4 **(a)** Y
(b) N
(c) Y
(d) N
(e) Y

5 **(a)**

General journal		
	$	$
Mandeep	9	
Bank		9
Sales returns	110	
Ahmet		110
Sales	450	
Office equipment		450
Bibek	14	
Lili		14
Bank	400	
Owner's equity		400

(b) Adjustments to assets:

- Bank decreased by $9
- Office equipment decreased by $450
- Bank increased by $400

Overall adjustment: assets decreased by $59

6 (a)

General journal		
	$	$
Purchases	220	
Suspense		220
Sales	630	
Suspense		630
Car	1000	
Owner's equity		1000
Office expenses	462	
Suspense		462

(b)

Suspense			
	$		$
Balance b/d	1312	Purchases	220
		Sales	630
		Office expenses	462
	1312		1312

(c)

Ander Statement of corrected profit		
	$	$
Profit		2114
Less:		
Purchases undercast	220	
Sales overcast	630	
Office expenses undercast	462	1312
Corrected profit		802

(d) Assets will be increased by $1000 due to the introduction of the owner's car into the business.

3.3 Bank reconciliation

Answers to knowledge check questions

1 D

2 C

3 D

4

Updated cash book					
		$			$
31 Aug	Interest received	8	31 Aug	Balance b/d	695
31 Aug	Credit transfer: Somchi	430	31 Aug	Standing order: Rachid	250
31 Aug	Dividends received	85	31 Aug	Direct debit: Faisal	89
31 Aug	Balance c/d	643	31 Aug	Dishonoured cheque	121
			31 Aug	Bank charges	11
		1166			1166
			1 Sept	Balance b/d	643

5 (a)

Updated cash book			
	$		$
30 Nov Dividends	44	30 Nov Balance b/d	332
30 Nov Balance c/d	408	30 Nov Bank charges	25
		30 Nov Direct debit: Telephone bill	95
	452		452
		30 Nov Balance b/d	408

(b)

Chun Bank reconciliation statement as at 30 November 2018	
	$
Balance on updated cash book	408 (O/D)
Add unpresented cheque: Salma	199
	209 (O/D)
Less uncredited deposit: Rajab	56
Balance on bank statement	265 (O/D)

3.4 Control accounts

Answers to knowledge check questions

1 C

2 C

3 B

4

Sales ledger control account			
	$		$
Balances b/d	6546	Payments received	43431
Credit sales	44205	Sales returns	877
		Discounts allowed	990
		Balances c/d	5453
	50751		50751

5

Purchases ledger control account			
	$		$
Payments made	18711	Balances b/d	2230
Purchases returns	1986	Credit purchases	20131
Discounts received	766		
Balances c/d	898		
	22361		22361

6

Sales ledger control account					
2018		$			$
1 March	Balance b/d	6225	31 March	Cashbook	72010
31 March	Sales daybook	74 554	31 March	Sales returns	2314
			31 March	Discounts allowed	651
			31 March	Set-offs	290
			31 March	Irrecoverable debts	291
			31 March	Balance b/d	5223
		80 779			80 779
1 April	Balance b/d	5223			

Purchases ledger control account					
2018		$	2018		$
31 March	Cashbook	39040	1 March	Balance b/d	3123
31 March	Discounts received	333	31 March	Purchases daybook	43545
31 March	Set-offs	290			
31 March	Purchases returns	1112			
31 March	Balance c/d	5893			
		46668			46668

7

			31 July	Irrecoverable debts	445
			31 July	Balance c/d	6224
		141 773			141 733
1 August	Balance b/d	6224			

Purchases ledger control account					
		$			$
31 July	Cashbook	90 020	1 July	Balance b/d	4370
31 July	Discounts received	2311	31 July	Purchases daybook	98 697
31 July	Set-offs	1890	31 July	Interest on overdue accounts	27
31 July	Purchases returns	1980			
31 July	Balance c/d	6893			
		103 094			103 894
			1 August	Balance c/d	6893

Answers to chapter review

1 B

2 D

3 A

4 D

5 C

6 B

7 A

8 D

9 C

10 A

11 (a)

Bibek Trial balance as at 31 December 2018 (1)		
	$	$
Revenue		**87588 (1)**
Purchases	**48998 (1)**	
Sales returns	541	
Purchases returns		4323
Machinery	**21000 (1)**	
Discounts received		**898 (1)**
General expenses	**14500 (1)**	
Equipment	18500	
Inventory at 1 January 2018	4342	
Trade payables		6456
Trade receivables	8787	
Bank	2466	
Office salaries	**23000 (1)**	
Discounts allowed	**1131 (1)**	
Owner's equity		**55000 (1)**
Drawings	11000	
	154265	154265

Additional information:

Inventory at 31 December 2018 was valued at $6544. (1)

Correct total balance figures **(1)**

(b) Two marks for each explanation up to a maximum of 4. Relevant points include:

- Makes it easier to prepare financial statements **(1)** having all balances together **(1)**
- Arithmetic check on ledgers **(1)** if trial balance totals are the same then a number of errors have been avoided **(1)**
- Gives information about state of business **(1)** – e.g. balances owing. **(1)**

(c) (i) Commission

(ii) It would only be in the incorrect account **(1)**, the amounts and the side the entry is made on are correct, so the trial balance wouldn't highlight this type of error **(1)**.

(iii) 1 mark for identification plus 1 mark for correct explanation from:

- Omission – transaction is not recorded at all in double entry accounts
- Complete reversal – the debit and credit entries are on the wrong side (but are the correct value and in correct accounts)

- Principle – entry is on the correct side but is in the wrong type of account, for example sale of asset recorded in the sale of inventory
- Original entry – entries are in correct accounts and on the correct sides but the value of each entry is incorrect (though the same for both debit and credit).

12 (a) (i) Receipt of money **(1)** paid automatically into the business bank account **(1)**

(ii) Regular/on-going payment **(1)** of varying amounts **(1)**

(iii) Cheque received and deposited by the business **(1)** from a payer who has insufficient funds and the bank will not credit the bank account with the amount **(1)**.

(b) Nominal (or general) ledger **(1)**.

(c)

Updated cash book					
		$			$
1 Oct	Balance b/d	234 **(1)**	1 Oct	Interest	22 **(1)**
1 Oct	Credit transfer	150 **(1)**	1 Oct	Standing order: Jian	335 **(1)**
1 Oct	Dividends	22 **(1)**	1 Oct	Direct debit: Insurance	89 **(1)**
1 Oct	Balance c/d	454 **(1)**	1 Oct	Cheque dishonoured: Sara	414 **(1)**
		860			860
			1 Oct	Balance b/d	454

(d)

Bintu Bank reconciliation statement as at 1 October 2018 (1)	
	$
Balance as on updated cash book	454 (O/D) **(1)**
Add: Unpresented cheques	146 **(1)**
	308 (O/D)
Less: Uncredited deposits	287 **(1)**
	595 (O/D) **(1)**

13 (a)

Purchases ledger control account					
		$			$
30 Apr	Cash book	396 987 **(1)**	01 Apr	Balances b/d	6670 **(1)**
30 Apr	Purchases returns	2311 **(1)**	30 Apr	Credit purchases	404 524 **(1)**
30 Apr	Discounts received	1 101 **(1)**	30 Apr	Interest owing	175 **(1)**
30 Apr	Contra entries	765 **(1)**			
30 Apr	Balance c/d	10 205 **(1)**			
		411 369			411 369

(b) (i) Purchases journal **(1)**

(ii) Cash book **(1)**

(c) This means a credit customer of the business is also a credit supplier and there are two accounts for this business **(1)** – one in the sales ledger and one in the purchases ledger. Debts between the two businesses are normally offset against one another **(1)**.

(d) Possible uses include:

- Checking the accuracy of the sales and purchases ledgers **(1)**. If the control account does not balance, mistakes are present **(1)**.
- Checking for fraud **(1)** as it can show if not all money received from sales was deposited **(1)**.
- Calculating missing figures **(1)**; if all other information is present, a missing figure can be calculated **(1)**.

(e) • They only expose certain types of error **(1)** – those that do not affect the trial balance **(1)**.

• It takes time to produce **(1)** and may not be that useful for businesses with only a limited number of credit customers or suppliers **(1)**.

14 (a)

General journal			
Date	**Details**	**Dr**	**Cr**
31 Dec		**$**	**$**
	Purchases	282 (1)	
	Suspense		282 (1)
	Suspense	90 (1)	
	Cashbook		90 (1)
	Suspense	11 (1)	
	E Li		11 (1)
	Cashbook	297 (1)	
	Drawings		297 (1)
	H Puni	42 (1)	
	Cashbook		42 (1)

(b)

Suspense					
		$			$
31 Dec	Balance b/d (1)	181	31 Dec	Purchases (1)	282
31 Dec	Cashbook (1)	90			
31 Dec	E Li (1)	11			
		282			282

(c) Possible answers include (1 mark for any reasonable statement):

- to act as a deterrent for late payments
- to encourage prompt payment
- to compensate for cash flow issues (such as business having to borrow money to cover shortfall).

(d) Any of the following (1 mark for each):

- entering two debits or credits for a transaction
- missing out the debit or credit 'half' of the transaction
- entering different amounts on one side of the transaction
- arithmetical mistakes.

(e) \$990 – \$282 (1) = \$708 (1) (2 for correct answer)

4 ACCOUNTING PROCEDURES

4.1 Capital and revenue expenditure and receipts

Answers to knowledge check questions

1 C

2 B

3 C

4 A

5 Capital expenditure: A, D

Revenue expenditure: B, C, E

6 (a) Capital expenditure $25 340

Revenue expenditure $2 612

(b) Profit for the year will be $25 340 higher.

(c) Assets of the business will be $25 340 higher.

4.2 Accounting for depreciation and disposal of non-current assets

Answers to knowledge check questions

1 A

2 B

3 C

4 D

5 (a)

	$
Cost	50 000
Depreciation: Year 1	12 500
Net book value at end of year 1	37 500
Depreciation: Year 2	12 500
Net book value at end of year 2	25 000
Depreciation: Year 3	12 500
Net book value at end of year 3	12 500
Depreciation: Year 4	12 500
Net book value at end of year 4	0

(b)

Provision for depreciation of equipment					
Year 1		$	Year 1		$
End of year	Balance c/d	12 500	End of year	Income statement	12 500
Year 2			Year 2		
End of year	Balance c/d	25 000	Start of year	Balance b/d	12 500
			End of year	Income statement	12 500
		25 000			25 000
			Year 3		
			Start of year	Balance b/d	25 000

6 (a)

	$
Cost	50 000
Depreciation: Year 1	25 000
Net book value at end of year 1	25 000
Depreciation: Year 2	12 500
Net book value at end of year 2	12 500
Depreciation: Year 3	6 250
Net book value at end of year 3	6 250
Depreciation: Year 4	3 125
Net book value at end of year 4	3 125

(b)

Provision for depreciation of equipment					
Year 1		**$**	**Year 1**		**$**
End of year	Balance c/d	25 000	End of year	Income statement	25 000
Year 2			**Year 2**		
End of year	Balance c/d	25 000	Start of year	Balance b/d	25 000
			End of year	Income statement	12 500
		37 500			37 500
			Year 3		
			Start of year	Balance b/d	37 500

7 (a)

General journal			
Date	**Details**	**Dr**	**Cr**
		$	$
	Van disposal	30 000	
	Van at cost		30 000
	Provision for depreciation of vans	20 000	
	Van disposal		20 000
	Bank	5000	
	Van disposal		5000
	Income statement	5000	
	Van disposal		5000

(b)

Van disposal			
	$		**$**
Van	30000	Provision for depreciation of van	20000
		Bank	5000
		Income statement	5000
	30000		30000

4.3 Other payables and other receivables

Answers to knowledge check questions

1 A

2 D

3 C

4 B

5 (a)

Office expenses					
2018		**$**	**2018**		**$**
31 Dec	Bank	640	31 Dec	Income statement	722
31 Dec	Balance c/d	82			
		722			722

(b)

Insurance					
2018		**$**	**2018**		**$**
31 Dec	Bank	1190	31 Dec	Income statement	980
			31 Dec	Balance c/d	210
		1190			1190

6 (a)

Administration					
2018		**$**	**2018**		**$**
31 Dec	Bank	450	31 Dec	Income statement	400
			31 Dec	Balance c/d	50
		450			450

(b)

Rent received					
2018		**$**	**2018**		**$**
31 Dec	Income statement	3950	31 Dec	Bank	3400
			31 Dec	Balance c/d	550
		3950			3950

7 (a)

Rent					
2018		**$**	**2018**		**$**
31 Dec	Bank	4355	1 Jan	Balance b/d	91
31 Dec	Balance c/d	145	31 Dec	Income statement	4409
		4500			4500
			2019		
			1 Jan	Balance c/d	145

(b)

Insurance					
2018		**$**	**2018**		**$**
1 Jan	Balance b/d	77	31 Dec	Income statement	940
31 Dec	Bank	844			
31 Dec	Balance c/d	19			
		940			940
			2019		
			1 Jan	Balance c/d	19

(c)

Commission received					
2018		**$**	**2018**		**$**
1 Jan	Balance b/d	112	1 Jan	Bank	922
31 Dec	Income statement	781			
31 Dec	Balance c/d	29			
		922			922
			2019		
			1 Jan	Balance c/d	29

4.4 Irrecoverable debts and provision for doubtful debts

Answers to knowledge check questions

1 B

2 D

3 C

4

Irrecoverable debts					
2018		**$**	**2018**		**$**
15 Apr	Rani	65	31 Dec	Income statement	262
8 May	Jana	56			
10 Nov	Fahad	141			
		262			262

5

Provision for doubtful debts					
2018		**$**	**2018**		**$**
31 Dec	Balance c/d	340	1 Jan	Balance b/d	250
			31 Dec	Income statement	90
		340			340

6

Provision for doubtful debts					
2018		**$**	**2018**		**$**
31 Dec	Balance c/d	1500	1 Jan	Balance b/d	980
			31 Dec	Income statement	520
		1500			1500
2019			**2019**		
31 Dec	Income statement	450	1 Jan	Balance b/d	1500
31 Dec	Balance c/d	1050			
		1500			1500
2020			**2020**		
			1 Jan	Balance b/d	1050

7

Jow					
2018		**$**			**$**
3 Nov	Recovery of debts written off	490	3 Nov	Bank	490

Recovery of debts written off					
2018		**$**			**$**
31 Dec	Income statement	490	3 Nov	Jow	490

4.5 Valuation of inventory

Answers to knowledge check questions

1 C

2 B

3 C

4 **(a)** $175

(b) Closing inventory was overvalued by \$5 so profit for the year will be \$5 lower than the value calculated before the correction. Assets (inventory) will also be \$5 lower than the value calculated before the correction.

5 (a) Produce B12: 25 × \$6 = \$150

Product ZX8: 35 × \$5 = \$175

Product S7: 18 × \$12 = \$216

Total value of inventory held = \$541

(b) Profit for the year has been overstated by \$566 – \$541 = \$25

Corrected profit for the year = \$3780 – \$25 = \$3755

Answers to chapter review questions

1 C

2 D

3 A

4 C

5 B

6 D

7 A

8 C

9 A

10 A

11 (a)

General journal		
	Dr.	Cr.
	\$	\$
(1) Irrecoverable debts	89	
(1) Kasi		89
(1) Income statement	180	
(1) Provision for doubtful debts		180
(1) Wages	380	
(1) Income statement		380
(1) Income statement	213	
(1) Heating costs		213
(1) Income statement	200	
(1) Depreciation on equipment		200

(b) \$4501 – \$89 – \$180 + \$380 – \$213 – \$200 = \$4199 (1 for each correct adjustment = 6 marks)

(c)

Statement of financial position (extract)		
Current assets	**\$**	**\$**
(1) Trade receivables	4500	
(1) Less provision for doubtful debts	180	4320

(1) for correct layout

(d) Profit would be lower/understated **(1)**.

12 (a) Any two from: wear and tear, depletion, advances in technology, changes in market trends **(2)**

(b) Reducing balance method **(1)**

(c) (i)

Machinery at cost					
2018		**$**	**2018**		**$**
1 Jan	**(1)** Balance b/d	18000	31 Dec	**(1)** Machinery disposal	12000
1 Jan	**(1)** Bank	12000	31 Dec	Balance c/d	32000
31 Aug	**(1)** Bank	9000			
30 Sep	**(1)** Bank	5000			
		44000			44000

(ii)

Provision for depreciation of machinery					
2018		**$**	**2018**		**$**
31 Dec	**(1)** Machinery disposal	1200	1 Jan	Balance b/d	8000
31 Dec	Balance c/d	10225	31 Dec	**(3)*** Income statement	3425
		11425			11425

* Workings for machinery depreciation as follows:

(1) $\$18000 + \$12000 = \$30000 \times \frac{1}{10} = \$3000$

(1) $\$9000 \times \frac{1}{10} \times \frac{4}{12} = \$300$

(1) $\$5000 \times \frac{1}{10} \times \frac{3}{12} = \$125$

(iii)

Machinery disposal [new query no 62]					
2018		**$**	**2018**		**$**
31 Dec	**(1)** Machinery at cost	12000	31 Dec	**(1)** Depreciation	1200
			31 Dec	**(1)** Bank	9000
			31 Dec	**(1)** Income statement	1800
		12000			12000

(iv)

Equipment at cost					
2018		**$**	**2018**		**$**
31 Mar	**(1)** Bank	8000	31 Dec	Balance c/d	15000
30 Jun	**(1)** Bank	7000			
		15000			15000

(v)

Provision for depreciation of equipment					
2018		**$**	**2018**		**$**
31 Dec	Balance c/d	3000	31 Dec	**(2)*** Income statement	3000

* Workings for depreciation of equipment: (\$8000 + \$7000) × 20% **(1)** = \$3000 **(1)**

13 (a)

	Dr.	**Cr.**
	$	**$**
Revenue		**(1)** 41341
Purchases	**(1)** 21313	
Irrecoverable debts	**(1)** 531	
Provision for doubtful debts		560
Machinery	**(1)** 36500	
Provision for depreciation on machinery		**(1)** 12500

	Dr. $	Cr. $
General expenses	(1) 14500	
Inventory at 1 January 2018	8870	
Trade payables		5211
Trade receivables	6700	
Bank	2121	
Office salaries	(1) 18677	
Owner's equity		(1) 65000
Drawings	15400	
	124612	124612

Additional information: Inventory at 31 December 2018 was valued at $11314 **(1)**

Correct total balance figures **(1)**

(b) Irrecoverable debts are those debts a business decides are unlikely to be collected and are written off as expenses for that period **(1)**. Provision for doubtful debts is an estimate of likely future irrecoverable debts (and therefore is an estimate of the likely reduction in the value of trade receivables) **(1)**.

(c) Although the business receives revenue when selling a non-current asset, it is the profit or loss made on the sale that is included in the income statement **(1)**. If the asset is sold for a loss, capital receipts will increase **(1)** but revenue expenditure increases to reflect the loss on the sale **(1)**.

(d) The provision may be increased due to any of the following: **(1 mark for each of two stated plus 1 each for explanation – total 4 marks)**

- Increase in the size of trade receivables – a business with more trade receivables will, on average, experience a larger value of irrecoverable debts.
- Economic factors – in economic downturns business failure is more common. This increases the likelihood of debts becoming irrecoverable.
- Increased age of trade receivables – debts are more likely to become irrecoverable the longer they remain outstanding.
- Possible change in who the business lends money to – a business may increasingly offer trade credit to businesses that have a higher risk of failing. This will lead to a higher risk of irrecoverable debts.
- A more cautious approach taken on the management of trade receivables – a business may wish to increase its estimate of the likely size of future irrecoverable debts.

(e) As a revenue receipt. **(1)**

14 (a) Irrecoverable debts are debts owing to the business that are not expected to be collected and have been written off against the profit for the year as revenue expenditure **[1]**. Provision for doubtful debts is an estimate of the likely value of future irrecoverable debts **[1]**.

(b)

Provision for doubtful debts					
2018		$	2018		$
31 Dec	Balance c/d	280 [1]	1 Jan	Balance b/d	245 [1]
			31 Dec	Income statement	35 [1]
		280			280
			2019		
			1 Jan	Balance b/d	280

(c) ($1100 + $100) **[1]** × 20% = $240 **[1]**

(d)

	$
Original profit	1780
Increase in provision for doubtful debts	(35) **[1]**
Irrecoverable debts	(235) **[1]**
Recovery of debts written off	54 **[1]**
Subtraction of capital expenditure included as revenue expenditure	1000 **[1]**
Depreciation of computer	(240) **[1]**
Adjustment to inventory	(18) **[2]***
Corrected profit	2306 **[1]**

[*Inventory should be valued at $35 – $8 = $27 which is $18 less than the value stated. Award one mark for subtracting the overstated value from profit and one mark for the correct value.]

(e)

Zhao Balance sheet extract as at 31 December 2018		
Current assets	**$**	**$**
Current assets		
Trade receivables	5600 **[1]**	
Less provision for doubtful debts	280 **[1]**	5320 **[1]**

(f) Inventory should be valued at the lower of **[1]** cost and net realisable value **[1]**.

5 PREPARATION OF FINANCIAL STATEMENTS

5.1 Sole traders

Answers to knowledge check questions

1 A

2 C

3 D

4

Advantages	Disadvantages
Small businesses are easy to set up.	
Low initial start-up costs. The owner is only required to find a small amount of capital.	Business growth is limited by the amount of capital available from the sole trader.
The sole trader is responsible for all business decisions.	The sole trader has no one to share the responsibility of running the business with.
The sole trader can choose their own working conditions, hours and holidays to be taken.	The sole trader often has to work long hours and may find it difficult to take holidays or find cover when they are unwell.
The sole trader does not need to share their profit with any other owner.	The sole trader will be liable for any debts that the business cannot pay; there is unlimited liability.
A sole trader has limited legal requirements for the preparation of financial records. Sole traders do need to register to pay tax. Also, if they employ workers, they are responsible for complying with tax, employee and health and safety legislation.	

5 Sole traders use their income statements and statements of financial position to assess the business's financial performance. This may include a review of their gross profit and profit for the year. They may use the details to support an application for finance or to assess how much they can take as drawings.

It is often useful for the sole trader to compare income statements over a period of several years. Businesses will analyse changes in revenue, cost of sales and expenses and make adjustments to their business practices as required.

6 A trading business buys goods with the intention of selling them to consumers and other businesses. Examples include supermarkets, clothes stores and other retail outlets.

A service business sells services to their customers rather than goods. Examples include hairdressers, travel agents and garden designers.

7

Rudd Antiques Trading account for the year ended 31 December 2018			
	$	$	$
Revenue		37950	
Sales returns		595	
			37355
Opening inventory	3950		
Purchases	29570		
Carriage inwards	650		
Less purchases returns	980		
		33190	
Closing inventory		5990	
Cost of sales			27200
Gross profit (or loss)			10155

8

Hedges and Edges Income statement for the year ended 31 March 2018		
	$	$
Revenue received		150 000
Additional income		
Decrease in provision for doubtful debts		100
		150 100
Less expenses		
Rent (20 000–550)	19 450	
Lighting and heating expenses (14 000 + 300)	14 300	
Salaries and wages	50 000	
Insurance	14 300	
General expenses	20 000	
Depreciation: equipment	3 500	
		121 550
Profit for the year		28 550

Hedges and Edges Statement of financial position as at 31 March 2018			
	$ Cost	$ Depreciation	$ Net book value
Non-current assets			
Equipment	35 000	10 500	24 500
	35 000	10 500	24 500
Current assets			
Trade receivables	1 000		
Less provision for doubtful debts	100	900	
Bank		6 000	
Other receivables (prepaid expenses)		550	

Hedges and Edges Statement of financial position as at 31 March 2018			
	$	$	$
	Cost	Depreciation	Net book value
			7 450
Total assets			31 950
Capital and liabilities			
Capital			22 400
Add profit for the year			28 550
			50 950
Less drawings			20 000
			30 950
Current liabilities			
Trade payables			700
Other payables (accrued expenses)			300
			1 000
Total liabilities			31 950

9

Bee music store Income statement for the year ended 31 August 2018		
	$	$
Revenue		89900
Sales returns		900
		89000
Less cost of sales		
Opening inventory	3500	
Purchases	34445	
	37945	
Closing inventory	15300	
Cost of sales		22645
Gross profit		66355
Additional income		
Commission received	175	175
		66530
Less expenses		
Rent	12000	
Lighting and heating expenses	8600	
Salaries and wages	18408	
Insurance	7500	
Irrecoverable debts	175	
Discounts allowed	750	
Provision for doubtful debts	555	
Motor vehicle expenses	175	

Bee music store Income statement for the year ended 31 August 2018		
	$	$
Depreciation: motor vehicles	4375	
Depreciation: fixtures and fittings	1100	
		53638
Profit for the year		12892

Bee music store Statement of financial position as at 31 August 2018			
	$	$	$
	Cost	Depreciation	Net book value
Non-current assets			
Motor vehicles	25000	11875	13125
Fixtures and fittings	11000	6100	4900
	36000	17975	18025
Current assets			
Inventory		15300	
Trade receivables	3525		
Less provision for doubtful debts	705	2820	
Bank		1500	
Other receivables (prepaid expenses)		575	
			20195
Total assets			38220
Capital and liabilities			
Capital			79528
Add Profit for the year			12892
			92420
Less Drawings			56305
			36115
Current liabilities			
Trade payables			1550
Other payables (accrued expenses)			555
			2105
Total liabilities			38220

5.2 Partnerships

Answers to knowledge check questions

1 B

2 D

3 D

4 Three each of the following:

Advantages	Disadvantages
Greater capital and resources can be raised from the partners.	Profits will need to be shared between the partners.
Spreads personal risk across all of the partners, meaning that, in the case of financial difficulty, there are more people able to share the debt burden.	All partners are responsible for the debts of the business.
Partners may bring additional skills and ideas to the business.	There are potential problems if partners disagree over the direction of the business.
Business responsibilities are shared among the partners.	The actions of one partner are binding on all of the other partners.
Partners can discuss issues before final decisions have to be taken.	Decision-making can be time-consuming.
Partnerships may have increased public image and credibility with customers and suppliers when compared with a sole trader.	There is the potential for disputes over workloads.

5 Five of the following:

- The amount of capital invested by each partner
- Details of how profits and losses will be divided between the partners
- The amount of interest payable on capital (paid before profits are shared)
- The amount of interest payable on drawings
- The value of partners' salaries
- Information on how many votes each partner has when decisions are to be made
- Rules on the admission of new partners
- Procedures for ending the partnership.

6 Partnership agreements will prevent disputes between the partners and provide a structure for the operation of the business.

7 An appropriation account shows how a partnership's profit or loss for the year is shared out between the partners.

8 To deter partners from taking excessive drawings.

9 The profit for the year for a partnership + interest on drawings – salaries and interest on capital is residual profit. It is shared between the partners in the agreed profit sharing ratio.

10 Partners often contribute different amounts of capital to a partnership. As a reward for contributing capital, partners are credited with interest on this capital.

11 This would mean that the partner has withdrawn more money from the partnership than they have 'earned'.

12

Capital account as 31 March 2018							
	Anton	Basil	Emir		Anton	Basil	Emir
	$	$	$		$	$	$
Balance c/d	150000	170000	190000	Balance b/d	150000	170000	190000
	150000	170000	190000		150000	170000	190000
				Balance b/d	150000	170000	190000

Current account as 31 March 2018							
	Anton	Basil	Emir		Anton	Basil	Emir
	$	$	$		$	$	$
Balance b/d		1930		Balance b/d	1195		1770
Drawings	25000	21000	27000	Interest on capital	5000	7000	9000
Interest on drawings	450	330	510	Salaries		19500	9550
Balance c/d	3745	36240	45810	Share of profit	23000	33000	53000
	29195	59500	73320		29195	59500	73320
				Balance b/d	3745	36240	45810

13 1. Profits and losses are shared equally.
2. Interest on capital is not allowed.
3. Interest on drawings will not be levied on drawings.
4. Partnership salaries are not allowed.
5. Any loans made by partners to the partnership should entitle partners to 5% interest on the loan.

14

Appropriation account as at 30 November 2018					
	Sundeep	Mihai		Sundeep	Mihai
	$	$		$	$
Balance b/d		300	Balance b/d	750	
Drawings	18100	28000	Interest on capital	1500	850
Balance c/d	4550	2750	Salaries	0	20000
			Share of profit	20400	10200
	22650	31050		22650	31050
			Balance b/d	4550	2750

Sundeep and Mihai Statement of financial position as at 30 November 2018			
	Cost	Depreciation	Net book value
	$	$	$
Non-current assets	50000	32000	18000
	50000	32000	18000
Current assets			
Trade receivables		57100	
Less provision for doubtful debts		3800	
			53300
Other receivables (prepaid expenses)			7000
Accrued income			3500
Cash in hand			1500
			65300
Total assets			**83300**
Capital			
Capital account: Sundeep			30000
Capital account: Mihai			17000
Current account: Sundeep			4550
Current account: Mihai			2750
			54300
Current liabilities			
Trade payables	5000		
Bank overdraft	17000		
Loan	7000		
		29000	
Total liabilities			**83300**

15

Li and Piao Appropriation account for the year ended 31 December 2018						
	1 Jan – 30 Jun		1 Jul – 31 Dec		Full year	
	$	$	$	$	$	$
Operating profit		34000		34000		68000
Less interest on capitals						
Li	3750		3750		7500	
Piao	2500	6250	2500	6250	5000	12500
		27750		27750		55500
Less Salary (Li)		7500				7500
		20250		27750		48000
Profit shares:						
Li	13500		13875		27375	
Piao	6750	20250	13875	27750	20625	48000

Current accounts					
	Li	Piao		Li	Piao
	$	$		$	$
Drawings	5500	3400	Balance b/d	18000	9000
Balance c/d	54875	31225	Salaries	7500	
			Interest on capital	7500	5000
			Profits	27375	20625
	60375	34625		60375	34625
			Balance b/d	54875	31225

5.3 Limited companies

Answers to knowledge check questions

1 A

2 D

3 C

4

Advantages	Disadvantages
Public limited companies have the ability to raise large amounts of capital via share issues.	Public limited companies that become too large may have issues with employee relations.
The benefit of economies of scale – due to their size, public limited companies are able to bulk buy products and employ specialist staff as required.	Conflicts of interest can occur between shareholders and the board of directors.
Due to their size, public limited companies are able to produce goods at lower unit costs.	There is a possibility of a takeover or merger as shares are freely available on the stock market.

5

Preference shares	Ordinary (equity) shares
receive a fixed percentage rate of dividend	receive a variable dividend each year or may not receive one at all
are not entitled to vote at a limited company's annual general meeting	are entitled to vote at shareholder meetings – one vote per share
receive their dividends before ordinary shareholders receive their dividends	receive their dividend payment after the preference shareholders have received their dividend payment
receive capital before ordinary shareholders in the event of the company closing	will be the last people to receive their share capital if the limited company goes bankrupt

6 Debentures provide an alternative to raising finance by an issue of ordinary shares. They are long-term loan capital and increase the debt capital of the company. Debenture holders receive a fixed rate of interest and the amount borrowed is charged on the assets of the company.

A debenture is one of the most common forms of long-term loan that a limited company can take. Sole traders and partnerships are not able to raise finance from debentures. Debentures need to be repaid on a specific date at a fixed interest rate.

7 Equity: the value of the shares issued by a limited company.

8 Issued share capital: the amount of share capital that has actually been sold by the company.

A limited company may not require all of the money due from its shares immediately. In this case, the limited company may allow shareholders to pay the amount they owe in instalments. The total amount of money that will be due to the limited company is known as called-up share capital. The amount of money that has actually been received by the limited company is known as paid-up share capital.

9 Shareholders of limited companies are not personally liable for the debts of the business.

10 In the case where a company goes into liquidation or becomes bankrupt, the shareholders would not be asked to pay the debts. They would however, lose the money that they have paid for their shares. If they had not paid in full for the shares that they owned they would be required to pay the balance.

11 A limited company rarely distributes all of its profits to its shareholders. It will usually keep part of the profit earned each year in the form of reserves. This allows the business to use the retained profits for other purposes within the business.

Even if a limited company would like to distribute all of the profit it had available to its shareholders, it is very unlikely that there would be sufficient cash available in the business to pay the dividends.

Any profit that is remaining after appropriation is carried forward to the next financial year. This profit, known as retained profit or retained earnings, remains as a balance on the income statement appropriation account and is carried forward to the next financial year to fund business plans. This figure appears in the statement of financial position as part of the reserves which are added to share capital.

In addition to leaving a balance of undistributed profit in the income statement, many companies will transfer an amount to a general reserve. This is another means of ploughing profits back into the company to help fund both future known and unknown obligations.

12 (a) 500 000 × $2.50 = $1 250 000

10% of $1 250 000 = $125 000

(b) 10% of $2.50 = $0.25

13 (a) 550 000 shares × $2 = $1 100 000

(b) 500 000 shares × $2 = $1 000 000

(c) 500 000 shares × $1 = $500 000

(d) 475 000 shares × $1 = $475 000

14

Ahmed Ltd Extract of statement of financial position as at 31 December 2017	
Capital and reserves	**$**
Ordinary share capital (100 000 $1 shares)	100 000
Preference share capital (50 000 7% non-redeemable preference shares $1)	50 000
General reserve	12 000
Retained earnings	41 900
	203 900

15

Tiga Stadium Supplies Limited Statement of financial position as at 30 April 2018	
	$m
Non-current assets	
Non-current assets	1446.75
Current assets	

Tiga Stadium Supplies Limited Statement of financial position as at 30 April 2018	
	$m
Inventory	558.9
Trade receivables	218.1
Short-term investments	5.85
Cash at bank	357.75
Total assets	**2587.35**
Capital and reserves	
Called-up share capital	246.9
General reserves	502.95
Profit and loss account	323.85
Non-current liabilities	
Loan repayable 2021	493.2
Current liabilities	
Trade payables	983.25
Loan repayable December 2018	37.2
Total liabilities	**2587.35**

5.4 Clubs and societies

Answers to knowledge check questions

1 B

2 C

3 B

4 Accumulated fund: Represents the difference in value between the assets and liabilities of the organisation.

5 Income and expenditure accounts are the equivalent of a profit-making organisation's income statement. These include non-cash transactions and adjustments, for example depreciation, accruals and prepayments.

An incomes and expenditure account lists all of the receipts and payments for the financial period adjusted for prepayments, accruals, irrecoverable debts, etc.

A receipts and payments account is a summarised cash book. The account applies double entry procedures:

- The debit side of the receipts and payments account details the income of the organisation.
- The credit side of the receipts and payments account details the expenditure of the organisation.

The balance carried down at the end of the period will be transferred to the next financial period.

6 An accrual of income is treated as a current asset as this is money that a club expects to receive.

7 An expense paid in advance is treated as a current asset in the statement of financial position. The prepaid amount is deducted from the relevant expense before inclusion in the income statement.

8

Snow Island ski club Subscriptions account			
	$		$
Balance b/d (accrued)	320	Balance b/d (prepaid)	550
Income and expenditure account	**7075**	Bank/cash	6795
		Irrecoverable debts	210
Balance c/d (prepaid)	510	Balance c/d (accrued)	350
	7905		7905
Balance b/d	350	Balance b/d	510

9

Western organic food association Receipts and payments account			
	$		$
Balance b/d	7250	Purchases of gardening equipment for resale	3150
Subscriptions received	19855	Wages – sales assistant	2770
Revenue from sales of organic food	12375	Wages – café staff	3158
Café revenue	6250	Rent and rates	2579
Entrance fees received	978	Heat and light	1235
		General expenses	795
		Purchase of gardening equipment	1650
		Cost of prizes	357
		Balance c/d	31014
	46708		46708
Balance b/d	31014		

10 (a) Depreciation = $3500 + $4000 – $6850 = $650

Accumulated fund at start of year = $87 + $32 + $3500 + $295 + $76 – $225 – $27 = $3738

Accumulated fund at start of year = $95 + $56 + $6850 – $43 + $55 – $118 – $22 – $4000 = $2873

Birkdale Snooker Club Statement of financial position as at 31 December 2018		
	$	$
Non-current assets		
Sports equipment		6850

(b)

Birkdale Snooker Club Statement of financial position as at 31 December 2018		
	$	$
Current assets		
Bar inventory	95	
Subscriptions owing	56	
Cash	55	
	206	
Current liabilities		
Payables on bar	118	
Subscriptions received in advance	22	
Bank	43	
	183	23
Less Non-current liabilities		
Bank loan		4000
		2873
Accumulated fund		
Balance at start of year		3738
Less Deficit		865
Balance at end of year		2873

5.5 Manufacturing accounts

Answers to knowledge check questions

1 B

2 B

3 A

4 Goods which are not finished are known as work in progress.

5 Royalties: a fee that is paid to the individual who originally invented the product being manufactured.

6 Direct costs: the costs incurred in physically making the products and related to the level of output.

Indirect costs: the costs involved in the operation of a factory that cannot be directly linked to the goods that are being produced.

7 The opening balance of work in progress is added to the production cost and the work in progress left at the end of the year will need subtracting to give the cost of the goods completed during the period being dealt with.

8 **(a)** Direct materials – the raw materials that are required to make the finished goods. The type of raw material will vary depending on the type of business. For example, a window manufacturer will require glass, a baker will need flour and a machinery production company requires metal.

(b) Direct labour – this is often referred to as direct wages. Direct labour is the cost of the wages that are paid to individuals who are employed to make the goods being produced.

(c) Prime cost – the total direct costs of physically making a product. For example, direct materials, direct labour and direct expenses.

(d) Factory overheads – also known as indirect costs or indirect manufacturing costs. These are costs involved in the operation of a factory that cannot be directly linked to the goods that are being produced.

This section includes all other expenses concerned with the production of output but not in a direct way. This means that if the level of production increases, these expenses may also increase but not by the same proportion.

Examples include indirect labour, factory rent and rates, and depreciation of factory machinery.

9 Opening inventory of raw materials

Add purchases of raw materials

Add carriage inwards on raw materials

Less purchases returns of raw materials

Less closing inventory of raw materials

Equals cost of raw materials consumed.

10

Opus manufacturers Manufacturing account for the year ended 30 April 2018			
	$	$	$
Raw materials			
Opening inventory		4000	
Purchases		48000	
		52000	
Less closing inventory		(4800)	
Cost of raw materials consumed			47200
Direct wages/labour			96000
Royalties paid			1200
PRIME COST			**144400**
Add factory overheads			
Factory rent		3400	
Depreciation of factory equipment		2000	

Opus manufacturers Manufacturing account for the year ended 30 April 2018			
	$	$	$
General indirect expenses		2200	
			7600
			152000
Add: Opening work in progress			16000
			168000
Less: Closing work in progress			(24000)
Manufacturing cost of goods completed			**144000**

11

Saigon boat manufacturers Manufacturing account for the year ended 31 December 2018			
	$	$	$
Raw materials			
Opening inventory		97292	
Purchases		492844	
		590136	
Less closing inventory		106704	
Cost of raw materials consumed			483432
Direct wages / labour			350744
Royalties paid			21372
PRIME COST			**855548**
Add factory overheads			
Supervisor's salaries		101808	
Factory lighting		49528	
Rent and rates		19616	
			170952
			1026500
Add: Opening work in progress			137296
			1163796
Less: Closing work in progress			213812
Manufacturing cost of goods completed			**949984**

5.6 Incomplete records

Answers to knowledge check questions

1 D

2 C

3 C

4 It may not be possible to produce a full set of financial statements. Without financial statements, the business may overpay the tax they owe and they have no evidence to support a loan application.

The cost of hiring an accountant to prepare financial statements from incomplete records will be considerably higher than for an organisation with double entry accounts.

5 A statement of affairs can be used to determine a business's capital. This can only be completed if the total amounts of assets and liabilities are known.

6 A single entry system does not differentiate between items such as drawings, expenses, purchases, capital or revenue expenditure.

7 Capital = assets – liabilities

Opening capital = 89 080 – 5120 = $83 960

Closing capital = 77 400 – 7890 = $69 510

Profit = closing capital – opening capital – capital introduced + drawings

Profit = 69 510 – 83 960 – 10 000 + 29 000 = $4550

8

Retailer Income statement for the year ended 31 December 2018			
	$	$	$
Revenue			80 000
Opening inventory	2600		
Purchases (56 000 + 2800 – 2600)	56 200		
		58 800	
Closing inventory		2800	
Cost of sales (80 000 – 24 000)			56 000
Gross profit (30% of 80 000)			24 000

9

Frederic Income statement for the year ended 31 October 2018			
	$	$	$
Revenue (880 000 + 220 000)			1 100 000
Opening inventory	45 000		
Purchases (880 000 + 65 000 – 45 000)	900 000		
		945 000	
Closing inventory		65 000	
Cost of sales			880 000
Gross profit (mark-up 25% × 880 000)			220 000

10

Agyei Income statement for the year ended 30 April 2018			
Revenue (135 000 + 10 500 + 13 000 – 7500 + 9000)			160 000
Less cost of sales			
Opening inventory	8000		
Purchases (124 000 – 6000 + 4000 + 1200)	123 200		
		131 200	
Less closing inventory		3200	
Cost of sales			128 000
Gross profit			**32 000**
Discounts received			1200
			33 200
Less expenses			
General expenses		12 000	

Agyei Income statement for the year ended 30 April 2018			
Wages		6050	
Rent		5050	
Depreciation		4500	
Irrecoverable debts		280	27880
Profit for the year			**5320**

Answers to chapter review questions

1 C

2 D

3 A

4 D

5 A

6 A

7 A

8 D

9 C

10 C

11 (a) There are a number of businesses that produce the goods that they sell. **(1)**

They purchase the raw materials and convert these into finished goods that they sell. **(1)**

If a business produces the goods that they sell there is no 'purchases' figure to include in the trading account section of the income statement. **(1)**

The costs incurred in the production of goods appear instead and these are calculated in a manufacturing account. **(1)**

A manufacturing account shows the cost of producing the goods that are sold during an accounting period. **(1)**

(b) (i) Prime cost – direct costs of physically making the products that are related to the level of output. **(1)**

These direct costs will include direct materials, direct labour and direct expenses. **(1)**

(ii) Goods which are not finished are known as work in progress. **(1)**

The opening balance of work in progress is added on to the production cost **(1)** and the work in progress left at the end of the year is subtracted to give the cost of the goods completed during the period being dealt with. **(1)**

(c)

Berenice manufacturing company Manufacturing account for the year ended 31 August 2018		
	$	$
Raw materials		
Opening inventory	14080	
Purchases	87640	
	101720 **(1)**	
Less closing inventory	12440	
Cost of raw materials consumed		89280 **(1)**
Direct wages/labour		80380 **(1)**
PRIME COST		**169660 (1)**
Add factory overheads		
Wages – factory managers	36800 **(1)**	
Depreciation of factory machinery	16800 **(1)**	
General expenses	10680 **(1)**	

Berenice manufacturing company Manufacturing account for the year ended 31 August 2018		
	$	$
Rates and Insurance	12000 (1)	
		76280
		245940
Add: Opening work in progress		1620 (1)
		247560
Less: Closing work in progress		1900 (1)
Manufacturing cost of goods completed		245660

12 (a)

Somerton home designs Income statement for the year ended 30 June 2018		
	$	$
Fees received		300000 (1)
Less expenses		
Advertising	4600 (1)	
Office expenses	164425 (1)	
Heat and light	7000 (1)	
Provision for depreciation: office equipment	8900 (1)	
Discounts allowed	3200 (1)	
Provision for doubtful debts	1180 (1)	
General expenses	74445 (1)	
		263750 (1)
Profit for the year		36250 (1)

(b)

Mathilda home designs Statement of financial position as at 30 June 2018			
	$	$	$
	Cost	Depreciation	Net book value
Non-current assets			
Premises	120000	0	120000
Office equipment	89000	17800	71200
	209000	17800	191200 (1)
Current assets			
Trade receivables	5900		
Less provision for doubtful debts	1180	4720 (1)	
Other receivables		575 (1)	
			5295
Total assets			196495
Capital			125600 (1)
Add profit for the year			36250 (1)
			161850
Less drawings			23000 (1)

Mathilda home designs Statement of financial position as at 30 June 2018			
	$ Cost	$ Depreciation	$ Net book value
Current liabilities			
Trade payables			6300 **(1)**
Short-term loan			50000 **(1)**
Bank overdraft			790 **(1)**
Other payables			555 **(1)**
			57645
Total liabilities			196495

13 (a)

Melissa and Chris Statement of financial position as at 31 October 2018			
	Cost $	Depreciation $	Net book value $
Non-current assets	170000	20000	150000
	170000	20000 (1)	150000 (1)
Current assets			
Inventory			16000 **(1)**
Trade receivables			28000 **(1)**
Bank			10000 **(1)**
			54000
Total assets			**204000**
Capital			
Capital account: Melissa			100000 **(1)**
Capital account: Christofor			60000 **(1)**
Current account: Melissa			30000 **(1)**
Current account: Christofor			– 10000 **(2)**
			180000
Current liabilities			
Trade payables			24000 **(1)**
Total liabilities			**204000** (1)

(b) 1 mark for the identification of an advantage and 1 mark for the explanation. Maximum of 6 marks for 3 advantages.

Greater capital **(1)** and resources **(1)** can be raised from the partners.

Spreads personal risk across all of the partners **(1)**, meaning that in the case of financial difficulty there are more people able to share the debt burden **(1)**.

Partners may bring additional skills **(1)** and ideas to the business **(1)**.

Business responsibilities are shared among the partners **(1)**, allowing them to discuss issues before final decisions have to be taken **(1)**.

Partnerships may have increased public image and credibility **(1)** with customers and suppliers when compared with a sole trader **(1)**.

(c) 1 mark for each correct item up to a maximum of 2

1. The amount of capital invested by each partner.
2. Details on how profits and losses will be divided between the partners.

3. The amount of interest payable on capital (paid before profits are shared).
4. The amount of interest payable on drawings.
5. The value of partners' salaries.
6. Information on how many votes each partner has when decisions are to be made.
7. Rules on the admission of new partners.
8. Procedures for the ending of the partnership.

14 (a)

Akira, Eito and Fumihiro Appropriation account for the year ended 30 November 2018			
	$	$	$
Profit for the year **[1]**			131500
Add interest on drawings:			
Akira **[1]**		950	
Eito **[1]**		800	
Fumihiro **[1]**		800	2550
			134050
Less salary: Akira **[1]**		15000	
Less interest on capital:			
Akira **[1]**	16000		
Eito **[1]**	12000		
Fumihiro **[1]**	12000		
		40000	
			(55000)
			79050
Balance of profits shared:			
Akira **[1]**		39525	
Eito **[1]**		26350	
Fumihiro **[1]**		13175	
			79050 **[1]**

(b) Additional capital is contributed to the partnership **[1]**

Non-current assets are revalued **[1]**

Goodwill is introduced **[1]**

A partnership is dissolved/ended **[1]**

(c) Fixed capital accounts record a fixed sum of capital, which the partners agree to maintain year on year **[1]**. All profits, salaries, interest on capital, and interest on drawings are recorded in a separate current account **[1]**. If a fluctuating capital account is used then all profits, drawings, etc. are charged to the capital account, **[1]** which will fluctuate on an ongoing basis **[1]** / which could result in a reduction in the capital contribution of a partner if drawings exceed appropriations **[1]**.

[Award a maximum of 4 marks]

15 (a) Subscriptions working:

Subscriptions			
	$		$
Balance b/d (Accrued)	1000	Bank / Cash	42600
Income and expenditure account	40000		
Balance c/d (Prepaid)	1600		
	42600		42600
		Balance b/d	1600

Oceana Golfing Club Income and expenditure account for the year ended 31 December 2017		
	$	$
Income		
Subscriptions	40000	
Competition income $3200 – $840	2360	
		42360
Expenditure		
General expenses	10580	
Travelling expenses	3320	
Rent $10 400 – $200 – $400	9800 **(2)**	
Loss on sale of motor van (8000–7000)	1000	
Depreciation of motor van	6000	
		30700
Surplus for the year		**11660**

(b)

Oceana Golfing Club Statement of financial position as at 31 December 2017			
	$	$	$
	Cost	**Depreciation**	**Net book value**
Non-current assets			
Motor van	40000	6000	34000
	40000	6000	34000
Current assets			
Bank		260	
Other receivables (rent)		400	
			660
Total assets			**34660**
Accumulated fund			21400
Add surplus for the year			11660
			33060
Current liabilities			
Subscriptions prepaid			1600
			1600
Total liabilities			**34660**

16

Gumia Manufacturing Ltd Manufacturing and trading account for the year ended 28 February 2018			
	$	$	$
Raw materials			
Opening inventory of raw materials		42500 **[1]**	
Purchases		620000 **[1]**	
		662500	

Gumia Manufacturing Ltd Manufacturing and trading account for the year ended 28 February 2018			
	$	$	$
Less: Closing inventory of raw materials		39300 [1]	
Cost of raw materials consumed			623200
Direct wages and salaries			153200 [1]
Direct expenses			73100 [1]
PRIME COST			**849500 [1]**
Add: Factory overheads			
Indirect wages and salaries		41000 [1]	
Rent		20000 [1]	
Insurance		1500 [1]	
Depreciation of buildings		5200 [1]	
Depreciation of plant and equipment		8050 [1]	
			75750
			925250
Add: Opening work in progress			84600 [1]
			1009850
Less: Closing work in progress			37550 [1]
Manufacturing cost of goods completed			**972300 [1]**
Revenue		1500000 [1]	
Less: Sales returns		4000 [1]	
			1496000
Less: Cost of sales			
Opening inventory of finished goods	52500 [1]		
Cost of goods produced	972300 [1]		
		1024800	
Less: Closing inventory of finished goods		78750 [1]	
Cost of sales			946050
Gross profit			**549950** [1]

17 (a) Shares that carry a fixed dividend **[1]**/that don't carry a vote at the AGM **[1]**/that receive their dividend before ordinary shareholders **[1]** plus that are eventually paid back to the shareholder **[1]** **[Must have last point in to gain 2 marks]**

(b) Dividends workings for year ending 31 December 2017:

Preference share dividends = 7% of $50000 = $3500 **[1]**

Ordinary share dividends = 4% of $100000 = $4000 **[1]**

Total dividends = $3500 + $4000 = $7500 **[2]** if presented as one total

Owl Traditional Toys Ltd Income statement (extract) for the year ended 31 December 2017	
Operating profit	92400 [1]
Other operating income	0
Finance costs	(31200) [1]
Profit for the year	61200 [1]

Owl Traditional Toys Ltd Income statement (extract) for the year ended 31 December 2017	
Dividends	(7500) **[2]**
Transfer to general reserve	(2000) **[1]**
Retained earnings	51700
Retained profit brought forward	0
Retained profit carried forward	51700

(c)

Owl Traditional Toys Ltd Statement of changes in equity for the year ended 31 December 2017					
	Ordinary share capital	**Preference share capital**	**General reserve**	**Retained earnings**	**Total**
	$	**$**	**$**	**$**	**$**
Opening balance	100000	50000	0	0	150000 **[1]**
Profit for the year				61200	61200 **[1]**
Dividend paid				(7500)	(7500) **[1]**
Transfer to general reserve			2000	(2000) **[1]**	
Share issue	0	0			0
Closing Balance	100000	50000	2000	51700	203700 **[1]** OFR

(d) Advantages could include:

- Owners now benefit from limited lability **[1]**, which means that their own personal possessions are not at risk if the business faces failure or claims from stakeholders of the business **[1]**.
- It allows for the chance of extra finance to be brought in **[1]**. Additional shareholders may be allowed to contribute capital to provide resources for the business **[1]**.
- Banks may be more willing to lend money to the business **[1]** due to a company existing separately from the owners. It may find it is charged lower interest rates as a result **[1]**.

Disadvantages could include:

- Costly to set up **[1]**. There are forms and procedures which must be fulfilled to convert to a company – these do not exist for partnerships **[1]**.
- Have to publish/supply more data **[1]**, which may expose more information than the partners would have been willing to release about the performance of the business **[1]**.

6 ANALYSIS AND INTERPRETATION

6.1 Calculation and understanding of ratios

Answers to knowledge check questions

1 B

2 C

3 C

4

	Store 1	Store 2	Store 3
(a)	38.46%	30%	66.67%
(b)	26.92%	24%	36.67%
(c)	63.64%	48%	157.14%

5 8.4 times

6

	Store 1	Store 2	Store 3
(a)	2 : 1	2.6 : 1	1.24 : 1
(b)	1.6 : 1	2 : 1	1.04 : 1

7 The current ratio is calculated by dividing current assets by current liabilities. The liquid (acid test) ratio excludes closing inventory from the current assets total.

8 Profitability ratios help to assess whether a business has met its objectives in relation to profits, whereas liquidity ratios evaluate the ability of a business to pay its short-term debts.

9 The return on capital employed ratio (ROCE) measures the profit (return) made by a business in relation to the capital that has been invested in the business.

10 The statement of financial position contains information about the current assets and current liabilities of a business. The information in the statement of financial position allows the calculation of both the current ratio and the liquid (acid test) ratio.

6.2 Interpretation of accounting ratios

Answers to knowledge check questions

1 C

2 D

3 A

4 The liquid ratio is a more severe test of a business's liquidity and its ability to pay short-term debts. The ratio assumes that inventory may be perishable, go out of date or become obsolete (due to changes in fashion or technology). This means that the business will be left with inventory that it cannot sell and will not be able to use to pay the business's short-term debts.

5 Opening and closing inventory is used in the calculation of cost of sales. Cost of sales is deducted from sales revenue to calculate gross profit.

6 By paying early, the business gains a good reputation with its suppliers. It may be offered cash discounts for early payment. However, the business will have less cash, which could affect its cash flow.

7 Current ratio and liquid (acid test) ratio.

8 The business could reduce its expenses, for example heat and light and wages. It could also attempt to reduce its cost of sales, for example by purchasing cheaper goods.

9 Inventory turnover may fall because of:

- a fall in sales level
- a reduction in business activity
- a falling demand in the current market
- a significant increase in selling prices
- the business purchasing too much inventory.

10 The supplier will be disappointed by its current collection period. The supplier needs to chase its credit customers so that they pay within the credit period.

11 Working capital = current assets – current liabilities. To improve working capital, the business needs to either increase current assets or reduce current liabilities.

12 (a)

Farnoud Statement to compare financial results		
	31 January 2017 $	31 January 2018 $
	'000	'000
Cost of sales (1)	1795	2300
Gross profit (2)	2205	2300
Profit for the year (3)	1450	990
Current assets (4)	1430	2605
Current liabilities (5)	650	620
Gross margin (6)	55.13%	50.00%
Profit margin (7)	36.25%	21.52%
Return on capital employed (8)	65.37%	57.13%

Farnoud Statement to compare financial results		
	31 January 2017	31 January 2018
	$	$
Current ratio (9)	2.20:1	4.20:1
Liquid (acid test) ratio (10)	0.80:1	3.5:1
Rate of inventory turnover (11)	2.24 times	3.42 times
Trade receivables turnover (12)	42.89 days	97.60 days
Trade payables turnover (13)	117.74 days	124.00 days

Workings (all answers to 2 decimal places):

	31 January 2017	31 January 2018
	$	$
	'000	'000
Cost of sales (1)	690 + 2015 – 910 = 1795	910 + 1825 – 435 = 2300
Gross profit (2)	4000 – 1795 = 2205	4600 – 2300 = 2300
Profit for the year (3)	2205 – 755 = 450	2300 – 1310 = 990
Current assets (4)	910 + 470 + 50 = 1430	435 + 1230 + 940 = 2605
Current liabilities (5)	650	620
Gross margin (6)	(2205 ÷ 4000) × 100 = 55.13%	(2300 ÷ 4600) × 100 = 50.00%
Profit margin (7)	(1450 ÷ 4000) × 100 = 36.25%	(990 ÷ 4600) × 100 = 21.52%
Return on capital employed (8)	(1450 ÷ 2218) × 100 = 65.37%	(990 ÷ 1733) × 100 = 57.13%
Current ratio (9)	1430 ÷ 650 = 2.20:1	2605 ÷ 620 = 4.20:1
Liquid (acid test) ratio (10)	(1430 – 910) ÷ 650 = 0.80:1	(2605 – 435) ÷ 620 = 3.5:1
Rate of inventory turnover (11)	1795 ÷ ([690 + 910] ÷ 2) = 2.24 times	2300 ÷ ([910 + 435] ÷ 2) = 3.42 times
Trade receivables turnover (12)	(470 ÷ 4000) × 365 = 42.89 days	(1230 ÷ 4600) × 365 = 97.60 days
Trade payables turnover (13)	(650 ÷ 2015) × 365 = 117.74 days	(620 ÷ 1825) × 365 = 124.00 days

(b)
- Farnoud's cost of sales has increased from 2017 to 2018.
- The business's gross profit has improved from 2017 to 2018 as it has increased by $95 000.
- Farnoud's profit for the year has deteriorated as his profit for the year has decreased from $1 430 000 to $990 000. This is due to the large increase in expenses.
- The business has had a large increase in current assets, due to the increase in trade receivables. Its current liabilities have slightly decreased.
- Farnoud's gross margin deteriorated in 2018. Together with the large increase in expenses, this has led to a fall in profit margin. This requires investigation by the management.
- The return on capital employed has worsened in 2018. The value decreased from 65.37% to 57.13%. Although the value has decreased, 57.13% is still an excellent return.
- The current ratio has increased. The value in 2018 is too high (the business should aim for 2 : 1) due to the large number of trade receivables. This follows through into the liquid (acid test) ratio. There has been an improvement in 2018. However, the value is too high and the business should attempt to reduce the level of trade receivables.
- The rate of inventory turnover improved in 2018 and helps to ensure that out of date inventory is not left unsold.
- The trade receivables turnover period has increased considerably. This has a negative impact on the business's working capital. The business needs to chase its credit customers and collect debts as soon as possible. The trade payables turnover period has remained relatively constant. In both years, it is in excess of the trade receivables turnover period. This is beneficial to allow the business to pay its debts after receiving payment from customers.

6.3 Inter-firm comparison

Answers to knowledge check questions

1 D

2 A

3 D

4 Inter-firm comparison: this is where a business compares its financial performance with another business of a similar size in the same business sector.

5
- A business may apply different **accounting principles** when preparing its financial statements.
- Financial statements are based on historical data and historic cost. They do not account for the effects of inflation.
- Non-monetary items do not appear in the accounting records of a business.
- The information provided for another business may be for one year only. Therefore, there is no opportunity to calculate business trends.
- Different businesses may apply different operating policies.
- It is not always possible to gain all of the information about another business that is required for a comprehensive comparison.
- Different businesses may have different financial year-ends.

6 (a)
- Zhongguo and Huaxia will be satisfied with their gross margin of 50%. This is considerably higher than their competitor's gross margin; Zhongguo and Huaxia's ratio is 15% higher than the competitor's.
- Zhongguo and Huaxia will also be satisfied with their profit margin. This is again higher than the local competitor's profit margin.
- Zhongguo and Huaxia will be extremely satisfied with their return on capital employed of 30%. This is considerably higher than the local competitor's ROCE. In comparison to other investment opportunities, 30% is very high. Zhongguo and Huaxia should have no problem in attracting an investor to their business.

(b) Zhongguo and Huaxia could have a higher closing inventory value or a higher amount of money owing from trade receivables.

(c) Zhongguo and Huaxia should be satisfied with their rate of inventory turnover as the current turnover rate is higher than the rate of the local competitor. As Zhongguo and Huaxia are selling perishable goods, the rate of inventory turnover ensures that their products do not go out of date.

(d) Although Zhongguo and Huaxia are more profitable and have better liquidity than their competitor, they could consider:
- increasing their selling price
- purchasing goods from a cheaper supplier
- increasing the amount of money spent on advertising and marketing.

Zhongguo and Huaxia will be able to assess their current performance. They will also be able to set targets for improvement in the future.

6.4 Interested parties

Answers to knowledge check questions

1 A

2 C

3 B

4

Stakeholder group	Financial interest in a business
Government	Profitability Tax liabilities
Owner of a small retail store	Profitability Efficiency Liquidity

Stakeholder group	Financial interest in a business
Manager in a private limited company	Profitability Efficiency Liquidity
Trade payable	Liquidity Ability to repay debts on time
Bank	Profitability Liquidity Assets available as security
Investor	Profitability Potential returns
Member of a local football club	Subscriptions/donations Expenditure Surplus/deficit

5 Trade payable

Owner

Bank

6 Prior to offering a business credit, a supplier should review the liquidity position of the business. In particular, it may review the trade payables turnover to evaluate current performance.

Following review, a supplier then decides on the credit limit and length of credit term that it will offer to a business.

7 Club members expect their subscription money to be used appropriately. The financial statements show how subscription money has been used.

6.5 Limitations of accounting statements

Answers to knowledge check questions

1 B

2 C

3 C

4 Historic cost / difficulties of definition / non-financial aspects.

5 Historic data: this is financial data or information from the past. In an income statement, this is traditionally the last year.

6
- Financial information, also known as quantitative information, is included in financial statements and is expressed in monetary terms.
- Non-financial information, also known as qualitative information, cannot be expressed in monetary terms and is therefore omitted from financial statements.

Answers to chapter review questions

1 A

2 D

3 B

4 D

5 B

6 D

7 C

8 A

9 C

10 C

11 **(a)** (i) 85 540

(ii) 22 834

(iii) Loss for the year

(iv) 1800

(v) liabilities

(vi) 600

(vii) overdraft

One mark for each term/number. **[7]**

(b) (i) Current ratio = 39684 **(1)** ÷ 38400 **(1)** = 1.03 : 1 (2 d.p.) **(1)** **[3]**

(ii) Liquid (acid test) ratio =

(39684 **(1)** – 16300 **(1)**) ÷ 38400 **(1)** = 0.61 : 1 (2 d.p.) **[3]**

(c) Working capital = 39684 **(1)** – 38400 **(1)** = 1284 **(1)** **[3]**

(d) Decrease in reputation **(1)** – withdrawal of credit from suppliers **(1)**.

Lack of funds to pay short-term debts **(1)** – cash discounts will be lost **(1)**. **[4]**

[Total 20]

12 (a)

- **The liquid or acid test ratio** measures the liquidity of a business.
- It compares current assets excluding closing inventory to current liabilities.
- This ratio is a more severe test of a business's liquidity and its ability to pay short-term debts.
- The ratio assumes that inventory may be perishable, go out of date or become obsolete (due to changes in fashion or technology).
- This would mean that the business is left with inventory that it cannot sell and therefore would not be able to use to pay the business's short-term debts.

Any four points – 1 mark per point. **[4]**

(b)

1. Businesses should be of a similar size. **(1)**
2. Businesses should be in the same trade. **(1)**
3. Businesses need to use the same policies, for example depreciation, inventory valuation. **(1)**
4. Businesses should have the same structure, for example, sole trader, partnerships, etc. **(1)** **[4]**

(c) (i) The only accepted way to record financial transactions is to use the original cost price. **(1)**

Financial accounting statements are produced using data from the past. **(1)** **[2]**

(ii) Different businesses will define accounting terms in different ways. **(1)**

Comparisons are only meaningful if like for like comparisons are made. **(1)** **[2]**

(iii) Only numerical data is included in the financial records of a businesses. **(1)**

Non-financial aspects are ignored. **(1)** **[2]**

(d) (i)

- Banks and other financial institutions use financial information to review the performance of a business prior to offering to lend money, via an overdraft, loan or mortgage.
- A bank needs to know if a business has sufficient security to cover the amount of any loan.
- Banks need to ensure that a business can repay any loan when it is due and that it has sufficient funds to pay the debt and any interest that has been charged.
- When making a mortgage offer, a bank needs to be sure that the non-current asset being purchased provides sufficient collateral in the unfortunate situation that the business cannot repay the debt.

Any two points – 1 mark per point. **[2]**

(ii)

- Trade payables are suppliers that provide businesses with goods and services on credit. They need to be repaid within the specified deadline.
- Prior to offering credit, a supplier should review the liquidity position of the business. In particular, they may review the trade payables turnover to review current performance.
- Following review, a supplier decides on the credit limit and length of credit term that will be offered to a business.

Any two points – 1 mark per point. **[2]**

(iii)

- Employees of any business need to be assured that it is likely to remain profitable and in operation for the foreseeable future.

- Any employee of a business expects to be fairly paid and have a long career with excellent working conditions.

  1 mark per point. **[2]**

[Total 20]

13 (a) (i) Trade receivables turnover =

15 000 **(1)** ÷ 134 250 **(1)** x 365 = 40.78 days (2 d.p.) **(1)** **[3]**

(ii) Trade payables turnover

10 100 **(1)** ÷ 121 250 **(1)** x 365 = 30.40 days (2 d.p.) **(1)** **[3]**

(b) State **and** explain whether Donald Maclean will be satisfied with the ratio results calculated in part (a).

Yes.

Donald Maclean will be satisfied that his trade receivables turnover is less than the 60 days that he offers to his customers.

Donald Maclean will be satisfied that he is just meeting the terms of the trade credit he has been offered by his suppliers.

Donald Maclean may be concerned that he is paying his debts before he receives the money from his trade receivables.

Any two points – one mark for stating the point and one mark for the explanation.

Maximum of 2 x 2 marks. **[4]**

(c) (i) Trade receivables turnover

1. Improve credit control within the business:

   send regular statements to all credit customers

   chase overdue accounts

   reduce the length of the credit period offered to credit customers
2. Offer cash discounts for early payment
3. Charge interest on overdue accounts
4. Offer cash sales only
5. Refuse further supplies until all accounts have been settled
6. Debt factoring

Any three points – 1 mark per point. **[3]**

(ii) Trade payables turnover

1. Reduce the value of credit purchases
2. Purchase goods for cash only
3. Take advantage of cash discounts offered
4. Pay debts as soon as possible.

Any three points – 1 mark per point. **[3]**

(d) A business aims to pay its trade payables after **(1)** the business has received money from its trade receivables. **(1)** **[2]**

(e)
- Different definitions of accounting policies and methods.
- Historic costs are used.
- Non-financial aspects are omitted.

Any two points – 1 mark per point. **[2]**

14 (a) **(i)** Current ratio = Current assets / Current liabilities **[1]**

- Jam Jar = $52 500 / $25 000 **[1]** = 2.1 **[1]**
- Fresh = $70 000 / $40 000 **(1)** = 1.75 **[1]** (or 1.8)

(ii) Acid test ratio = Current assets – Inventory / Current liabilities **[1]**

- Jam Jar = $52 500 – $30 000 / $25 000 **[1]** = 0.9 **[1]**
- Fresh = $70 000 – $10 000 / $40 000 **[1]** = 1.5 **[1]**

(b) Possible reasons include:

- Selling price is lower **[1]**, which means that less profit is earned n each item sold **[1]**
- Costs of raw materials (or any other aspect of cost of sales) is higher **[1]** and therefore less profit is earned on each item sold **[1]**
- Jam Jar may use higher quality ingredients **[1]** which means that they have less profit on each item sold **[1]**
- Jam Jar may be aiming to boost sales by keeping selling price lower **[1]**, which means less profit is earned on each sold **[1]**

(c) Possible reasons include:

- May have cash flow shortages **[1]**, which means the business may face difficulties in continuing trading **[1]**
- May need to arrange short-term finance (borrowing) **[1]**, which incurs an interest charge **[1]**
- May need to 'call in' receivables **[1]**, which may mean credit customers are not happy and Jam Jar loses their loyalty **[1]**

May need to sell inventory of cheaply **[1]** to generate cash flow if needed **[1]**

(d) Possible reasons include:

- Fresh may set a higher selling price **[1]** which means inventory is sold at a lower rate **[1]**
- Fresh may hold higher levels of inventory **[1]**, which means it needs to replace inventory less often **[1]**
- Fresh may hold items which are less perishable **[1]**, which means it can hold on to inventory a longer period **[1]**

15 (a) Gross margin = gross profit / revenue × 100 **[1]**

= 87 000 / 150 000 × 100 **[1]** = 58% **[1]**

Profit margin = profit for the year / revenue × 100 **[1]**

= 87 000 – 37 500 / 150 000 × 100 **[1]** = 33% **[1]**

Return on capital employed = profit for the year / capital employed × 100 **[1]**

= 87 000 – 37 500 / 95 000 × 100 **[1]** = 52.11% (2 decimal places) **[1]**

(b) Limitations could include:

historic cost **[1]** – The only accepted way to record financial transactions is to use the original cost price. Financial statements are produced using data from the past. **[1]**

non-financial aspects **[1]** – Only numerical data are included in the financial records of a business. Non-financial aspects are ignored. **[1]**

difficulties of definition **[1]** – Different businesses define accounting terms in different ways. Comparisons are only meaningful if like for like comparisons are made. **[1]**

[Total 20]

7 ACCOUNTING PRINCIPLES AND POLICIES

7.1 Accounting principles

Answers to knowledge check questions

1 A

2 C

3 C

4 Accounting principles are rules that accountants use when preparing their financial records.

5 The application of accounting principles ensures that financial records are consistently produced and can be compared.

6 In accordance with the money measurement principle, only transactions that can be expressed in monetary terms can be recorded in a business's financial records.

7 The matching principle ensures that incomes are matched to expenses in a particular accounting period. Income and expenses need to be entered into a business's financial statements as they are earned or incurred, not when the money is received.

8 The depreciation method cannot be changed to increase profit for the year due to the consistency principle. When faced with a choice between different accounting techniques, an accountant should not change accounting policies without good reason.

9 Business entity – the financial affairs of a business must be maintained separately from those of the owner.

10 Prudence

11 Materiality – accountants should not spend time trying to accurately record items that are immaterial. A desk calculator's value is immaterial to a public limited company and should therefore be recorded as an expense.

12 The realisation principle states that revenue should be recognised when the exchange of goods or services takes place.

13 Historic cost

14 Yes. In accordance with the going concern principle, when preparing financial statements, there is an assumption that a business will continue to trade for the foreseeable future.

7.2 Accounting policies

Answers to knowledge check questions

1 C

2 D

3 C

4 In order to make meaningful comparisons, financial statement users need to:

- be aware of the accounting principles used by the businesses
- consider the accounting policies and principles applied when producing the statements
- identify similarities and differences between the businesses being compared.

5 A non-numerical characteristic in accounting. Relevance is associated with accounting information that is timely, useful and will make a difference to an interested party when making a decision.

6 Comparability

Relevance

Reliability

Understandability

7 An accounting policy that states that a business's financial information should be presented in such a way that an individual with a reasonable knowledge of business and finance and a willingness to study the information provided should be able to understand it.

Answers to chapter review questions

1 D

2 A

3 A

4 A

5 C

6 A

7 D

8 A

9 B

10 C

11 (a) (i) A quality of accounting information that allows the comparison of the financial statements **(1)** of one business to be compared with another business **(1)**. **[2]**

(ii) Accounting reliability refers to whether financial information can be verified **(1)** and used dependably for all interested parties **(1)**. **[2]**

(b) Business entity **(1)** – the financial affairs of a business must be maintained separately from those of the owner **(1)**.

The financial records of a business only relate to the business's transactions **(1)**, for example rent on business premises, purchases of goods, sales revenue **(1)**. **[4]**

(c) A cash discount is a deduction allowed **(1)** by a supplier to a customer if the customer pays within a specified period of time **(1)**. **[2]**

(d) To ensure the customers pay within a certain period of time **(1)**. This will improve the business's working capital **(1)**. **[2]**

(e) Recognising revenue or profit **(1)** only when they are achieved **(1)**. **[2]**

(f) Profit for the year **(1)** will be overstated **(1)**.

Trade receivables in the statement of financial position **(1)** will not be shown at a realistic level **(1)**. **[4]**

(g) Matching principle **(1)** – this principle ensures that revenues are matched to expenses in a particular accounting period. Income and expenses need to be entered into a business's financial statements as they are earned or incurred, not when the money is received or paid **(1)**. **[2]**

[Total 20]

12 (a) 1. Business entity **(1)** – the financial affairs of a business must be maintained separately from those of the owner **(1)**.

2. Money measurement **(1)** – this principle states that only transactions that can be expressed in monetary terms should be recorded in a business's accounts **(1)**.

3. Materiality **(1)** – accountants should not spend time trying to accurately record items that are immaterial **(1)**. **[6]**

(b) 1. Comparability **(1)**

2. Reliability **(1)**

3. Relevance **(1)**

4. Understandability **(1)** **[4]**

(c) (i) The bank statement is a copy of the account of the business as it appears in the books of the bank.

This is from the viewpoint of the bank – the business depositing money is a trade payable of the bank.

The bank account in the cash book is prepared from the viewpoint of the business.
The bank is a trade receivable of the business which has deposited the money. **[3]**

(ii) Every financial transaction has two effects on the business and requires two entries, one debit and one credit, to be made in the accounts. **[1]**

(iii) The cash book has a debit and credit side **(1)**. Every transaction placed in the cash book will have an equal and opposite entry in another account **(1)**. **[2]**

(d) A sole trader business is small **(1)** and easy to set up **(1)**.

There are low initial start-up costs **(1)**. Peter would only be required to find a small amount of capital **(1)**.

Peter is responsible for all business decisions **(1)**, therefore he can choose his own working conditions, hours and holidays to be taken **(1)**.

2 marks per advantage – maximum of 4 marks. **[4]**

[Total 20]

13 (a)
- To spread the cost of non-current assets over their useful lives.
- To apply the matching principle – recognising the time difference between payment for the non-current asset and the period over which it is used.
- To provide a more realistic view of the non-current assets.
- To record the part of the cost of the non-current asset consumed during the period of its use.

1 mark per reason – maximum of 3 marks. **[3]**

(b) When faced with a choice between different accounting techniques **(1)**, an accountant should not change accounting policies without good reason **(1)**. **[2]**

(c) Inventory valuation **(1)** – the use of the same inventory valuation method each year **(1)**. **[2]**

(d) (i) Relevance requires that the financial accounting information **(1)** should be useful to the users and that it will affect the decisions that they make **(1)**. **[2]**

(ii) An accounting term that states that a business's financial information should be presented **(1)** in such a way that any individual with a reasonable knowledge of business and finance should be able to understand it **(1)**. **[2]**

(e) Partnerships use their income statements and statements of financial position to assess their business's financial performance **(1)**.

This may include a review of their gross profit and profit for the year **(1)**. They may use the details to assess how the profit for the year can be appropriated at the year-end **(1)**. They use these statements as evidence to support an application for finance, for example a business loan or mortgage **(1)**.

It is often useful for business managers and owners to compare income statements over a period of several years **(1)**. Partnerships will analyse changes in revenue, cost of sales and expenses and make adjustments to their business practices as required **(1)**. **[6]**

(f)
- The amount of capital invested by each partner
- Details of how profits and losses will be divided between the partners
- The amount of interest payable on capital (paid before profits are shared)
- The amount of interest payable on drawings
- The value of partners' salaries
- Information on how many votes each partner has when decisions are to be made
- Rules on the admission of new partners
- Procedures for the ending of the partnership

1 mark per item – maximum of 3 marks. **[3]**

[Total 20]

Workbook answers

1 THE FUNDAMENTALS OF ACCOUNTING

1.1 The purpose of accounting

Answers – Support

1 (a), (d) and (e)

Answers – Practice

2 $46 000

Answers – Stretch

3 Reasons why profit may not be considered important could be:

- Business has charitable or social objectives as its main reason for existing.
- Survival is seen as more important.
- Profit is sacrificed in order to gain market share (i.e. price reduction in order to increase the volume of sales).

Answers – Unit review

1 D

2 D

1.2 The accounting equation

Answers – Support

1 Owner's equity = $65 500

2 Assets = $58 700

3 Owner's equity = $1680 – $260 = $1420

Answers – Practice

4 Owner's equity = $22 500 – $6110 = $16 390

5

Statement of financial position			
	$		$
Assets:		Liabilities and owner's equity:	
Business van	11 900	Owner's equity	12 000
Equipment	4 155	Bank loan	4 500
Inventory	656	Trade payables	2 310
Trade receivables	990		
Bank	1 109		
	18 810		18 810

Answers – Stretch

6 Assets would fall by the value of the cash taken out of the business by the owner. The owner's equity would also be reduced by the amount withdrawn. This means the statement of financial position would still balance.

7

	$		$
Assets:		Liabilities and Owner's equity:	
Machinery	32000	Owner's equity	25000
Inventory	1640	Bank loan	10000
Trade receivables	1390	Trade payables	920
Bank	890		
	35920		35920

Answers – Unit review

1 B

2 D

3 C

4 A

Chapter 1 review

Answers

1 D

2 C

3 D

4 A

5 C

6 A

7 C

8 B

9 Assets = $165000 **[1]** + $18900 **[1]** + $5542 **[1]** + $9991 **[1]** + $1010 **[1]** + $5000 **[1]** + $7600 **[1]**
= $213043

Liabilities = $50000 **[1]** + $8756 **[1]** = $58756

Owner's equity = $213043 – $58756 = $154287 **[1]**

10

Bonika Statement of financial position as at 31 December 2018 [1]			
	$		$
Assets:		Liability and owner's equity:	
Premises	**[1]** 250000	Owner's equity	**[1]** 129396
Equipment	**[1]** 34000	Mortgage on premises	**[1]** 175000
Motor vehicle	**[1]** 11000	Trade payables	**[1]** 3141
Cash in till	**[1]** 43		
Inventory	**[1]** 5550		
Trade receivables	**[1]** 4544		
Bank balance	**[1]** 2400		
	307537		307537

11

Statement of financial position					
		$			$
Premises		120000	Owner's equity	[1]	81380
Equipment		12500	Bank loan		60000
Inventory	[1]	6980	Trade payables	[1]	5720
Trade receivables		6780			
Bank balance	[1]	840			
	[1]	147100		[1]	147100

2 SOURCES AND RECORDING OF DATA

2.1 The double entry system of book-keeping

Answers – Support

1 T, F, F, T, T

Answers – Practice

2

Owner's equity					
		$			$
			1 Aug	Cash	500
			4 Aug	Bank	3000

Cash					
		$			$
1 Aug	Owner's equity	900			

Bank					
		$			$
4 Aug	Owner's equity	3000	7 Aug	Machinery	500
			22 Aug	Bracha	750

Machinery					
		$			$
7 Aug	Bank	600			

Equipment					
		$			$
15 Aug	Bracha	750			

Bracha					
		$			$
22 Aug	Bank	750	15 Aug	Equipment	750

Motor car					
		$			$
19 Aug	Chidike	2400			

Chidike					
		$			$
			19 Aug	Motor car	2400

3

Owner's equity					
		$	2009		$
			6 Oct	Bank	19 000

Bank					
2009		$	2009		$
6 Oct	Owner's equity	19 000	10 Oct	Premises	15 000
			15 Oct	Cash	1000

Premises					
2009		$			$
10 Oct	Bank	15 000			

Cash					
2009		$	2009		$
15 Oct	Bank	1000	21 Oct	Office equipment	500

Fixtures and fittings					
2009		$	2009		$
18 Oct	Citra	3 500	24 Oct	Dalitso	750

Office equipment					
2009		$			$
21 Oct	Cash	500			

Dalitso					
2009		$			$
24 Oct	Fixtures and fittings	750			

4

Purchases					
		$			$
1 July	Youssef	77			
3 July	Mila	54			

Purchases returns					
		$			$
			9 July	Youssef	14

Mila					
		$			$
14 July	Bank	54	3 July	Purchases	54

Cash					
		$			$
			15 July	Youssef	63

Bank					
		$			$
			14 July	Mila	54

Youssef					
		$			$
9 July	Returns out	14	1 July	Purchases	77
15 July	Cash	63			

5

Owner's equity					
		$			$
30 Sept	Balance c/d	900	1 Sept	Bank	900
			1 Oct	Balance b/d	900

Bank					
		$			$
1 Sept	Owner's equity	900	27 Sept	Drawings	100
			29 Sept	Wages	240
			30 Sept	Balance c/d	560
		900			900
1 Oct	Balance b/d	560			

Purchases					
		$			$
3 Sept	Oscar	102	30 Sept	Balance c/d	165
6 Sept	Wassane	75			
		177			177
1 Oct	Balance b/d	177			

Oscar					
		$			$
30 Sept	Balance c/d	102	3 Sept	Purchases	102
			1 Oct	Balance b/d	102

Wassane					
		$			$
13 Sept	Purchases returns	34	6 Sept	Purchases	75
30 Sept	Balance c/d	76			
		75			75
			1 Oct	Balance b/d	76

Sales					
		$			$
30 Sept		417	10 Sept	Gabriela	99
			22 Sept	Khatia	318
		417			417
			1 Oct	Balance b/d	417

Purchases returns					
		$			$
30 Sept	Balance c/d	34	13 Sept	Wassane	34
			1 Oct	Balance b/d	34

Commission received					
		$			$
30 Sept	Balance c/d	65	19 Sept	Cash	65
			1 Oct	Balance b/d	65

Cash					
		$			$
19 Sept	Commission received	65	30 Sept	Balance c/d	115
27 Sept	Gabriela	50			
		115			115
1 Oct	Balance b/d	115			

Gabriela					
		$			$
10 Sept	Sales	99	27 Sept	Cash	50
			30 Sept	Balance c/d	49
		99			99
1 Oct	Balance b/d	49			

Khatia					
		$			$
22 Sept	Sales	318	25 Sept	Sales returns	58
			30 Sept	Balance c/d	260
		318			318
1 Oct	Balance b/d	260			

Sales returns					
		$			$
25 Sept	Khatia	58	30 Sept	Balance c/d	58
1 Oct	Balance b/d	58			

Wages					
		$			$
29 Sept	Bank	240	30 Sept	Balance c/d	240
1 Oct	Balance b/d	240			

Drawings					
		$			$
26 Sept	Bank	100	30 Sept	Balance c/d	100
1 Oct	Balance b/d	100			

6

Anit					
		$			$
1 Dec	Sales	800	4 Dec	Sales returns	75
10 Dec	Sales	1200	18 Dec	Bank	700
			29 Dec	Computer	350
			31 Dec	Balance c/d	875
		2000			2000
1 Jan	Balance b/d	875			

Answers – Stretch

7 The profit made on the sale of inventory is added to the owner's equity in the owner's equity account. However, it is the profit for the year that is added to the ledger account for owner's equity rather than each individual sale of inventory. In effect, profits are the owner's reward so they would increase the owner's stake within the business.

8 Every double entry transaction will always involve equal amounts being added to the debit and to the credit side of the ledger accounts (even if the accounts are in different places). This means when the accounts are totalled and balanced, there should be equal amounts on both sides of the total of all accounts and hence, the totals of the balances of all the accounts should be the same.

Answers – Unit review

1 C

2 B

3 D

4 A

2.2 Business documents

Answers – Support

1 **(a)** Sales

(b) Bank

(c) Purchases

(d) Sales returns

(e) Cash

2

L BOALER
31 Seagrave Road
CARCHESTER
CR1 7TG

INVOICE

To:
Claude
12 Hollins Street
CARCHESTER
CR8 0RD

Invoice no: 013
Date: 1 June 2018

Quantity	Description	Unit price ($)	Total ($)
40	A4 Lever arch files	1.20	48.00
60	Exercise books (A5)	0.40	24.00
200	Pens (blue ink)	0.20	40.00
Less 20% Trade discount			112.00 11.20
TOTAL			108.80

3

Date:
14 / 09 / 2018

Payee
Sampson

Amount:
$ 650-00

A/c 1448908

Nanchester Bank
High Street Branch

Date:
14 / 09 / 2018

$ 650-00

Pay Sampson
Six hundred and fifty
dollars only

A Student

Cheque number	Branch sort code	Account number
00025	04-01-26	1448908

4

MIGUEL'S SANDWICH SHOP
11 Head Street
Oldtown
OT4 1SN

INVOICE

To:
Hamman Business Conferences
Unit 12, Business Park
Oldtown
OT4 7XJ

Invoice no: 001
Date: 1 June 2018

Quantity	Description	Unit price ($)	Total ($)
50	Mixed vegetarian	1.20	60.00
25	Fish	1.40	35.00
20	Savoury platters	3.00	60.00
Less 10% Trade discount			155.00 15.50
TOTAL			139.50

Answers – Stretch

5 This is based on the research of the student.

Answers – Unit review

1 D

2 C

3 B

4 C

2.3 Books of prime entry

Answers – Support

1 **(a)** T

(b) F

(c) F

(d) T

(e) F

2 **(a)** Sales

(b) General journal

(c) General journal

(d) Purchases

(e) Purchases returns

3

Cash book							
2010		Cash	Bank	2010		Cash	Bank
		$	$			$	$
1 Mar	Balances b/d	60	320	9 Mar	Sorin		110
2 Mar	Shanaya		560	15 Mar	Wages		250
6 Mar	Sales	50		21 Mar	Purchases		440
18 Mar	Commission received	88		25 Mar	Telephone	32	
				31 Mar	Balances c/d	166	80
		198	880			198	880
1 Apr	Balances b/d	166	80				

Answers – Practice

4

Petty cash book					
Receipts	**Date**	**Details**	**Total**	**Travel expenses**	**Office expenses**
$			**$**	**$**	**$**
100	1 June	Cash			
	2 June	Rail fares	21	21	
	7 June	Bus fares	9	9	
	8 June	Paper for printer	6		6
	15 June	Bus fares	5	5	
	22 June	Pens and pencils	12		12
	29 June	Petrol	27	27	
80	30 June	Cash			
	31 June	Balance c/d	100		
180			180	62	18
100	1 Sep	Balance b/d			

5

Cash book									
		Discount	**Cash**	**Bank**			**Discount**	**Cash**	**Bank**
2018		**$**	**$**	**$**	**2102**		**$**	**$**	**$**
1 Nov	Balance b/d		29		1 Nov	Balance b/d			210
5 Nov	Isodore	14		546	9 Nov	Rent			285
5 Nov	Irina	8		312	16 Nov	Cash			70
16 Nov	Bank		70		20 Nov	Rajinder	20		380
24 Nov	Sales		111		20 Nov	Nelu	16		624
28 Nov	Cash			50	21 Nov	Purchases		44	
					28 Nov	Bank		50	
30 Nov	Balance c/d			661	30 Nov	Balance c/d		116	
		22	210	1569			36	210	1569
1 Dec	Balance c/d				1 Dec	Balance c/d			661

6

Sales journal		
		$
1 June	Farzana	230
9 June	Julien	155
20 June	Farzana	101
30 June	Total for month	486

Purchases journal		
		$
13 June	Khamisi	47
24 June	Vendula	95
30 June	Total for month	142

Sales ledger Farzana					
		$			**$**
1 June	Sales	230			
20 June	Sales	101			

Julien					
		$			$
9 June	Sales	155			

Purchases ledger Khamisi					
					$
			13 June	Purchases	47

Vendula					
					$
			24 June	Purchases	95

Nominal ledger Sales					
		$			$
			30 June	Total sales for month	486

Purchases					
		$			
30 June	Total purchases for month	142			

7

General journal			
		Dr	Cr
		$	$
1 Oct	Amerdeep	560	
	Machinery		560
5 Oct	Van	5200	
	Owner's equity		5200
13 Oct	Gerda	80	
	Horaci		80
19 Oct	Clemente	400	
	Computer		400
23 Oct	Equipment	290	
	Eduard		290

Answers – Stretch

8

Sales journal		
		$
5 July	Natalia	314
19 July	Dian	167
25 July	Dian	182
31 July	Total for month	663

Purchases journal		
		$
1 July	Stefano	86
3 July	Yannick	63
15 July	Proclus	92
31 July	Total for month	241

Sales returns journal		
		$
10 July	Natalia	31
28 July	Dian	41
31 July	Total for month	72

Purchases returns journal		
		$
7 July	Stefano	31
20 July	Proclus	19
31 July	Total for month	50

Nominal ladger Sales					
		$			$
			31 July	Total credit sales for month	663

Purchases					
		$			
31 July	Total credit purchases for month	241			

Sales returns					
		$			
31 July	Total sales returns for month	72			

Purchases returns					
					$
			31 July	Total purchases returns for month	50

Sales ledger Natalia					
		$			$
5 July	Sales	314	10 July	Sales returns	31

Dian					
		$			$
19 July	Sales	167	28 July	Sales returns	41
25 July	Sales	182			

Purchases ledger Stefano					
		$			$
7 July	Purchases returns	31	1 July	Purchases	86

Yannick					
					$
			3 July	Purchases	63

Proclus					
		$			$
20 July	Purchases returns	19	15 July	Purchases	92

Answers – Unit review

1 D

2 A

3 C

4 A

Chapter 2 review

Answers

1 C

2 B

3 A

4 B

5 D

6 C

7 A

8 B

9 C

10 D

11

	Account to be debited	Account to be credited
(a) Wages paid from bank account	**Wages**	**Bank**
(b) Car purchased on credit from Bhutta	Car	Bhutta
(c) Inventory sent back by business to Sahi	Sahi	Purchases returns
(d) Rent received in cash	Cash	Rent received
(e) Cash paid into business bank account	Bank	Cash
(f) Sale of inventory on credit to Viktor	Viktor	Sales
(g) Owner takes money out of bank for personal use	Drawings	Bank

A [1 mark for each correct entry from (b) onwards]

Kassar					
2018		**$**	**2018**		**$**
18 March	Bank [1]	1800	1 March	Balance b/d	720
24 March	Purchases returns [1]	380	5 March	Purchases [1]	2230
28 March	Bank [1]	400	26 March	Purchases [1]	490
31 March	Balance c/d [1]	860			
		3440			3440
			1 April	Balance b/d [1]	860

B Purchases ledger **[1]**

12 A

Cash book									
		Discount allowed $	**Bank $**	**Cash $**			**Discount rec. $**	**Bank $**	**Cash $**
1 May	Balances b/d [1]		1250	88	3 May	Purchases [1]		152	
5 May	Commission rec. [1]			45	8 May	Bernat	16 [1]	304 [1]	
12 May	Sahar	26 [1]	344 [1]		8 May	Julia	6 [1]	114 [1]	
					14 May	Drawings [1]			50
					24 May	Juan	10 [1]	390 [1]	
					24 May	Ariel	5 [1]	195 [1]	
					31 May	Balance c/d		439 [1]	38 [1]
		26	1594	133			37	1594	88
1 June	Balances b/d		439	38					

B [1 mark for each valid reason (max 2 marks)]

- Stops cash book becoming crowded with many small items of expenditure
- Allows book-keeper who maintains cash book to delegate petty cash book to a junior member of staff
- Allows analysis of items of expenditure as a means of keeping control of spending.

C Nominal ledger **[1]**

D **[1 mark for any valid reason**, such as:**]**

- To attract customers
- To generate loyalty of existing customers
- As a reciprocal arrangement as business may benefit from trade credit from suppliers
- Other businesses offer trade credit and would lose sales otherwise.

13 A

General journal			
		Dr	Cr
		$	$
4 April	Machinery **[1]**	2500	
	Equipment **[1]**		2500
8 April	Cash **[1]**	450	
	Computer **[1]**	450	
	Hania **[1]**		900
17 April	Office furniture **[1]**	400	
	Owner's equity **[1]**		400
23 April	Fixtures and fittings **[1]**	250	
	Bulan **[1]**		250
25 April	Drawings **[1]**	5300	
	Car **[1]**		5300

B

Business document	Account to be debited	Account to be credited	Recorded in the following book of prime entry
(i) Cheque counterfoil showing cheque written to Igor	***Igor***	***Bank (or cash book)***	***Cash book***
(ii) Sales invoice sent to Miron **[1]**	Miron **[1]**	Sales **[1]**	Sales journal **[1]**
(iii) Paying-in slip for cheque deposited from Nyoman **[1]**	Bank **[1]**	Nyoman **[1]**	Cash book **[1]**
(iv) Credit note sent to Caesar **[1]**	Sales returns **[1]**	Caesar **[1]**	Sales returns journal **[1]**

1 mark for each correct entry. [Answer to **(i)** is already filled in]

3 VERIFICATION OF ACCOUNTING RECORDS

3.1 The trial balance

Answers – Support

1 Debit balances: (a), (b), (c), (e)

Credit balances: (d), (f)

2 **(a)** T

(b) T

(c) F

(d) F

(e) F

Answers – Practice

3 **(a)** Omission

(b) Original entry

(c) Principle

(d) Complete reversal

(e) Commission

4

	Dr	Cr
	$	$
Sales		41480
Purchases	26790	
Wages and salaries	5600	
Discounts received		300
Inventory as at 1 Jan 2018	1015	
Office expenses	1875	
Vehicles	6600	
Owner's equity		9000
Equipment	8900	
	50780	50780

Inventory as at 31 December 2018 is valued at $999

5

Wayan Trial balance as at 31 December 2018		
	Dr	Cr
	$	$
Sales		48900
Purchases	13726	
Sales returns	411	
Purchases returns		238
Motor vehicles	17500	
Discounts received		340
Office expenses	14500	
Office equipment	25940	
Inventory at 1 January 2018	8312	
Trade payables		7681
Trade receivables	10190	
Bank	756	
Office salaries	22300	
Discounts allowed	564	
Owner's equity		66600
Drawings	9560	
	123759	123759

Inventory as at 31 December 2018 is valued at $5670

Answers – Stretch

6

Trial balance		
	Dr	Cr
	$	$
Capital		20000
Machinery	10300	
Bank	4055	
Machinery insurance	156	
Purchases	990	
Ling		55
Returns outwards		113
Vehicle	7557	
Sales		1590
Bank loan		2000
Drawings	500	
Cash	200	
	23758	23758

Answers – Unit review

1 A

2 D

3 B

4 D

3.2 Correction of errors

Answers – Support

1 **(a)** Original entry
(b) Commission
(c) Principle
(d) Complete reversal

2 **(a)** Omission
(b) Principle
(c) Complete reversal
(d) Compensating

3 **(a)** Yes
(b) Yes
(c) No
(d) Yes
(e) Yes

Answers – Practice

4

General journal		
	$	$
Tina	112	
Thea		112
Car	2000	
Sales returns		2000
Bank (or cash book)	45	
Adrien		45
Agatho	103	
Bank (or cash book)		103
Serge	170	
Purchases returns		170

5

General journal		
	$	$
Insurance	9	
Cash (book)		9
Georgia	220	
Sales		220
Bank (or cash book)	320	
Rent received		320
Drawings	150	
Heating costs		150
Cash (book)	100	
Wages		100

6

General journal		
	$	$
Suspense	300	
Bank		300
Cash	18	
Durga		18
Suspense	90	
Rashmi		90
Suspense	89	
Purchases returns		89

Suspense			
	$		$
Bank	300	Balance b/d	479
Rashmi	90		
Purchases returns	89		
	479		479

7

	$	$
Net loss		(55)
Add:		
Discounts allowed overcast	335	
Drawings	33	368
		313
Less:		
Purchases	450	
Wages omitted	100	550
Corrected loss for the year		(237)

Answers – Stretch

8

General journal		
	$	$
Suspense	150	
Discounts allowed		75
Discounts received		75
Suspense	616	
Bank		616
Purchases	145	
Suspense		145

Suspense			
	$		$
Discounts	150	Balance b/d	621
Bank	616	Purchases	145
	766		766

9 a

General Journal		
	$	$
Suspense	109	
Sales		109
General expenses	90	
Suspense		90
Drawings	17	
Phone expenses		17
Osanna	100	
Purchases		100

b

Suspense			
	$		$
Sales	109	Balance b/d	19
		General expenses	90
	109		109

c

Statement of corrected profit		
	$	$
Profit		250
Add:		
Sales undercast	109	
Phone expenses overcast	17	126
		376
Less:		
General expenses undercast	90	
Purchases overcast	100	190
Corrected profit		186

Answers – Unit review

1 B

2 D

3 C

4 B

3.3 Bank reconciliation

Answers – Support

1 Debit entries: (a), (d), (e)

Credit entries: (b), (c), (f), (g), (h)

2

Cash book					
		$			$
30 Nov	Balance b/d	247	30 Nov	Interest paid	12
30 Nov	Credit transfer received	250	30 Nov	Direct debits paid	310
			30 Nov	Balance c/d	175
		497			497
1 Dec	Balance b/d	175			

Answers – Practice

3

Cash book					
		$			$
31 Mar	Balance b/d	474	31 Mar	Dividends received	45
31 Mar	Bank charges	36	31 Mar	Standing order: Zikmund	290
31 Mar	Interest paid	34	31 Mar	Direct debit	130
31 Mar	Credit transfer	350	31 Mar	Balance c/d	429
		894			894
1 Apr	Balance b/d	429			

4

Sebastian Bank reconciliation statement as at 30 June 2018	
	$
Balance as per cash book	116
Add: Unpresented cheques	564
	680
Less: Lodgements	670
Balance as per bank statement	10

5

Javed Bank reconciliation statement		
	$	$
Balance as per cash book		89.45
Add unpresented cheques:		
100341	40.11	
100344	91.14	131.25
		220.70
Less: Uncredited deposit		296.36
Bank statement balance (overdrawn)		(75.66)

6

Updated cash book					
		$			$
30 June	Balance b/d	104	30 June	Standing order	65
30 June	Interest	12	30 June	Direct debit	47
			30 June	Balance b/d	4
		116			116

Bank reconciliation statement as at 30 June	
	$
Balance as per cash book	4
Add: Unpresented cheques	177
	181
Less: Uncredited deposits	119
Balance as per bank statement	62

Answers – Stretch

7

Liddle Cash book as at 31 July 2018					
2018		$	2018		$
31 July	Balance b/d	90	31 July	Interest	19
31 July	Credit transfer	260	31 July	Direct debit	95
31 July	Balance c/d	74	31 July	Standing order	105
			31 July	Dishonoured cheque	125
			31 July	Error correction	80
		424			424
			1 Aug	Balance b/d	74

Liddle Bank reconciliation statement as at 31 July 2018		
	$	$
Balance on updated cash book		74 (Cr)
Add unpresented cheques:		
Ana	335	
Emil	210	545
		471
Less uncredited deposits:		
Alexandra	615	
Efrem	219	834
Balance on bank statement		363 O/D

Answers – Unit review

1 D

2 A

3 D

4 C

3.4 Control accounts

Answers – Support

1

Sales ledger control account			
	$		$
Balance b/d	421	Sales returns	78
Credit sales for month	2341	Discounts allowed	23
		Bank	2010
		Irrecoverable debts	95
		Balance c/d	556
	2762		2762

2

Purchases ledger control account			
	$		$
Purchases returns	454	Balance b/d	890
Cash book payments	9201	Credit purchases for January	10005
Discounts received	230		
Balance c/d	1010		
	10895		10895

Answers – Practice

3

Purchases ledger control account					
		$			$
30 Nov	Cash book	141411	1 Nov	Balances b/d	10190
30 Nov	Purchases returns	2400	30 Nov	Credit purchases	146550
30 Nov	Discounts received	3122			
30 Nov	Balance c/d	9807			
		156740			156740

4

Sales ledger control account					
		$			$
1 Nov	Balances b/d	21406	30 Nov	Cash book	224009
30 Nov	Credit sales	234000	30 Nov	Sales returns	5109
30 Nov	Dishonoured cheques	448	30 Nov	Discounts allowed	6101
			30 Nov	Irrecoverable debts	875
			30 Nov	Balance c/d	19760
		255854			255854

5

Sales ledger control account					
		$			$
1 Nov	Balances b/d	2480	30 Nov	Cash book	48800
30 Nov	Credit sales	54234	30 Nov	Sales returns	1870
30 Nov	Contra entries	460	30 Nov	Discounts allowed	1020
30 Nov	Dishonoured cheques	140	30 Nov	Contra entries	460
			30 Nov	Irrecoverable debts	985
			30 Nov	Balance c/d	4179
		57314			57314

6

Purchases ledger control account					
		$			$
30 Nov	Cash book	21010	1 Nov	Balances b/d	1314
30 Nov	Purchases returns	311	30 Nov	Credit purchases	22410
30 Nov	Discounts received	448	30 Nov	Interest owing	56
30 Nov	Contra entries	101			
30 Nov	Balance c/d	1910			
		23780			23780

Answers – Stretch

7

Purchases ledger control account			
	$		$
Balances b/d	111	Balances b/d	2418
Cashbook	32990	Credit purchases	34387
Contra entries	187		
Purchases returns	341		
Discounts received	300		
Balances c/d	2876		
	36805		36805

Sales ledger control account			
	$		$
Balances b/d	4141	Cashbook	70900
Credit sales	78999	Contra entries	187
Dishonoured cheques	290	Sales returns	441
Refunds to customers	88	Discounts allowed	770
		Irrecoverable debts	1250
		Balances c/d	9461
	83518		83009

Given the discrepancy of $509 on the sales ledger control account totals, it appears the chief accountant is correct.

8

Sales ledger control account					
		$			$
1 Aug	Balances b/d	4152	31 Aug	Balance b/d	282
31 Aug	Credit sales for month	177800	31 Aug	Cash and bank receipts	168045
31 Aug	Dishonoured cheques	890	31 Aug	Discounts allowed	1291
31 Aug	Refunds to customers	111	31 Aug	Bad debts	2450
			31 Aug	Returns inwards	1317
			31 Aug	Contra entries	660
			31 Aug	**Balances c/d**	8908
		182953			182953

Purchases ledger control account					
		$			$
31 Aug	Payments for credit purchases	95670	1 Aug	Balances b/d	3123
31 Aug	Discounts received	678	31 Aug	Credit purchases for Aug	101450
31 Aug	Returns outwards	850	31 Aug	Interest on overdue accounts	78
31 Aug	Contra entries	660			
31 Aug	Balances c/d	6793			
		104651			104651

Answers – Unit review

1 C

2 A

3 B

4 D

Chapter 3 review

Answers

1 C

2 A

3 C

4 A

5 B

6 B

7 C

8 B

9 B

10 A

11 A Principle **[1]**

B

General journal		
July 2018	**$**	**$**
Rent [1]	1320	
Suspense [1]		1320
Commission received [1]	715	
Suspense [1]		715
Suspense [1]	215	
Purchases returns [1]		215
Sales [1]	1230	
Owner's equity [1]		1230

C

Suspense					
		$			**$**
1 Jul	Balance b/d **[1]**	1820	31 Jul	Rent **[1]**	1320
31 Jul	Purchases returns **[1]**	215	31 Jul	Commission received **[1]**	715
		2035			2035

D Corrected profit for the year = \$6580 – \$1320 **[1]** + \$715 **[1]** + \$215 **[1]** – \$1230 **[1]** = \$4960 **[1]**

E Some errors do not prevent the trial balance totals from being the same **[1]**. This means no suspense account entry is needed for these errors and yet these may still exist **[1]**.

12 A

Updated cash book					
2004	**Dr**	**$**	**2004**	**Cr**	**$**
30 Apr	Balance c/d **[1]**	451	30 Apr	Direct debit **[1]**	67
30 Apr	Dividends **[1]**	25	30 Apr	Standing order **[1]**	75
			30 Apr	Balance c/d **[1]**	334
		476			476

B

Dalitso Bank reconciliation statement as at 30 April 2018 [1]		
	$	**$**
Balance as per updated cash book		334 [1]
Add Unpresented cheques		
Tiberiu		155 [1]
		489
Less Uncredited deposits		
Devdas	280 [1]	
Amelia	315 [1]	595
Balance as per bank statement		106 (Dr) [1]

C **(i)** Cheque deposited for which the payer has insufficient funds **[1]** and the amount received and credited to the bank account is cancelled **[1]**

(ii) Regular payment of varying amounts **[1]** made automatically from bank account **[1]**

(iii) Regular payment of fixed amount **[1]** made automatically from bank account **[1]**

D
- Error by business **[1]**
- Error by bank **[1]**
- Fraud or embezzlement **[1 – do not allow as separate reasons]**

13 A

Purchases ledger control account					
2016		**$**	**2016**		**$**
31 July	Cash and bank payments **[1]**	40100	1 July	Balances b/d **[1]**	3870
31 July	Discounts received **[1]**	487	31 July	Credit purchases for July **[1]**	43005
31 July	Purchases returns **[1]**	289	31 July	Interest on overdue accounts owed to suppliers **[1]**	65
31 July	Contra entries **[1]**	120			
31 July	Balances c/d **[1]**	5944			
		46940			46940

B

Sales ledger control account					
2016		**$**	**2016**		**$**
1 July	Balances b/d **[1]**	5422	31 July	Cash and bank receipts **[1]**	59012
31 July	Credit sales for month **[1]**	65780	31 July	Discounts allowed **[1]**	755
31 July	Dishonoured cheques **[1]**	400	31 July	Irrecoverable debts **[1]**	50
			31 July	Sales returns **[1]**	890
			31 July	Contra entries **[1]**	120
			31 July	Balances c/d **[1]**	8775
		71602			69602

C $2000 **[1]**

D **(i)** Cash book **[1]**

(ii) General journal **[1]**

E Omission, original entry, commission **[1 for any]**

4 ACCOUNTING PROCEDURES

4.1 Capital and revenue expenditure and receipts

Answers – Support

1 Capital expenditure: (a), (d), (f)

Revenue expenditure: (b), (c), (e)

2 Capital receipts: (b), (c), (e)

Revenue receipts: (a), (d)

3 Capital expenditure: (i), (j), (k)

Capital receipts: (b), (f),

Revenue expenditure: (c), (d), (e), (g), (h)

Revenue receipts: (a), (l)

Answers – Practice

4 Capital expenditure: $1870 + $280 + $55 = $2205

Revenue expenditure: $190 + $485 + $224 = $899

5 Capital expenditure = $3000 + $575 + $520 = $4095

6 Capital expenditure: (b), (g), (i) = $5450

Revenue expenditure: (a), (c), (d), (e), (f), (h) = $20 786

Answers – Stretch

7 **(a)**

	$	$
Gross profit		16250
Less: proceeds from sale of asset		550
		15700
Add: rent received		2310
		18010
Less expenses:		
Insurance	875	
Wages	12500	
Transport of goods to customers	260	
Marketing costs	450	14085
Profit for the year		3925

(b) Profit for the year, after corrections, is $315 lower.

(c) Assets, after corrections, will be: $345 + $1890 – $550 = $1685 higher (assuming assets appearing in the income statement were not adjusted for on the balance sheet)

Answers – Unit review

1 C

2 B

3 C

4 A

4.2 Accounting for depreciation and disposal of non-current assets

Answers – Support

1 \$80 000/5 = \$16 000 each year

2 Year 1 = 20% of \$100 000 = \$20 000

Year 2 = 20% of \$80 000 = \$16 000

3 Net book value = \$12 000 – \$6000 = \$6000

Profit on disposal = \$6700 – \$6000 = \$700

Answers – Practice

4 Yearly depreciation = (\$25 000 – \$5000)/4 = \$5000

Net book value at end of year 1 = \$25 000 – \$5000 = \$20 000

Net book value at end of year 2 = \$25 000 – \$10 0000 = \$15 000

5

	Straight line \$	Reducing balance \$
	60 000	60 000
Year 1 depreciation	6000	6000
Net book value at end of year 1	54 000	54 000
Year 2 depreciation	6000	5400
Net book value at end of year 2	48 000	48 600
Year 3 depreciation	6000	4860
Net book value at end of year 3	42 000	43 740
Year 4 depreciation	6000	4374
Net book value at end of year 4	36 000	39 366
Year 5 depreciation	6000	3937
Net book value at end of year 5	30 000	35 429

6

Provision for depreciation on van

2018		\$	2018		\$
31 Dec	Balance c/d	12 000	31 Dec	Income statement	12 000
2019			**2019**		
31 Dec	Balance c/d	21 000	1 Jan	Balance c/d	12 000
			31 Dec	Income statement	9000
		21 000			21 000
2020			**2020**		
31 Dec	Balance c/d	27 750	1 Jan	Balance c/d	21 000
			31 Dec	Income statement	6750
		27 750			27 750

7 (a)

Machinery disposal			
	$		$
Machinery at cost	42000	Provision for depreciation of machinery	36750
		Bank	5000
		Income statement	250
	42000		42000

(b)

General journal		
	Dr ($)	Cr ($)
Asset disposal	42000	
Machinery		42000
Asset sold – transfer to disposal account made		
Provision for depreciation of machinery	36750	
Asset disposal		36750
Depreciation on machinery transferred to disposal account		
Bank	5000	
Asset disposal		5000
Proceeds from sale of machinery		
Income statement	250	
Asset disposal		250
Loss on disposal of asset transferred to income statement		

Answers – Stretch

8 (a) (i)

Equipment					
2018		$	2018		$
1 Jan	Bank	20000	31 Dec	Balance c/d	92000
30 Apr	Bank	12000			
30 Jun	Bank	40000			
1 Oct	Bank	20000			
		92000			92000

Workings:

\$20000/5 = \$4000

\$12000/5 = \$2400 x (2/3) = \$1600

\$40000/5 = \$8000 x (1/2) = \$4000

\$20000/5 = \$4000 x (1/4) = \$1000

Total depreciation for 2018 = \$10600

(ii)

Provision for depreciation of equipment					
2018		$	2018		$
31 Dec	Balance c/d	10600	31 Dec	Income statement	10600

(iii)

Equipment disposal					
2019		$	2019		$
30 Jun	Equipment	12000	30 Jun	Provision for depreciation	2800
			30 Jun	Bank	8300
			30 Jun	Income statement	900
		12000			12000

(b)

General journal		
	Dr ($)	Cr ($)
Asset disposal	12000	
Equipment		12000
Provision for depreciation of equipment	2800	
Asset disposal		2800
Bank	8300	
Asset disposal		8300
Income statement	900	
Asset disposal		900

Answers – Unit review

1 D

2 A

3 B

4 C

4.3 Other payables and other receivables

Answers – Support

1 (a) $4955

(b) $730

(c) $22650

2 (a) $10060

(b) $725

(c) $370

Answers – Practice

3 (a)

Heating and lighting					
2018		$	2018		$
31 Dec	Bank	985	31 Dec	Income statement	1061
31 Dec	Balance c/d	76			
		1061			1061

General journal			
2018		Dr ($)	Cr ($)
31 Dec	Income statement	1061	
	Heating and lighting		1061
	Transfer of yearly expense to income statement		
31 Dec	Heating and lighting	76	
	Accrued expenses (heating and lighting owing)		76
	Unpaid heating and lighting for year to 31 Dec 2018		

(b)

Rent paid					
2018		$	2018		$
31 Dec	Bank	8900	31 Dec	Income statement	8125
			31 Dec	Balance c/d	775
		8900			8900

General journal			
2018		Dr ($)	Cr ($)
31 Dec	Income statement	8125	
	Rent		8125
	Transfer of yearly expense to income statement		
31 Dec	Prepaid expenses (rent paid in advance)	775	
	Rent		775
	Prepaid rent for period beginning 1 January 2019		

4 (a)

Insurance					
2018		$	2018		$
31 Dec	Bank	1010	31 Dec	Income statement	911
			31 Dec	Balance c/d	99
		1010			1010

General journal			
2018		Dr ($)	Cr ($)
31 Dec	Income statement	911	
	Insurance		911
	Transfer of yearly expense to income statement		
31 Dec	Prepaid expenses (insurance paid in advance)	99	
	Insurance		99
	Prepaid insurance for period beginning 1 January 2019		

(b)

Commission received					
2018		$	2010		$
31 Dec	Income statement	2320	31 Dec	Bank	2090
			31 Dec	Balance c/d	230
		2320			2320

General journal			
2018		Dr ($)	Cr ($)
31 Dec	Commission received	2320	
	Income statement		2320
	Transfer of yearly commission received to income statement		
31 Dec	Accrued income (income still owing to business)	230	
	Commission received		230
	Income owing as at 31 December 2018		

5

Electricity					
2018		$	2018		$
4 Jan	Bank	500	31 Dec	Income statement	1200
29 May	Bank	500	31 Dec	Balance c/d	300
18 Nov	Bank	500			
		1500			1500

6

	$	
Wages	22760	($22300 – $450 + $910)
Commission received	4301	($4500 – $86 – $113)
Gas and electricity	3956	($3670 + $199 + $87)

Answers – Stretch

7 (a)

General expenses					
2018		$	2018		$
31 Dec	Bank	754	1 Jan	Balance b/d	44
31 Dec	Balance c/d	81	31 Dec	Income statement	791
		835			835

(b)

Marketing costs					
2018		$	2018		$
31 Dec	Bank	1243	1 Jan	Balance b/d	55
			31 Dec	Income statement	1166
			31 Dec	Balance c/d	22
		1243			1243

(c)

Insurance					
2018		$	2018		$
1 Jan	Balance b/d	310	31 Dec	Income statement	4910
31 Dec	Bank	4190			
31 Dec	Balance c/d	410			
		4910			4910

(d)

Rent received					
2018		**$**	**2018**		**$**
1 Jan	Balance b/d	387	31 Dec	Bank	2840
31 Dec	Income statement	2571	31 Dec	Balance c/d	118
		2958			2958

Answers – Unit review

1 D

2 C

3 C

4 A

4.4 Irrecoverable debts and provision for doubtful debts

Answers – Support

1

Irrecoverable debts					
2018		**$**	**2018**		**$**
31 Mar	Adebisi	89	31 Dec	Income statement	279
27 June	Pedro	190			
		279			279

2 New provision = 5% × $20 000 = $1000

Entry in income statement (as an expense) is $1000 – $820 = $180.

Answers – Practice

3

Irrecoverable debts					
2018		**$**	**2018**		**$**
26 July	Ariel	75	31 Dec	Income statement	180
31 Aug	Luiz	81			
8 Nov	Javiera	24			
		180			180

4

Yuuma			
	$		**$**
Balance b/d	960	Bank	240
		Irrecoverable debts	720
	960		960

5

Provision for doubtful debts					
2018		**$**	**2018**		**$**
31 Dec	Balance c/d	620	1 Jan	Balance b/d	450
			31 Dec	Income statement	170
		620			620

2018		Dr ($)	Cr ($)
31 Dec	Income statement	170	
	Provision for doubtful debts		170
	Increase in provision for doubtful debts		

6

Benet					
2018		$	2018		$
23 Feb	Recovery of irrecoverable debts	317	23 Feb	Bank	317

Recovery of debts written off					
2018		$	2018		$
31 Dec	Income statement	317	11 May	Benet	317

Answers – Stretch

7

Provision for doubtful debts					
2018		$	2018		$
31 Dec	Balance c/d	740	31 Dec	Income statement	740
2019			2019		
31 Dec	Balance c/d	840	1 Jan	Balance b/d	740
			31 Dec	Income statement	100
		840			840
2020			2020		
31 Dec	Balance c/d	1150	1 Jan	Balance b/d	840
			31 Dec	Income statement	310
		1150			1150
2021			2021		
31 Dec	Income statement	125	1 Jan	Balance b/d	1150
31 Dec	Balance c/d	1025			
		1150			1150

General journal			
2018		Dr ($)	Cr ($)
31 Dec	Income statement	740	
	Provision for doubtful debts		740
31 Dec	Income statement	100	
	Provision for doubtful debts		100
31 Dec	Income statement	310	
	Provision for doubtful debts		310
31 Dec	Provision for doubtful debts	125	
	Income statement		125

Answers – Unit review

1 D

2 A

3 B

4 C

4.5 Valuation of inventory

Answers – Support

1 Inventory should be valued at cost or net **realisable** value, whichever is **lowest**.

2 $39

3 **(a)** $450

(b) $390

(c) $390

4 overvalued, undervalued

Answers – Practice

5 $47

6 $140

7 Product X, $40

Product Y, $96

Product Z, $220

Total = $356

Answers – Stretch

8 Correct value of inventory is $25 000. Closing inventory is $2000 overvalued. This means profit for the year is $2000 overvalued and should be reduced by this amount.

9 **(a)** $583 – see table below

(b) Assets will be lower in value by $33 ($616 – $583)

	Value at cost ($)	Value at NRV ($)	Appropriate value (Cost or NRV) ($)
AK3	48	78	48 (cost)
KE4	90	55	55 (NRV)
MA8	220	230	220 (cost)
EB33	76	78	78 (cost)
BN18	182	202	182 (cost)
Total	**616**	**643**	**583**

(c) The value for equity will be lowered. If closing inventory is lowered in value, then the cost of sales will increase, and this leads to lower profits. Once profit for the year – which is lower – is added on to the opening equity balance, the new equity balance will be lower than it would have been with the higher inventory valuation.

Answers – Unit review

1 A

2 D

3 D

Chapter 4 review

Answers

1 C

2 C

3 B

4 C

5 A

6 D

7 B

8 B

9 A

10 C

11 (a)

Gas and electricity costs					
2018		**$**	**2018**		**$**
1 Jan	Balance b/d (E)	350 **[1]**	1 Jan	Balance b/d (G)	43 **[1]**
31 Dec	Bank (G)	1650 **[1]**	31 Dec	Income statement (G)	1800 **[1]**
31 Dec	Bank (E)	1980 **[1]**	31 Dec	Income statement (E)	2100 **[1]**
31 Dec	Balance c/d (G)	193	31 Dec	Balance c/d (E)	230
		4173			4173
2019			2019		
1 Jan	Balance b/d (E)	230 **[1]**	1 Jan	Balance b/d (G)	193 **[1]**

(b) Current assets **[1]**. The business is owed money **[1]**

(c)

Commission received					
2018		**$**	**2018**		**$**
31 Dec	Income statement	1030 **[1]**	1 Jan	Balance b/d	75 **[1]**
			7 Aug	Bank	340 **[1]**
			11 Sep	Bank	560 **[1]**
			31 Dec	Balance c/d	55 **[1]**
		1030			1030
2019			**2019**		
1 Jan	Balance b/d	55			

(d) Any of the following. 1 mark for each:

- More of the sales are on credit terms
- Worsening economic outlook
- Business manages poor credit control
- Offers credit terms to 'riskier' customers

(e) Account to be debited: Irrecoverable debts **[1]**

Account to be credited: Customer/business that owes commission **[1]**

12 (a)

Didi Trial balance as at 30 April 2018	Dr $	Cr $
Inventory as at 1 April 2018	5245 **[1]**	
Revenue (sales)		79656 **[1]**
Purchases	42511 **[1]**	
Recovery of debts written off		213 **[1]**
Irrecoverable debts	545 **[1]**	
Provision for doubtful debts		660 **[1]**
Provision for depreciation of machinery		8750 **[1]**
Machinery	25900 **[1]**	
Trade receivables	7555 **[1]**	
Trade payables		2432 **[1]**
Wages	11212 **[1]**	
General expenses	8785 **[1]**	
Owner's equity		10042 **[2*]**
	101753	101753

[* 1 mark for correct side and 1 mark for correct value (OFR)]

(b) ($25 900 – $8750) **[1]** × 20% = $3430 **[1]**. [**2** for correct answer]

(c) Nominal (or general) **[1]**

(d) NBV of machinery = $25 900 – $8750 – $3430 = $13 690.

Loss on disposal **[1]** = $11 000 – $13 690 **[1]** = $2690.

(e) General journal **[1]**

13 (a) Profit for the year = $9900 – $90 **[2]** – $2055 **[2]** – $300 **[1]** + $120 **[1]** = $7575 **[1]**

(b)

	$	$
Irrecoverable debts	300 **[1]**	
Matheus		300 **[1]**
Income statement	90 **[1]**	
Provision for doubtful debts		90 **[1]**
Income statement	2055 **[1]**	
Provision for depreciation on equipment		2055 **[1]**

(c) Cash book **[1]**

(d)

	Capital expenditure	Revenue expenditure
Purchase of business premises	**[1]**	
Repairs to brickwork		**[1]**
Purchase of office furniture	**[1]**	
Transport costs of office furniture to business	**[1]**	
Wage costs		**[1]**
Depreciation on office furniture		**[1]**

5 PREPARATION OF FINANCIAL STATEMENTS

5.1 Sole traders

Answers – Support

1 The owner/s of a business is/are personally liable for the debts of the business if the business is unable to repay them. A sole trader has limited legal requirements for the preparation of financial records. Sole traders do need to register to pay tax. Also, if they employ workers, they are responsible for complying with tax, employee and health and safety legislation.

2

Abid Trading account for the year ended 30 April 2018			
	$	$	$
Revenue		45663	
Sales returns		(2300)	
			43363
Opening inventory	15723		
Purchases	29361		
Carriage inwards	1563		
Purchases returns	(1089)		
		45558	
Closing inventory		(4077)	
Cost of sales			(41481)
Gross profit (or loss)			1882

3

Bina Income statement for the year ended 31 January 2018		
	$	$
Revenue		25582
Less cost of sales		
Opening inventory	325	
Purchases	7980	
	8305	
Closing inventory	(153)	
Cost of sales		8152
Gross profit		17430
Less expenses		
Wages and salaries	7850	
Delivery expenses	3150	
Rent	2130	
Insurance	320	
General expenses	290	
		13740
Profit for the year		3690

Answers – Practice

4

BFC book store Trading account for the year ended 30 April 2018		
	$	$
Sales		170000
Cost of sales		
Opening inventory	20000	
Purchases	50000	
Closing inventory	(10000)	
		60000
Gross profit		110000

5

Hasan Income statement for the year ended 31 May 2018		
	$	$
Commission received (39500 + 2055)		41555
Less expenses		
Stationery and printing costs	3940	
Insurance (1900 – 300)	1600	
Administration expenses	10700	
Office rent	7514	
General expenses	3900	
Office equipment depreciation (30000 × 20%)	6000	
		33654
Profit for the year		7901

6

Dolphins bakery Income statement for the year ended 30 April 2018		
	$	$
Revenue		57588
Less cost of sales		
Opening inventory	3000	
Purchases	47606	
	50606	
Closing inventory	18000	
Cost of sales		32606
Gross profit		24982
Less expenses		
Lighting and heating (844 – 250)	594	
Delivery vehicle expenses (2266 + 500)	2766	
Salaries and wages	6328	
Insurance	210	
Delivery vehicle depreciation	2020	
Office expenses	1708	
		13626
Profit for the year		11356

Dolphins bakery Statement of financial position as at 30 April 2018			
	$ Cost	$ Depreciation	$ Net book value
Non-current assets			
Buildings	103012	0	103012
Delivery vehicles	10100	4040	6060
	113112	4040	109072
Current assets			
Inventory		18000	
Trade receivables	6332		
Less provision for doubtful debts	0	6332	
Bank		4694	
Other receivables (prepaid expenses)		250	
			29276
Total assets			138348
Capital and liabilities			
Capital			130000
Add profit for the year			11356
			141356
Less drawings			(5700)
			135656
Current liabilities			
Trade payables		2192	
Other payables (accrued expenses)		500	2692
Total liabilities			138348

Answers – Stretch

7 There are a number of ways to calculate the missing capital. The students could use the accounting equation, produce a trial balance or prepare a statement of financial position.

Aadi Trial balance as at 31 March 2018		
	Dr $	Cr $
Motor vehicle	23500	
Office equipment	15750	
Inventory	3500	
Cash at bank	2500	
Trade receivables	5000	
Trade payables		3000
Bank overdraft		1500
Drawings	9500	
Capital		55250
	59750	59750

8 The statement of financial position contains information about the current assets, current liabilities and working capital of the sole trader business. The income statement provides information about the business's cost of sales, gross profit and profit for the year. The sole trader is able to review their performance over a number of years.

Answers – Unit review

1 C

2 A

3 C

4 D

5.2 Partnerships

Answers – Support

1 An agreement that outlines the conditions that partners have consented to. It may also be referred to as a partnership agreement.

2 A partner's claim to the assets and liabilities of a partnership are recorded in partners' capital and current accounts.

The capital of a sole trader is recorded in a capital account. This obeys the double entry accounting rules. The same principle applies to partners. Each partner will have a separate capital account. It is usual for all partners to keep current accounts in addition to their capital accounts.

Adjustments are required to a partner's capital account when:

1 additional capital is contributed to the partnership

2 non-current assets are revalued

3 goodwill is introduced

4 a partnership is dissolved (ended).

All other adjustments made to the partners' capital are entered in the current accounts.

The capital account of each partner includes their original contribution to the partnership and is adjusted when changes take place that involve structural adjustments to the business. These capital accounts are known as fixed capital accounts. When maintaining a fixed capital account, partners are also required to prepare a current account. The current account records all entries relating to drawings, interest on capital, interest on drawings and profit or loss share.

A current account is a form of capital account that obeys the same double entry rules as a capital account. A current account includes adjustments to a partner's capital that arise from day-to-day trading operations. This is in contrast to the capital account that only adjusts for one-off structural changes to the partnership.

3

Alfredo, Giovanni and Katya Appropriation account for the year ended 31 December 2018			
	$	$	$
Profit or loss for the year			63000
Add interest on drawings:			
Alfredo		900	
Giovanni		600	
Katya		600	
			2100
			65100
Less salary: Alfredo		10000	
Less interest on capital:			
Alfredo	3200		
Giovanni	2400		
Katya	2400		
		8000	
			(18000)
			47100
Balance of profits/losses shared:			
Alfredo		23550	
Giovanni		15700	
Katya		7850	
			47100

4

Amir and Harman Appropriation account for the year ended 31 December 2018		
	$	$
Profit for the year		40000
Add interest on drawings:		
Amir	728	
Harman	550	1278
		38722
Less salaries:		
Amir		12000
		26722
Less interest on capital:		
Amir	1500	
Harman	1000	2500
		24222
Balance of profits shared:		
Amir	16148	
Harman	8074	
		24222

Amir and Harman Current accounts for the year ended 31 October 2018					
	Amir $	Harman $		Amir $	Harman $
Drawings	18200	13750	Balances b/d	8100	9320
Interest on drawings	728	550	Salaries	12000	
Balances c/d	18820	4094	Interest on capital	1500	1000
			Profits	16148	8074
	37748	18394		37748	18394
			Balances b/d	18820	4094

5

Capital account as at 31 October 2018							
	Xi $	Yorath $	Zane $		Xi $	Yorath $	Zane $
Balance c/d	100000	140000	180000	Balance b/d	100000	140000	180000
	100000	140000	180000		100000	140000	180000
				Balance b/d	100000	140000	180000

Current account as at 31 October 2018							
	Xi $	Yorath $	Zane $		Xi $	Yorath $	Zane $
Balance b/d		1860		Balance b/d	390		1540
Drawings	30000	22000	34000	Interest on capital	10000	14000	18000
Interest on drawings	900	660	1020	Salaries		19000	
Balance c/d	29490	108480	134520	Share of profit	50000	100000	150000
	60390	133000	169540		60390	133000	169540
				Balance b/d	29490	108480	134520

Xi, Yorath and Zane Balance sheet extract as at 31 October 2018		
	$	$
Capital account balances:		
Xi	100000	
Yorath	140000	
Zane	180000	420000
Current account balances:		
Xi	29490	
Yorath	108480	
Zane	134520	272490
		692490

Answers – Stretch

6 • The amount of capital invested by each partner.

- Details of how profits and losses will be divided between the partners – Benjamin may argue for a higher profit share given his greater experience, but his experience could be rewarded with a partnership salary. Melinda may argue for a higher profit share given her higher capital contribution but the interest on capital could be adjusted to a percentage that rewards her for this extra contribution.
- The amount of interest payable on capital (paid before profits are shared) – Interest on capital may provide compensation for using their capital in this business rather than for alternative uses.
- The amount of interest payable on drawings – Both may want to allow interest on drawings to ensure there is a deterrent for taking excessive drawings.
- The value of partners' salaries, if applicable.
- Information on how many votes each partner has when decisions are to be made.
- Rules on the admission of new partners.
- Procedures for ending the partnership.

7 The balance on a partner's current account usually has a credit balance. It is possible, however, for the partner to have a debit balance on their current account. This would mean that the partner has withdrawn more money from the partnership than they have 'earned'. If this persists, the partner would need to transfer capital from their fixed capital account to the current account.

Answers – Unit review

1 B

2 C

3 C

4 A

5.3 Limited companies

Answers – Support

1 $0.055 × 700000 = $38500

2 $0.03 × 350000 = $10500

Ordinary dividend = $0.02 × 500000 = $10000

Preference dividend = 4% × 220000 = $8800

Total dividend = $18800

Answers – Practice

3 **(a)** 500 000 shares × $1.50 = $750 000

(b) 350 000 shares × $1.50 = $525 000

(c) 350 000 shares × $0.75 = $262 500

(d) 200 000 shares × $0.75 = $150 000

4

Atom Enterprises Ltd Income statement for the year ended 31 December 2018		
	$	$
Revenue		210500
Less cost of goods sold:		
Opening inventory	17800	
Add purchases	130000	
	147800	
Less closing inventory	34500	113300
Gross profit		97200
Less expenses:		
Distribution costs	11500	
Administration costs	8800	
Depreciation on non-current assets	38100	
Debenture interest	2400	
Directors remuneration	6750	67550
Profit before tax		29650
Finance costs		3400
Profit for year		26250
Ordinary dividends	2000	
Preference dividends	1500	3500
		22750
Transfer to general reserve		5000
Retained earnings		17750
Retained earnings b/d		20000
Retained earnings c/f		37750

Atom Enterprises Ltd Balance sheet as at 31 December 2018			
	$ Cost	$ Depreciation	$ NBV
Non-current assets	195000	42600	152400
Current assets			
Inventory		34500	
Trade receivables		16900	
Cash and cash equivalents		25700	
		77100	
Current liabilities			
Trade payables		10950	
Finance costs owing		3400	
Debenture interest owing		2400	
		16750	
Working capital			60350
			212750
Non-current liabilities			
Debentures			40000
NET ASSETS			172750
Capital and reserves			
Ordinary share capital			100000
Preference share capital			30000
General reserve			5000
Retained earnings			37750
			172750

Answers – Stretch

5 Arguments in favour of Weishuan's idea:

- It would allow her to access more capital, which will be needed to expand.
- Dividends do not have to be paid (if she issues ordinary shares).

Arguments against her idea:

- She may lose control over the company if she issues shares and dilutes her own stake in the business.
- Share issues are often expensive to arrange.
- Shareholders may wish her to pursue profits instead of personal objectives she may have.

Overall it will depend on how much and by how far she wishes to expand. If interest rates are low, then a loan would be easier to arrange and may allow her to retain control over decision-making.

6 Any profits earned by the shareholders that are not given out as dividends are retained and reinvested into the company. This will allow a company access to retained earnings which can be used for expansion (or repayment of debt). This should allow the business to become more efficient, to expand and hopefully to become more profitable. In this case, the market share price is likely to rise, and the investor can sell the shares for a profit (a capital gain) – which may not be possible if profits are distributed as dividends instead.

7 The share premium exists when a company issues shares that are likely to be very popular. This could be when a business has issued its share capital in several stages. If the market price of a share has risen from its original par value by the time of the next stage of the share issue, it is likely that the business would want to ensure the new issue of shares are not sold cheaply, and the share premium is a way of ensuring any new shares issued are sold for a price that they are seen to be worth and not at an out-of-date par value.

Answers – Unit review

1 D

2 D

3 A

4 C

5.4 Clubs and societies

Answers – Support

1 • Subscriptions or membership fees
- Donations
- Life memberships
- Grants
- Revenue received from activities, for example sale of refreshments
- Money received from club/society events

2 • Receipts and payments account
- Income statement (also known as a trading account)
- Subscriptions account
- Income and expenditure account
- Statement of financial position

3

Profit-making organisations	Non-profit making organisations
Income statement	Income and expenditure account
Capital	Accumulated fund
Profit	Surplus
Loss	Deficit
Cash book	Receipts and payments account

4

Ylber craft club Receipts and payments account for the year ended 28 February 2018			
	$		$
Balance b/d	10500	Purchases of craft materials for resale	2000
Subscriptions received	10000	Wages – knitting coach	1500
Revenue from sales of craft materials and supplies	6000	Wages – sales assistant	3500
Café revenue	8900	Wages – café staff	2750
National knitting and sewing competition: entrance fees received	3500	Rent and rates	2900
		Heat and light	1000
		General expenses	300
		Purchase of craft equipment	2000
		National knitting and sewing competition: cost of prizes	750
		Balance c/d	22200
	38900		38900
Balance b/d	22200		

5

Highlands steam railway society Subscriptions account as at 31 March 2018			
	$		$
Balance b/d (accrued)	350	Balance b/d (prepaid)	330
Income and expenditure account	3452	Bank/cash	3522
Balance c/d (prepaid)	370	Balance c/d (accrued)	320
	4172		4172
Balance b/d	320	Balance b/d	370

6

Bali football society Subscriptions account as at 30 April 2018			
	$		$
Balance b/d (accrued)	1120	Balance b/d (prepaid)	1350
Income and expenditure account	14675	Bank/cash	13595
		Irrecoverable debts	1100
Balance c/d (prepaid)	1500	Balance c/d (accrued)	1250
	17295		17295
Balance b/d	1250	Balance b/d	1500

7

Sweet Treats baking club café Income statement for the year ended 31 July 2018		
	$	$
Revenue		33865
Less cost of sales		
Opening inventory	1190	
Purchases	11488	
	12678	
Closing inventory	197	
Cost of sales		12481
Gross profit		21384
Less expenses		
Food store wages	11100	
		11100
Profit for the year		10284

Answers – Practice

8 (a)

Blue Harbour Tennis Club Subscriptions account			
	$		$
Balance b/d	800	Balance b/d	250
Income and expenditure	1570	Bank	1300
Balance c/d	480	Balance c/d	1300
	2850		2850

(b)

Calculation of profit/loss on snack bar		
	$	$
Snack bar sales		940
Less cost of snack bar:		
Opening inventory	260	
Add purchases ($920 – $120 + $90)	890	
	1150	
Less closing inventory	160	990
Loss on snack bar		50

Calculations for income from events		
	$	$
Income from events		2460
Less expenses:		
Hire of equipment	378	
Other expenses	222	600
Profit on events		1860

Blue Harbour Tennis Club Income and expenditure account for year ended 31 December 2018		
	$	$
Income		
Subscriptions	1570	
Profit on events	1860	3430
Expenditure		
Rent of clubhouse ($4600 + $1080 – $720)	4960	
Telephone	230	
Transport costs	500	
Loss on snack bar	50	
Stationery	150	
Heating and lighting	500	
Depreciation on equipment (see calculation below)	600	6990
Excess of expenditure over income		3560

Depreciation of equipment is calculated as follows:

	$
Equipment at start of year	10000
Add equipment bought	1000
	11000
Less equipment at end of year	10400
Equals depreciation	600

(c)

Blue Harbour Tennis Club Statement of affairs as at 1 January 2018		
	$	$
Equipment	10000	
Subscriptions owing	800	
Cash at bank	1400	
Snack bar inventory	260	12460
Subscriptions paid in advance	250	
Payables for snack bar purchases	120	
Accrued rent	720	1090
Accumulated fund as at 1 January 2018		11370

(d)

Blue Harbour Tennis Club Statement of financial position as at 31 December 2018			
	$	$	$
Non-current assets			
Equipment			10400
Current assets			
Inventory		160	
Subscriptions owing		1300	
		1460	
Current liabilities			
Snack bar payables	90		
Subscriptions in advance	480		
Accrued rent	1080		
Overdraft	2400	4050	(2590)
			7810
Accumulated fund			
Balance as at 1 January 2018			11370
Less deficit			3560
			7810

Answers – Stretch

9 The debit side of the receipts and payments account details the money received by the organisation.

The credit side of the receipts and payments account details the money paid out by the organisation.

The balance carried down at the end of the period is transferred to the next financial period.

A debit balance represents money that is owned by the organisation and is recorded as an asset in the statement of financial position.

A credit balance represents money that is owed by the organisation and is recorded as a liability in the statement of financial position. This is also known as an overdrawn balance.

10 Subscriptions received need to be adjusted in accordance with the matching principle to calculate the amount to be included in the financial statements.

The subscriptions total needs to be adjusted for members who have not paid their subscriptions on time or have paid in advance for their membership.

The production of a subscriptions account allows the club or society to adjust the amount received for prepayments and accruals at both the start and end of the financial period.

Clubs and societies produce a subscriptions account at the end of each financial period. This calculates the amount of subscriptions to be included in the income and expenditure account.

11 This would largely depend on how many years to expect the average member to be an active member of the club and use the facilities of the club. For example, if most members paying for life membership are involved in the activities of the club for 10 years on average then it would seem sensible to include $\frac{1}{10}$ of the life membership fund each year in the income and expenditure account. If the average duration of membership is lower or higher, then the fraction included could be adjusted accordingly.

12 It would be prudent to write off the amount owing as irrecoverable. The need to write off the debt is perhaps not as pressing as it would be for a company owned by shareholders. However, it would be sensible not to include the amount as a current asset when it is highly likely that the money will not be received, so writing the debt off is advisable.

Answers – Unit review

1 B

2 C

3 C

4 A

5.5 Manufacturing accounts

Answers – Support

1 **Prime cost**:

Direct wages

Purchases of raw materials

Royalties

Factory overheads:

Depreciation of equipment

Wages of factory manager

Factory rent

Expenses in income statement:

Office rent

Depreciation of office equipment

Carriage outwards

2

	$
Inventory of raw materials as at 1 April 2017	5670
Add purchases	45655
	51325
Add carriage inwards	290
	51615
Less purchases returns	1125
	50490
Inventory of raw materials as at 31 March 2018	6910
Cost of raw materials consumed	43580

3

Prime cost for the year ended 31 May 2018	
	$
Inventory of raw materials as at 1 June 2017	8070
Purchases of raw materials	99405
	107475
Inventory of raw materials as at 31 May 2018	7986
Cost of raw materials consumed	99489
Direct wages	87560
Royalties	2311
Prime cost	189360

Answers – Practice

4
- There is no information regarding efficient use of resources – it is not a performance indicator.
- There is no comparison of costs and revenues.
- It is a general account which does not relate to the costing of individual products.
- There may be an arbitrary apportionment of costs between the factory and the office.
- It may be difficult to decide which costs are direct and which are indirect to determine prime cost and total production cost.

5
- To see whether the manufacturing section of the business is cost effective compared with the external purchase price of the goods produced – part of the control system.
- To compare relative profitability levels of the business's manufacturing and retailing sections.
- To give credit to the factory workforce and management for their efforts, perhaps in the form of bonuses.
- To charge the retailing section a more realistic price for the goods it receives.

6

Arboleda manufacturers Manufacturing account for the year ended 30 November 2018		
	$	$
Raw materials:		
Opening inventory	12000	
Purchases	124000	
	136000	
Less closing inventory	(12600)	
Cost of raw materials consumed		123400
Direct wages/labour		148000
Royalties paid		1600
PRIME COST		273000
Add factory overheads:		
Factory rent	11700	
Depreciation of factory equipment	11000	
General indirect expenses	11100	
		33800
		306800
Add opening work in progress		18000
		324800
Less closing work in progress		(12000)
Manufacturing cost of goods completed		312800

7

Manufacturing account for the year ended 31 December 2018		
	$	$
Opening inventory of raw materials		29670
Add purchases	235500	
Add carriage inwards	369	
	235869	
Less purchases returns	3369	232500
		262170
Less closing inventory of raw materials		23529
Cost of raw materials consumed		238641
Direct wages		203025
Royalties		5250
Prime cost		446916
Add factory overheads:		
Indirect wages	118500	
Rent ($22950 + $1170) × 0.75	18090	
Factory running costs ($16470 – $570)	15900	
Depreciation of equipment	8220	160710
		607626
Add opening work in progress		37020
		644646
Less closing work in progress		42699
Manufacturing cost of goods completed		601947

Answer – Stretch

8

Manufacturing account for the year ended 31 December 2018		
	$	$
Opening inventory of raw materials		28480
Add: Purchases	270000	
Less: Returns outwards	2426	267574
		296054
Less: Closing inventory of raw materials		31308
Cost of raw material consumed		264746
Direct wages		290600
Royalties		8468
Prime cost		563814
Add: Factory overheads		
Indirect wages	177136	
Heating expenses ($13572 + $432) × $\frac{2}{3}$	9336	
Depreciation: Factory machinery	41082	
Depreciation: Factory property	10000	
Rent ($29048 – $1580) ÷ 2	13734	251288
		815102
Add: Opening work in progress		34662
		849764
Less: Closing work in progress		33088
Manufacturing cost of goods completed		816676

Income statement for the year ended 31 December 2018		
	$	$
Sales		1134000
Less: Cost of goods sold		
Opening inventory of finished goods	57956	
Add: Manufacturing cost of goods completed	816676	
	874632	
Less: Closing inventory of goods completed	68820	805812
Gross profit		328188
Less: Expenses		
Office administration ($87000 + $10900)	97900	
Rent ($29048 – $1580) ÷ 2	13734	
Distribution costs	70000	
Heating expenses ($13572 + $432) x $\frac{1}{3}$	4668	186302
Net profit		141886

Answers – Unit review

1 C

2 B

3 A

5.6 Incomplete records

Answers – Support

1 A statement of affairs is a list of a business's assets and liabilities at a given date; it is similar to a statement of financial position. It can be used to determine a business's capital. This can be completed only if the total amount of assets and liabilities is known.

2 Profit for the year = closing capital – opening capital – capital introduced + drawings

3 **(a)** Capital = assets – liabilities

Opening capital = 157 080 – 14 200 = $142 880

Closing capital = 167 400 – 16 980 = $150 420

(b) Profit = closing capital – opening capital – capital introduced + drawings

Profit = 150 420 – 142 880 – 0 + 129 000 = $136 540

4

Income statement for the year ended 31 March 2018			
	$	$	$
Revenue			179 600
Opening inventory	14 890		
Purchases	154 000		
		158 890	
Closing inventory		15 210	
Cost of sales			143 680
Gross profit			35 920

5

Credit sales:	$
Receipts from trade receivables	1 663 200
Less	
Opening balance for trade receivables	147 600
Add	
Closing balance for trade receivables	153 600
Equals	
Credit sales for the year	1 669 200
Credit purchases:	
Payments to trade payables	1 498 800
Less	
Opening balance for trade payables	139 400
Add	
Closing balance for trade payables	140 400
Equals	
Credit purchases for the year	1 499 800
(a) Total sales = $1 669 200 + $124 000 = **$1 793 200**	
(b) Total purchases = $1 499 800 + $315 300 = **$1 815 100**	

6

Theba's bank account as at 30 June 2018			
	$		$
Balance b/d	25400	Payments to trade payables	1498800
Receipts from trade receivables	1663200	Administration expenses	139240
Cash sales	124000	Drawings	176800
Balance c/d	329640	Salaries	180000
		Heat and light	17600
		Insurance	13800
		Equipment	116000
	2142240		2142240
		Balance b/d	329640

Answers – Practice

7

Afaaq's profit for the year	$
Capital as at 31 December 2018	4912
Capital as at 1 January 2018	4697
Change in capital	215
Add drawings	32000
Profit for the year	32215

8 If the mark-up is $\frac{1}{3}$ then the gross margin used must be $\frac{1}{4}$.

From sales revenue of $1000 the gross profit would be $\frac{1}{4}$ x $1000 = $250, which implies that the cost of sales is $750.

If the cost of sales is $750, it is also equal to $130 + $980 – Closing inventory

$130 + $980 – ? = $750

The closing inventory should therefore be $360, but it is only $30.

This means that ($360 – $30) golfing shoes worth $330 were stolen.

Answers – Stretch

9 Calculation for credit sales and credit purchases:

Sales control account			
	$		$
Balance b/d	8708	Receipts	75680
Credit sales	**78873**	Balance c/d	11901
	87581		87581

Purchases control account			
	$		$
Payments	62455	Balance b/d	4802
Balance c/d	6660	**Credit purchases**	**64313**
	69115		69115

Total sales:	$
Cash sales banked	32100
Add: Drawings	6240
Cash sales	38340
Add: Credit sales	78873
	117213

Income statement for the year ended 31 December 2018		
	$	$
Sales		117213
Less cost of goods sold:		
Opening inventory	4890	
Add: Purchases	64313	
	69203	
Less: Closing inventory	6122	63081
Gross profit		54132
General expenses	7455	
Rent	1736	
Depreciation: Equipment	8900	
Depreciation: Motor cars	2800	20891
Net profit		33241

Statement of financial position as at 31 December 2018		
	$	$
Non-current assets		
Premises	140000	
Equipment	21700	
Motor cars	9700	171400
Current assets		
Inventory	6122	
Trade receivables	11901	
Prepayments	110	
Bank	34704	
	52837	
Current liabilities		
Trade payables	6660	
Accruals	555	
	7215	
Working capital		45622
Net assets		217022
Capital		190021
Add: Net profit		33241
		223262
Less: Drawings		6240
		217022

Answers – Unit review

1 B

2 D

3 B

Chapter 5 review

Answers

1 D

2 A

3 C

4 C

5 A

6 B

7 C

8 C

9 C

10 B

11 (a)

	Item	Trading account	Income statement	Appropriation account	Statement of financial position
(i)	Interest on capital			√	
(ii)	Premises				√ **[1]**
(iii)	Revenue	√ [1]			
(iv)	Opening inventory	√ [1]			
(v)	Trade receivables				√ [1]
(vi)	Interest on drawings			√ [1]	
(vii)	Residual profit			√ [1]	
(viii)	Commission received		√ [1]		
(ix)	Carriage outwards		√ [1]		

(b)

Alejo Current account as at 1 January 2019			
	$		$
Balance b/d	1500 **[1]**	Interest on capital	4000 **[1]**
Drawings	2000 **[1]**	Salaries	8000 **[1]**
Interest on drawings	500 **[1]**	Share of profit	15000 **[1]**
Balance c/d	23000		
	27000		27000
		Balance b/d	23000 **[1]**

(c) The interest on capital rewards partners for taking risk and investing in the business **[1]**.

The interest balances the rights of the partners where profits are not shared in the proportions of the capital introduced by the individual partners **[1]**.

Interest on drawings is a penalty for taking drawings out of the business **[1]**.

It is in the best interests of the partnership that the profits should be kept in the business **[1]**.

The interest will discourage partners from taking too much money out of the business, particularly early in the year in anticipation of profits **[1]**.

12 (a) (i) Depreciation for Machinery: $186 000 / 5 = $37 200 **[1]**

(ii) Depreciation for Fixtures: ($54 000 – $15 600) **[1]** × 20% = $7680 **[1] [or 2 for correct figure]**

(iii) Provision for doubtful debts 5% × $30 600 = $1530 **[1]** – $840 = $690 **[1] [or 2 for correct figure]**

(b)

Pietrek Statement of financial position as at 31 December 2018			
	$	$	$
Non-current assets			
Machinery		186000 [1]	
Less Provision for depreciation		65700 **[1]**	120300
Fixtures		54000 **[1]**	
Less Provision for depreciation		23280 **[1]**	30720
			151020
Current assets			
Inventory		57366 **[1]**	
Trade receivables	30600 **[1]**		
Less Provision for doubtful debts	1530 **[1]**	29070	
Prepayments		2295 **[1]**	
Bank		25500 **[1]**	
		114231	
Less Current Liabilities			
Trade payables	23400 **[1]**		
Accruals	17241 **(2)**	40641	73590
			224610
Capital			216000 **[1]**
Add Operating profit			71610 **[1]**
			287 610
Less Drawings			63000 **[1]**
			224610

13 (a) Dividend for ordinary shares:

$600 000 × 80% = $480 000 **[1]**

$480 000 × $0.03 = $14 400 **[1]**

Dividend for preference shares:

$500 000 × 50% = $250 000; $250 000 × 4% = $10 000 **[1]**

Total dividend:

$14 400 + $10 000 = $24 000 **[1]**

[Award all 4 marks for correct answer of $24 000 without workings]

(b)

FFG Ltd Balance sheet extract as at 31 December 2018	
	$
Capital and reserves:	
Ordinary share capital	480 000 **[1]**
Preference share capital	250 000 **[1]**
General reserve	20 650 **[2]**
Retained earnings	35 000 **[4]**

[Calculation for general reserve: Allow 1 mark for $17 650 + $3000 seen]

[Calculation for retained earnings: $62 400 **[1]** – $3000 **[1]** – $24 400 **[1]** = $35 000 **[1]**]

(c)

General journal		
	Dr	Cr
	$	$
Receivables from investors	120 000 **[1]**	
Ordinary share capital		120 000 **[1]**
Receivables from investors	250 000 **[1]**	
Preference share capital		250 000 **[1]**

(d) Reasons may include:

- Debenture issue does not dilute control **[1]** – issuing more shares may mean directors lose control over voting capital of business **[1]**
- Interest rates may be lower **[1]** – this may be unlikely for the long term, but interest rates may remain low in the short term, meaning that the cost of 'servicing' the debentures is less than the likely dividend **[1]**
- A debenture issue may be less expensive to arrange **[1]** – share issues may cost more to administer and arrange in terms of publicity and finance costs **[1]**.

14 (a)

Grenhill Board Games Club Subscriptions			
	$		$
Balance b/d	23 **[1]**	Balance b/d	44 **[1]**
Income and expenditure	1871 **[1]**	Receipts	1780 **[1]**
Balance c/d	18	Balance c/d	88
	1912		1912

(b)

Grenhill Board Games Club Snack bar sales		
	$	$
Snack bar sales		1530 **[1]**
Less: Cost of snack bar sales		
Opening inventory	98 **[1]**	
Add: Purchases ($774 + $99 – $111)	762 **[3]**	
	860	
Less: Closing inventory	214 **[1]**	646
Profit on snack bar		884 **[1]**

(c)

Grenhill Board Games Club Income and expenditure account for the year ended 31 December 2018		
	$	$
Income:		
Subscriptions	1871 **[1]**	
Profit on snack bar	884 **[1]**	
Profit on raffle	70 **[1]**	2825
Expenditure:		
Electricity	616 **[3]**	
Premises depreciation	500 **[1]**	
Rent	1980 **[1]**	3096
Excess of expenditure over income		271 **[1]**

15 (a)

Bertels Ltd Manufacturing account for the year ended 31 December 2018		
	$	$
Opening inventory of raw materials		3241 **[1]**
Add purchases		52454 **[1]**
		55695 **[1]**
Less purchases returns		114 **[1]**
		55581
Less closing inventory of raw materials		4556 **[1]**
Cost of raw materials consumed		51025
Direct labour		50880 **[2]**
Manufacturing royalties		556 **[1]**
Prime cost		102461
Add factory overheads:		
Factory rent	8030	**[1]**
Factory heating costs	2141	10171 **[2]**
		112632
Add opening work in progress		6574 **[1]**
		119206
Less closing work in progress		5558 **[1]**
Manufacturing cost of goods completed		113648 **[1]**

(b)

Bertels Ltd Income statement extract for the year ended 31 December 2018		
	$	$
Sales		148000 **[1]**
Less sales returns		231 **[1]**
		147769
Less cost of sales:		
Opening inventory	11411	**[1]**
Add manufacturing cost	113648	**[1]**
	125059	
Less closing inventory	14550	110509 **[1]**
Gross profit		37260 **[1]**

(c) Current assets **[1]**

16 (a)

Kareem Trading account for the year ended 31 December 2018		
	$	**$**
Sales		79261 **[5*]**
Less cost of sales		
Opening inventory	9990 **[1]**	
Add purchases ($54 890 + $9101 – $8771 **[2]**)	55220 **[3]**	
	65210	
Less closing inventory	10443 **[1]**	54767 **[1]**
Gross profit		24494 **[1]**

*Sales calculation:

Drawings = 52 × $180 = $9360 **[1]**

Cash sales = $41414 + $9360 = $50774 **[1]**

Credit sales = $29900 + $12767 – $14180 **[1]** = $28487 **[1]**

Total sales = $50774 + $28487 = $79261 **[1]**

(b)

Kareem Trading account for the year ended 31 December 2017		
	$	**$**
Sales		150000 **[3]**
Less cost of sales:		
Opening inventory	7960 **[1]**	
Add purchases	122030 **[1]**	
	129990	
Less closing inventory	9990 **[1]**	120000 **[1]**
Gross profit		30000 **[1]**

Sales = $135640 + $9360 + $5000 **[2]** = $150000 **[1]**

17 (a)

Seo-yun Income statement for the year ended 31 December 2017			
	$	$	$
Revenue		260000	
Sales returns		8000 [1]	
			252000
Opening inventory	20000 [1]		
Purchases	235000		
Carriage inwards	5000 [1]		
Less purchases returns	34850 [1]		
		225150	
Closing inventory		41000	
Cost of sales			184150 [1]
Gross profit			67850 [1]
Additional income			
Discounts received		2000 [1]	
Rent received		6000 [1]	
			8000
			75850
Less expenses			
Sundry expenses		16000 [1]	
Wages and salaries		35000 [1]	
Insurance		24000 [1]	
Loan interest		4000 [1]	
Carriage outwards		3000 [1]	
Provision for doubtful debts		41 [1]	
Discounts allowed		3500 [1]	
Irrecoverable debts		450 [1]	
			85991
Net profit/(loss)			(10141)

(b) To apply the matching/accruals principle **[1]**

To prevent profit for the year being overstated **[1]**

To ensure non-current asset values are not overstated **[1]**

To apply the prudence principle **[1]**

(Any two points: 1 mark each + 1 mark each for development)

6 ANALYSIS AND INTERPRETATION

6.1 Calculation and understanding of ratios

Answers – Support

1 **(a)** Gross margin, profit margin, return on capital employed

(b) Rate of inventory turnover, trade receivables turnover, trade payables turnover

(c) Current ratio, liquid (acid test) ratio

Answers – Practice

2 **(a)** Current ratio = current assets ÷ current liabilities

24 600 ÷ 16 400 = 1.5 : 1

(b) Acid test ratio = (current assets – closing inventory) ÷ current liabilities

(24 600 – 8200) ÷ 16 400 = 1 : 1

(c) Rate of inventory turnover = cost of sales ÷ average inventory

(6350 + 89 150 – 8200) ÷ [(6350 + 8200) ÷ 2]

87 300 ÷ 7275 = 12 times

3 **(a)** Current ratio = 24 000 ÷ 12 000 = 2 : 1

(b) Liquid (acid test) ratio = (24 000 – 7000) ÷ 12 000 = 1.42 : 1 (to two decimal places)

4 **(a)** Trade receivables collection period = trade receivables ÷ credit sales × 365

Store 1 = 130 000 ÷ 235 000 × 365 = 201.91 days

Store 2 = 250 000 ÷ 260 000 × 365 = 350.96 days

Store 3 = 150 000 ÷ 255 000 × 365 = 214.71 days

(b) Trade payables payment period = trade payables ÷ credit purchases × 365

Store 1 = 50 000 ÷ 155 000 × 365 = 117.74 days

Store 2 = 75 000 ÷ 125 000 × 365 = 219 days

Store 3 = 100 000 ÷ 135 000 × 365 = 270.37 days

5 Café 1

(a) 38.46%

(b) 26.92%

(c) 63.64%

Café 2

(a) 30%

(b) 24%

(c) 48%

Café 3

(a) 66.67%

(b) 36.67%

(c) 157.14%

Answers – Stretch

6 The statement of financial position contains information about the current assets, current liabilities and working capital of the sole trader business. The owner will be able to calculate and analyse the results of both the current ratio and the liquid (acid test) ratio.

7 Gym 1

(a) 2 : 1

(b) 1.6 : 1

Gym 2

(a) 2.6 : 1

(b) 2 : 1

Gym 3

(a) 1.24 : 1

(b) 1.04 : 1

8 **(a)** $\frac{120\,000 - 60\,000 - 30\,000}{120\,000} \times 100 = 25\%$

(b) $\frac{120\,000 - 60\,000 - 30\,000}{100\,000} \times 100 = 30\%$

Answers – Unit review

1 A

2 B

3 C

4 B

6.2 Interpretation of accounting ratios

Answers – Support

1 **(a)** The gross profit that is earned for every $100 of sales revenue.

(b) The profit for the year that is earned for every $100 of sales revenue.

(c) ROCE is a very important ratio. The higher the ratio value, the more efficiently the capital invested into the business organisation is being employed.

(d) Calculates the number of times a business organisation sells and replaces its inventory over a period of time. The rate of inventory turnover will vary depending on the type of business.

(e) Measures the average time it takes trade receivables to pay their accounts. This needs to be compared with the credit terms that were offered to the customers when they made their purchases.

(f) Measures the average time that it takes a business organisation to pay its trade payables. The same business may have a similar trade payables turnover period from one year to the next.

(g) This can be referred to as the working capital ratio. It indicates the management of a business's current assets.

(h) Compares assets that are in the form of money or those which can be quickly converted into money, for example trade receivables with current liabilities.

2
- Damaging business reputation with the supplier
- Loss of any cash discount offered for early payment
- Suppliers refusing to offer a business organisation future credit terms
- Suppliers refusing to supply future goods to a business

Answers – Practice

3

	2017	2018
Trade receivables turnover period	25 days	37 days
Trade payables turnover period	36 days	40 days

- The trade receivables turnover period is rising – which means it is taking longer to collect money from customers.
- The trade payables turnover period is rising – which means it is taking longer to pay suppliers.
- The receivables ratio has risen faster than the payables ratios meaning the gap between the time taken to collect and the time taken to pay has narrowed significantly which could lead to cash flow shortages.

4 **(a)** Castleland will be satisfied with its rate of inventory turnover. The turnover rate is higher than the industry average. This will mean that it will not be left with out of date inventory, which is important due to the business sector Castleland is operating within.

(b) Castleland could consider:

- using a cheaper supplier for raw materials
- increasing the amount of advertising that it does to enhance its brand image.

5 **(a)** Gross margin = $\frac{\text{gross profit}}{\text{sales}} \times 100$

Year ended 31 March 2017: Gross margin = $\frac{220\ 000}{400\ 000} \times 100 = 55\%$

Year ended 31 March 2018: Gross margin = $\frac{250\ 000}{420\ 000} \times 100 = 59.52\%$ (to 2 d.p.)

Profit margin = $\frac{\text{profit for the year}}{\text{sales}} \times 100$

Year ended 31 March 2017: Profit margin = $\frac{(220\ 000 - 150\ 000)}{400\ 000} \times 100$

$= 17.5\%$

Year ended 31 March 2018: Profit margin = $\frac{(250\ 000 - 180\ 000)}{420\ 000} \times 100$

$= 16.67\%$ (to 2 d.p.)

(b) Abhi will be satisfied that his gross margin has increased by 4.52%. This indicates that his profitability has improved. However, he will be concerned that his profit margin has decreased by 0.83%. This has been caused by an increase in business expenses.

(c) To increase his profit margin, Abhi needs to control his business expenses. For example, he could consider reducing his spending on advertisements, heat and light or travel expenses.

6 A business could not meet its liabilities when they were due, meaning that it is unlikely that suppliers would be prepared to offer trade credit to the business.

Answers – Stretch

7 Answers may include:

- It may be hard for Aadesh to increase selling prices due to intense competition.
- It may be difficult for him to cut wage costs due to minimum wage laws.
- It may be difficult for him to cut cost of sales due to a need to maintain a certain level of quality.

8 A business organisation needs to consider the difference between their gross margin and the profit margin. This will indicate the business's efficiency. Any changes in gross margin will have a direct effect on profit margin. The profit margin will be affected by different types of business expenses.

9 The current ratio of 1.5 : 1 is lower than would be expected for this type of business. As has been identified, the sector average is 2 : 1.

This could be caused by having very little cash in the bank and therefore a low value of current assets.

The liquid (acid test) ratio is at the required level of 1 : 1. This means that Wickets cricket store would be able to pay all of its debts should they need repaying. The liquid (acid test) ratio is at the same level as the sector average.

Answers – Unit review

1 D

2 D

3 A

4 C

6.3 Inter-firm comparison

Answers – Support

1
- Higher profit margins (both gross margin and profit margin) for A–Z Sounds
- Slightly higher ROCE for 123 Music
- Higher current ratio and acid test for 123 Music – which is safer
- Faster rate of inventory turnover for 123 Music
- Faster collection of debts for A-Z Sounds (32 vs 44 days)
- Shorter payments of debts for A-Z Sounds (45 vs 51 days)
- The ratios are inconclusive. ROCE is often seen as the main measure of success, but different ratios would support either firm as performing better.

Answers – Practice

2 Hill top runners will be disappointed that its gross margin is 15% lower than that of Summit hiking supplies. This may have occurred if Hill top runners reduced its mark-up in order to encourage sales. Alternatively, Hill top runners may have purchased goods for resale that cost more to buy to improve the quality of the goods for sale.

Although Hill top runners' profit margin is lower than that of Summit hiking supplies, the difference is smaller than that of the gross margin. The difference in profit margins is 5%. This means that Hill top runners is managing its expenses more effectively.

Hill top runners' return on capital employed is 4% lower than Summit hiking supplies'. This may mean that it will find it difficult to encourage individuals to invest in its business.

Hill top runners needs to consider increasing its selling price; however, this may mean that customers will go to Summit hiking supplies. It could consider purchasing goods from a cheaper supplier. However, this may mean that the quality of goods being sold may decline, causing its customers to take their custom elsewhere. Hill top runners could increase the amount of advertising and marketing to encourage more sales but this will increase expenses.

3 Current ratio = current assets ÷ current liabilities

ABC Manufacturers: Current ratio = $\frac{(60000 + 110000 + 200000)}{190000}$

= 1.95 : 1 (2 d.p.)

DEF Production: Current ratio = $\frac{(170000 + 250000)}{(126000 + 50000)}$

= 2.39 : 1 (2 d.p.)

Liquid (acid test) ratio = current assets – closing inventory ÷ current liabilities

ABC Manufacturers: Liquid (acid test) ratio = $\frac{(110000 + 200000 - 60000)}{190000}$

= 1.32 : 1 (2 d.p.)

DEF Production: Liquid (acid test) ratio = $\frac{250000 - 170000}{(126000 + 50000)}$

= 0.45 : 1 (2 d.p.)

The current ratio of ABC Manufacturers, 1.95 : 1, is slightly lower than the benchmark of 2 : 1 and lower than the result for DEF Production. This appears to have been caused by a high level of trade payables.

DEF Production's current ratio is considerably above the benchmark. It has a considerable amount of inventory and money owing from trade receivables. It would be beneficial if it could reduce its inventory levels to prevent these going out of date and collect the money from its trade receivables.

The liquid (acid test) ratio of ABC Manufacturers of 1.32 : 1 is above the required level of 1 : 1. This means that it would be able to pay all of its debts should they need repaying. ABC Manufacturers' liquid (acid test) ratio value is above that of DEF Production. DEF Production's result is considerably below the benchmark and is lower than ABC.

Based on the liquidity ratios, it would be advisable to purchase ABC Manufacturers.

4 Arguments in favour of Fashion Supplies Ltd:

- It collects amounts from trade receivables more quickly than Quality Clothing (by almost two weeks)
- The gap between the receivables and payables is more than one week compared with only one day for Quality Clothing Ltd.

Arguments in favour of Quality Clothing Ltd:

- It takes longer to pay its trade payables – which frees up cash flow for business use
- It turns over its inventory twice per month on average (which may mean a faster rate of sales).

Overall:

- Difficult to tell – it would be necessary to know if Fashion Supplies Ltd deliberately orders large volumes of inventory, which means a lower rate of inventory turnover
- The gap between receivables and payables matters if the business struggles with cash flow – in this case Quality Clothing Ltd should try to collect receivables more quickly.

Answer – Stretch

5 Argo plc will be satisfied with its gross margin of 59%. This is considerably higher than its competitor. Argo plc's ratio is 27% higher than its competitor's.

Argo plc will also be satisfied with its profit margin. This is again considerably (14%) higher than the local competitor's.

However, the difference between gross margin and profit margin is 12% for the local competitor but 25% for Argo plc. This would imply that Argo plc is not managing its expenses effectively.

Argo plc will be extremely satisfied with its return on capital employed of 53%. This is considerably higher than the local competitor's. In comparison to other investment opportunities, 53% is very high. Argo plc would have no problem in attracting an investor to purchase shares or to invest in its business.

Answers – Unit review

1 B

2 D

3 D

4 B

6.4 Interested parties

Answers – Support

1 Owners, managers, employees, leisure centre guests, banks.

2 Annual memberships fees – this will bring money into the club which can be spent on improvements.

Surplus or deficit – a surplus will allow the club to spend money on improving facilities and maintaining the club. A deficit may suggest that the club may not continue operating in the future.

Answers – Practice

3 Banks will use financial information to review the performance of a sole trader prior to agreeing to lend money, via an overdraft, loan or mortgage. A bank will need to know if the sole trader has sufficient security to cover the amount of any loan. Banks will need to ensure that the sole trader can repay any loan when it is due and that they have sufficient funds to pay the debt and any interest that has been charged.

In terms of a mortgage, a bank will need to be sure that the non-current asset being purchased provides sufficient collateral in the unfortunate situation that the sole trader cannot repay the debt.

4 (a) Owners will have an interest in all aspects of the operation. In particular, they will be interested in the profitability, liquidity and efficiency of the business. This information allows the owners to evaluate the business's performance and progress.

In a sole trader business, the owner will be interested in the amount of profit for the year that is generated. This allows the owner to decide how many drawings they can take from the business organisation.

Financial information allows an owner to make informed decisions about expansion, business growth or future opportunities.

Potential partners considering joining a partnership will be interested in the profitability of a business and will want to be assured that the business is likely to continue for the foreseeable future.

(b) Managers and employees will need to be assured that it is likely to remain profitable and in operation for the foreseeable future. Any manager or employee will expect to be fairly paid, and have a long career with excellent working conditions.

Managers will also have an interest in all aspects of the operation. In particular, they will be interested in the profitability, liquidity and efficiency of the business.

A review of financial accounts and the use of ratio analysis will allow managers to evaluate past performance, plan for the future and take action to solve problems if required.

(c) Trade payables are suppliers that provide businesses with goods and services. The goods and services will have been provided on credit and will need to be repaid within the specified period.

Prior to offering trade credit, a supplier will review the liquidity position of the business. In particular, they may review the trade payables turnover to review current performance.

Following review, a supplier will decide on the credit limit and length of credit term that will be offered to a business.

(d) Club members are individuals that have paid a subscription or membership fee to a club in order to benefit from the club's services. For example, an individual may pay an annual subscription to a gym and leisure centre. This will allow them to use the gym and all of the facilities at the leisure centre for a twelve-month period.

Club members will be keen to see that their subscription money is being used appropriately. The financial statements will show how subscription money has been used.

(e) Central and local governments are key stakeholders of a business. The business is legally required to pay taxes on a regular basis and ensure that it complies with national and international laws.

Government departments will also compile business organisation statistics for national review.

Answers – Stretch

5 Shareholders hold shares in a limited company; this means that they own part of the business organisation.

Stakeholders have an interest in a business organisation but do not necessarily own it.

In many cases, the aims and objectives of the stakeholders are not the same as those of shareholders. This causes conflict.

For example, shareholders will wish to maximise their investment and receive the highest possible dividend. This is possible if a business organisation is able to maximise its profit for the year. However, an employee will desire a high wage, which will reduce the profit for the year. This reduction would mean that dividends to shareholders will be lower.

6 Potential investors will be interested in the profitability, liquidity and efficiency of the business. They will need to know the amount of return they can expect to gain from their investment, whether their money is safe and the possible amount of dividends or return that they may earn.

Answers – Unit review

1 B

2 A

3 D

6.5 Limitations of accounting statements

Answers – Support

1 The location of a business is likely to be a major factor in its success. An appropriately located business will attract more customers and will encourage customer loyalty. However, this benefit is difficult to value and cannot be accurately recorded in the accounting statements. The value would be classed as subjective.

Answers – Practice

2 Quantitative information is factual information and data that is not based on opinions.

Qualitative information is information collected based on an individual's opinions and views.

3 Customer satisfaction

Management skills

Business location

Customer loyalty

Motivation of workforce

4 Examples of conflicting accounting definitions include:

- The calculation of profit – some businesses adjust for loan interest, other businesses do not.
- Calculation of depreciation – one business organisation may depreciate its office equipment using a reducing balance method, whereas a competitor may use a straight line method.

5 This is financial data or information from the past. In an income statement, this is traditionally the last year.

Income statements contain numerical data from the past financial period. This is usually one year. A statement of financial position is based on a snapshot at a particular moment in time. This takes place on the last day of the financial year. At this time, a business will value its assets and liabilities.

By the time these accounting statements and records have been prepared and published, the material is out of date. This means that the accounting statements may not be a reliable prediction of what may be happening currently or in the future.

For example, during the financial year, a business completed a 'one-off' project earning a considerable amount of profit. This was not to be repeated in future years. This would inflate the amount of profit for the year, but would not impact on future years' accounts. This would give interested parties an incorrect view of the business's potential.

Answers – Stretch

6 Financial statements are based on historic costs. Financial transactions need to be recorded using their original cost price. Financial accounting statements are produced using data from the past. This does not necessarily predict the future.

Different businesses will define accounting terms in different ways. Comparisons are only meaningful if like for like comparisons are made. For example, if Taj plans to compare his financial statements with those of another business, he will need to ensure the same depreciation methods have been used.

Only numerical data is included in the financial records of a business. Non-financial aspects, for example customer loyalty, cannot be valued and included in the financial statements.

7 Premises are valued at their historic cost less any depreciation to date.

8

	2017	2018
Gross margin	43.8%	58.5%
Profit margin	27%	28.7%

- Profitability ratios have improved – quite significantly on gross margin.
- The profit margin is only slightly higher and this is because of the large increase in expenses.
- The higher rate of staff leaving the business has probably had an impact on expenses (recruitment costs) and there may also have been a cost associated with moving to a new system of payment.

- Sales have fallen. This may have been caused by a decline in staff morale causing them to be less effective at selling.
- Overall – the profitability ratios show improvement, but this may not be long-lasting and may disguise other issues with staff motivation and morale.

Answers – Unit review

1 C

2 D

3 B

4 B

Chapter 6 review

Answers

1 D

2 D

3 A

4 A

5 B

6 D

7 A

8 A

9 B

10 D

11 (a)
- Business growth is limited by the amount of capital Hua has available **[1]**.
- Hua has no one to share the responsibility of running the business **[1]**.
- She often has to work long hours and may find it difficult to take holidays or find cover when she is unwell **[1]**.
- Hua will be liable for any debts that the business cannot pay; there is unlimited liability **[1]**.

(b) **(i)** Historic cost **[1]**. The only accepted way to record financial transactions is to use the original cost price **[1]**. Financial accounting statements are produced using data from the past **[1]**.

(ii) Difficulties of definition **[1]**. Different businesses will define accounting terms in different ways **[1]**. Comparisons are meaningful only if like for like comparisons are made **[1]**.

(iii) Non-financial aspects **[1]**. Only numerical data is included in a business's financial records **[1]**. Non-financial aspects are ignored **[1]**.

(c) Gross margin **[1]**, profit margin **[1]**, return on capital employed **[1]**.

(d) Decrease in reputation **[1]** – withdrawal of credit from suppliers **[1]**. Lack of funds to pay short-term debts, for example repairs **[1]** – cash discounts will be lost **[1]**.

12 (a) **(i)** Gross margin $= \frac{\text{gross profit}}{\text{revenue}} \times 100$ **[1]**

$= \frac{100\,000}{260\,000} \times 100$ **[1]**

$= 38.46\%$ (to 2 d.p.) **[1]**

(ii) Profit margin $= \frac{\text{profit for the year}}{\text{revenue}} \times 100$ **[1]**

$= \frac{70\,000}{260\,000} \times 100$ **[1]** $= 26.92\%$ (to 2 d.p.) **[1]**

(iii) Return on capital employed = $\frac{\text{profit for the year}}{\text{capital employed}} \times 100$ **[1]**

$= \frac{70\,000}{110\,000} \times 100$ **[1]**

= 63.64% (to 2 d.p.) **[1]**

(b)
- Ludwig might have a lower selling price **[1]** which would mean a lower gross margin than his competitors **[1]**
- Gross margin may be lower because Ludwig might pay more for his supplies (instruments, music) **[1]** which are of higher quality – and this may be a selling point of his business **[1]**
- Profit margin may be lower due to him paying higher wages **[1]** which means costs are higher than high competitors' business.
- Ludwig may sell his inventory more quickly **[1]** which means he can operate with a lower profit margin on each sale **[1]**.

(c) Current ratio = $\frac{\text{current assets}}{\text{current liabilities}}$ **[1]**

$= \frac{11\,000 + 4000 + 3500}{12\,500}$ **[1]**

= 1.48 **[1]**

[Award all 3 marks for correct answer without workings]

(d) Suggested answers:

- Yes, because the current ratio is close to 1.5 and this normally indicates sufficient current assets to pay current liabilities.
- Yes, because the current ratio is 1.48 and normally not all the trade payables would require payment at the same time.
- No, because his inventory is not likely to be very liquid.
- No, because his liquid (acid test) ratio is very low (0.6).
- No, because inventory is very high and this isn't always easily converted into liquid assets.

[Award 1 mark for stating whether Ludwig should be happy or not and 1 mark for a suitable justification]

13 (a) $975 **[1]**

(b) Cash discount **[1]**

(c) To ensure prompt payment **[1]** and therefore sufficient cash flow **[1]**.

(d) **(i)** Current ratio = $\frac{\text{current assets}}{\text{current liabilities}}$ **[1]**

Current ratio = $\frac{24\,000}{12\,000}$ **[1]**

= 2 : 1 **[1]**

(ii) Liquid (acid test) ratio = $\frac{\text{current assets} - \text{closing inventory}}{\text{current liabilities}}$ **[1]**

Liquid (acid test) ratio = $\frac{24\,000 - 12\,000}{12\,000}$ **[1]** = 1 : 1 **[1]**

(e) Managers of any business need to be assured that it is likely to remain profitable **[1]** and in operation for the foreseeable future **[1]**.

Any manager of a business expects to be fairly paid, and have a long career with excellent working conditions **[1]**.

Managers also have an interest in all aspects of the operation. In particular, they are interested in the profitability, liquidity and efficiency of the business **[1]**.

A review of financial accounts and the use of ratio analysis allows managers to evaluate past performance **[1]**, plan for the future **[1]** and take action to solve problems if required **[1]**.

(f)
- Over time **[1]**. By only looking at one year's financial records the figures may hide a longer-term issue. Comparisons over several years allow interested parties to identify any key trends **[1]**.
- Against other businesses **[1]**. Interested parties may compare a business's financial records with those of a competitor. As long as the information that is available is detailed, meaningful comparisons can be made **[1]**.
- Against a benchmark **[1]**. Comparison against a benchmark can be useful for a business. However, the benchmark data may include very different businesses, making any comparison meaningless **[1]**.

[Two marks per comparison method – maximum of 4 marks]

7 ACCOUNTING PRINCIPLES AND POLICIES

7.1 Accounting principles

Answers – Support

1 In accordance with the materiality principle, accountants should not spend time trying to accurately record items that are immaterial. The curtains' value is immaterial to a public limited company and should therefore be recorded as an expense.

2 **(a)** The sole trader is required to include this transaction in his drawings account.

(b) The principle being applied is business entity – the financial affairs of a business must be maintained separately from those of the owner.

3 Adjustments for prepayments and accruals of income and expenditure need to be made in a business's income statement and statement of financial position.

Expenses

- An accrued expense is added to the relevant expense in the income statement and shown as a current liability (other payables) in the statement of financial position.
- A prepaid expense is deducted from the relevant expense in the income statement and shown as a current asset (other receivables) in the statement of financial position.

Income

- A prepaid income is deducted from the relevant additional income in the income statement and shown as a current liability in the statement of financial position.
- An accrued income is added to the relevant additional income in the income statement and shown as a current asset in the statement of financial position.

4 Workforce skills, management competency, local community residents and staff morale.

Answers – Practice

5 **(a)** The principle of consistency must be considered. Jabar should continue to use the straight line method. It does not matter if the asset values are unrealistic – that is not the point of depreciation. Using the same method is important as it ensures that comparisons with previous years are more meaningful if the same method is used.

(b) The realisation principle must be considered. Sales should only be recognised once the sale has been made with certainty. Once the goods have been transferred to the customer the sale can be recognised in the income statement but not before. He should therefore not include the sales in December.

(c) The matching principle means that expenses must be matched to the period in which they were incurred. This means if the electricity bill belongs to the current year it must appear in the income statement as an expense for the current year. It does not matter when the expense is paid, just when it was incurred.

Answers – Stretch

6 International Accounting Standard Number 1 (IAS 1) provides details of the accounting principles that accountants should apply when preparing financial accounts. Applying these principles ensures that financial records are consistently produced and can be compared.

If every business and accountant applied their own rules to the production of financial records, the records would become meaningless and make inter-firm comparisons impossible.

7 2 and 3 only. 1 is incorrect – a credit balance c/d will occur.

Answers – Unit review

1 D

2 A

3 B

4 C

7.2 Accounting policies

Answers – Support

1 In order to be reliable, financial statements should:

(a) be free from bias

(b) be free from errors

(c) be dependable for all interested parties

(d) represent a true and fair view

(e) be independently verifiable.

2 Financial statements produced by a business provide information about its performance and position in the market. These statements are used to make informed business decisions.

It is vital that the information is provided on time to enable these important decisions to be made. If the information is too late, then the information is of no use to the user.

It is very important that the data and information contained in any financial statement is relevant to the user. This means the information contained in the statements must:

- confirm expectations of historic events
- correct prior expectations of historic events
- form, revise or confirm expectations for the future.

3 Understandability depends on the clarity of the information provided by the business. It also depends on the ability of the interest party reading the financial information.

Answers – Practice

4 By using agreed accounting policies and principles, accountants can avoid confusion and inconsistencies. This allows accounting records to be effectively compared and analysed. The use of such policies and principles helps businesses present financial information that is 'true and fair' and ensure that none of the information is misleading.

Answers – Stretch

5 **(a)** IAS 1: Presentation of Financial Statements

(b) IAS 2: Inventories

(c) IAS 7: Statement of Cash Flows

(d) IAS 16: Property, Plant and Equipment

(e) IAS 33: Earnings Per Share

(f) IAS 38: Intangible Assets

Answers – Unit review

1 B

2 D

Chapter 7 review

Answers

1 B

2 A

3 C

4 C

5 C

6 D

7 D

8 D

9 B

10 A

11 **(a)** A statement of ledger balances **[1]** at a particular date **[1]**.

(b) Duality principle **[1]**: this states that a business transaction always has two effects on the business and requires two entries **[1]**, one debit and one credit, to be made in the accounts; also known as double entry **[1]**.

(c) Checks arithmetical accuracy **[1]**

Provides a list of balances **[1]**

Useful in preparing final accounts **[1]**

[Accept any two points]

(d) See next page

(e) Error of omission – a transaction is completely omitted from the books.

Error of commission – the correct amount is entered in the wrong person's account.

Error of principle – where an item is entered in the wrong class of account, e.g. motor expenses rather than motor van.

Compensating error – where errors cancel each other out.

Error of original entry – where the original figure is incorrect yet the double entry is still observed using this incorrect figure.

Complete reversal of entries – where the correct account is used but each item is shown on the wrong side of the account.

Transposition error – where the wrong sequence of individual characters within a number has been entered, e.g. 142 instead of 124.

[Any three errors – 1 each for the identification of an error + 1 each for the explanation]

(d)

Iram Trial balance as at 31 December 2018		
	Dr	Cr
	$	$
Cash at bank	6400 **[1]**	
Carriage inwards	1400 **[1]**	
Trade payables		17200
Trade receivables	29600	
Provision for depreciation: motor vehicles		5600 **[1]**
Drawings	48000	
General expenses	780	
Insurance	820	
Lighting and heating	1200	
Motor vehicles	35200 **[1]**	
Motor expenses	1720	
Office expenses	560	
Rent and rates	1800 **[1]**	
Purchases	151200	
Revenue		204000
Capital		179180 **[1]**
Inventory as at 31 December 2017	16800 **[1]**	
Wages and salaries	10500	
Freehold land	100000	
	405980	405980

12 (a) Duality principle **[1]**. Every financial transaction has two effects on the business and requires two entries, one debit and one credit, to be made in the accounts **[1]**.

(b)

	Transaction	Account to be debited	Account to be credited
(i)	*Purchase of fixtures and fittings, paying by cheque*	*Fixtures and fittings*	*Bank*
(ii)	Payment of employee wages by cash	Wages **[1]**	Cash **[1]**
(iii)	Cash sales	Cash **[1]**	Sales **[1]**
(iv)	Receipt of commission by cheque	Bank **[1]**	Commission received **[1]**
(v)	Fatima withdrew cash from the bank for her own use	Drawings **[1]**	Cash **[1]**
(vi)	Sale of goods on credit to Arjun	Arjun **[1]**	Sales **[1]**

(c) **(i)** Accounting reliability refers to whether financial information can be verified **[1]** and used dependably for all interested parties **[1]**.

(ii) Relevance requires that the financial accounting information **[1]** should be useful to the users and that it will affect the decisions that they make **[1]**.

(d) Business entity **[1]** – the financial affairs of a business must be maintained separately from those of the owner **[1]**. The financial records of a business only relate to the business's transactions **[1]**, for example rent on business premises, purchases of goods, sales revenue **[1]**.

